"Up The Hammers!"

The West Ham Battalion in the Great War

"Up The Hammers!"
The West Ham Battalion in the Great War
1914-1918

First published in 2012

All rights reserved

© Elliott Taylor & Barney Alston, 2012

Elliott Taylor and Barney Alston are hereby identified as author of this work in accordance withSection 77 of the Copyright, Designs and Patents Act 1988

ISBN 9 781479 279463

"Up The Hammers!"

The West Ham Battalion in the Great War

A History Of
**The 13th (*Service*) Battalion (West Ham)
The Essex Regiment
1914 – 1918**

Elliott Taylor
and
Barney Alston

Part 1 Formation
West Ham 1914 – France 1915

	Page
1 - Exigencies of Service	11
2 - The First Three Hundred	15
3 - On Wanstead Flats	18
4 - "Who is going to march on Berlin?"	21
5 - "For the Honour of the Borough"	24
6 - "Like a joyous crowd of excursionists..."	28
7 - Familiar Faces	32
8 - A Bad Omen	35
9 - Baptism	39
10 – "Itching for a Smack at the Germans!"	42
11 – Desperate Actions	45
12 – To the Islands	48
13 – Artois Tragedy	53
14 – Leave!	57
15 – In search of tranquillity	63

Part 2 Reinforced
The Somme 1916 – The Ancre 1917

16 – "Your loss is ours too..."	81
17 – Seeing red	85
18 – Gongs	92
19 – The Devil's Wood	95
20 – Hell at High Holborn	101
21 – "Anywhere sooner than France..."	104
22 – A new broom	110
23 – The Quadrilateral	115
24 – Missing, presumed...	120
25 – Be Prepared	124
26 – Another bloody year	126
27 – Home fires	128

Part 3 Moving Shadows
Oppy & Cambrai 1917 – West Ham 1919

28 "No friends out here!"	147
29 – Midfield Mayhem	151
30 – Mundane routine	155
31 – Enter the Lock	159
32 – "Most noteworthy courage"	162
33 – One last shout	168
34 – Goodbyee	172
35 – Captivity	178
Back Home Again	184
Muster Roll of the West Ham Battalion	187
Visiting the Battlefields	208
Acknowledgements	210
Illustrations	67-78, 133-144

"Cockney feet mark the beat of history..."
Noel Coward, 'London Pride'

This is a true story: of commitment, sacrifice, selflessness and camaraderie. It's about the people of the old East End, the area from which more men volunteered to fight in the Great War than anywhere else in the entire country.

A story of men, some of whom had just about become totally forgotten. Local men who followed in the footsteps of the county volunteer militias, the pride of Victorian society: defending their blood-line and their homes, their nation and, ultimately, Civilisation itself.

It was a harsh reality requiring stout courage in the face of unspeakable horror, cheerfulness in spite of extreme discomfort, making the best of it and struggling on - characteristics which some might argue are almost unrecognisable in parts of today's civilian population. I doubt we will ever see the likes of that generation again.

As you read of their individual and collective battles you will perhaps, like me, come to deeply appreciate just what they gave up for us all those generations ago. They are the ancestral blood, our cockney spirit and the very essence of local pride, serving as an example to us all.

It has been an honour researching the fascinating story of the West Ham Battalion.

Elliott Taylor
Spring 2012
London

Part 1

Formation

West Ham, 1914 – France, 1915

Chapter 1

Exigencies of Service

The County Borough of West Ham was created in 1889. Its footprint covered an enormous urban area, including Forest Gate, Stratford, Plaistow, Canning Town, Silvertown, Custom House and most of the incredibly busy Royal Victoria Docks. Over the years large families in huge communities had grown and, according to the 1911 census, it was the most heavily populated area of Essex. Every trade, vocation or calling was now represented throughout a Borough of just over a quarter of a million residents. The streets ranged from well lit avenues of recently constructed fine architecture occupied by the educated and prosperous, through to the vilest alleyways of worthless hovels containing the deepest deprivations imaginable. In places it was persistently grimy and tangibly smelly with the constant clamour of industry in the background. Others were pleasantly green and leafy, tranquil and civic-minded but in all areas its innumerable schools, pubs and churches shared a very local congregation. It was just one hectic portion of a rapidly expanding metropolis and at its heart were the docks.

Trade steamed and sailed in and out the docks on every tide. All manner of goods from the four corners of the Empire were landed and unloaded. Men worked deep in the treacherous holds of ships or sat aloft in high steam driven cranes. More men and some boys were engaged in the very same tasks their grandfathers had done on the hundreds of barges, filling them until they sat low in the water and were nudged and buffeted by hefty river tugs. Yet more dockers shifted cargo into warehouses already brimming to the rafters with global produce. This was all then distributed within the docks to other ships, to trains, lorries or to the thousands of carmen, with his single horse and cart, for final delivery.

The streets of West Ham were extremely busy, often congested in places and could at times be very dangerous. As the docks rapidly grew in importance huge businesses developed along the Thames and its tributaries. In Victoria Dock, three massive grain mills stood upright, noticeable from the river as a navigation landmark. Yet the towers were merely one element on this powerful skyline, projecting the peak of non-stop industrialisation. In Silvertown, Venesta opened a huge factory producing millions of wood veneer packing cases for the tea traders. Moore and Nettlefolds, the Gas Light and Coke Co Ltd, Loisiers and Nicolines, RH Greens and Silley Weir Co together with Yardley Perfumes in Carpenters Road, Stratford, were others with a very large workforce.

But by far the biggest employer in the area had been the Thames Ironworks, formerly CJ Mare & Co, at Canning Town by the mouth of the River Lea where it runs into the Thames.

The Thames Ironworks shipyard was responsible for building over a thousand craft of all types, from lifeboats to warships, including HMS Albion in 1898 and HMS Black Prince in 1904. Its workforce of thirty-thousand contained a plethora of craftsmen, many skilled in shaping iron and riveting it together with hammers. The Ironworks chairman, Arnold Hill, believed passionately in the general health and well being of his employees. There were agreements about working hours and conditions. They had a large brass band for entertainment and Hill actively encouraged the "sport-for-all' ethos in his workforce. He also promoted temperance, especially in drinking and smoking. Although personally inclined towards cycling, Hill encouraged his foreman David Taylor to establish a works team to play the increasingly popular sport, football. Formed in 1895, the team played its first match against a side from the Royal Artillery. From that moment onwards the sports mad workers, closely followed by local residents, could be heard supporting "the Irons" with deep throated roars. Fortune, usually hiding, then awkwardly stepped in. The football team flourished and became West Ham United in 1900. It is still one of England's top teams with a larger, diverse and more passionate support. By contrast, the Thames Ironworks fell on very hard times. In a last glorious achievement, the men built HMS Thunderer, the largest battleship then afloat in 1911 but the gates finally clanged shut the following year after the yard lost critical government contracts. The closure caused catastrophic levels of unemployment from which the Borough would never fully recover. Ironically, it also released a huge number of fit, healthy and hardworking men.

In August 1914, the residents of West Ham and the whole nation watched confusedly as the assassination of an unknown prince in a faraway backwater exploded into a full scale European conflict. Six days after war with Germany was declared, an urgent proclamation went out: "Your King and Country Needs You" featuring the face of Lord Kitchener, a military icon of the South African wars at the turn of the century. Copies of the poster were stuck on every bright red pillar box in Great Britain. More were pasted up at every town hall, sports ground, cinema and theatre nationwide. Ten days later 'Army Order 324' confirmed the formation of six Divisions for Kitchener's 'new army', made up of civilian volunteers with or without military experience. Almost at once, communities up and down the country clamoured to raise battalions for the fight, each proudly bearing the name of their city, borough or affiliation. Many northern counties and cities famously raised battalions in this way, made up of men with a common affinity, whether it was where they worked or where they lived and the understanding on enlistment was that they would always serve together. Serving alongside your chums was seen to be good for morale and these units were quickly dubbed "Pals Battalions" in the press, although officially they were known as *"Service"* Battalions. Sadly, not much thought was given to what possible effects might be inflicted on small communities left behind if anything went wrong at the front. Nevertheless, the Pals' proved a hugely popular recruitment tool and in the East End of London William Crow, the Mayor of West Ham, promptly enquired at the War Office about raising a battalion of his own local men. On the 15th September 1914, at an open meeting of West Ham Council, Mayor Crow detailed their reply. The new battalion *"must be raised on a Regular [Army] basis"*, volunteers must be aged between nineteen and thirty-five and any enlistment must be *"for three years or the duration of the war..."* It was also made clear that *"no special privileges or considerations can be given"* while *"the number offering to enlist must be [...] one thousand men after a medical examination has been held."* In addition, *"the individual or community responsible for raising the Battalion must be willing and able to clothe, house and feed it [...] and to arrange for its local training."* Lastly, it was noted that *"the Battalion will form part of the local County Regiment."* The Mayor then gave his personal undertaking to pay for any expense *"beyond that provided by the War Office..."* His proposal was seconded by Alderman White, the motion was carried *'nemine contradicente'* and the decision was reported that evening with journalistic excitement in the local newspaper with the largest readership, the Stratford Express.

The following day, the Borough buzzed with the news. One resident, Henry Palmer, a retired Army Colonel and stern Magistrate living in Stratford, instantly knew what the unit would require first and foremost. He wrote to the MP for West Ham, Baron de Forest, asking if he might *"be inclined to contribute to the cost of the Colours?"* The 'Colour' is a flag carried at the head of a battalion or regiment and in earlier eras of warfare was a recognisable symbol of the commander's location on the battlefield; essentially it was, and still is, emblazoned with a list of any battle honours around the regiment's insignia, usually on top of a Union Flag. Henry Palmer estimated the cost of the flag to be about sixty pounds, which was quite an amount, and concluded his letter with the hope that *"you will see your way to help."* He needn't have worried in these euphoric times. Baron de Forest immediately agreed, by telegram. And he was not the only one to offer instant support. Mr and Mrs E Wild of Garden Court at Lincoln's Inn, whose legal chambers had provided the council with its official Recorder for the last few years, wrote directly to the Stratford Express with their best wishes for the West Ham Battalion and offering to pay *"half the cost"* of the Colours.

By the time of the next Council meeting, nearly two hundred men had rushed to volunteer for service. Unfortunately this patriotic fervour proved slightly premature. Mayor Crow had some bad news for his residents. The War Office had just written to him stating that *"no more local battalions were to be raised, at least in the foreseeable future"*, and that *"the raising of a West Ham Battalion could not be sanctioned..."* The news caused great disappointment, not only within the Council Chamber, but throughout the Borough. In this time of heightened patriotism, whipped up by the newspapers, the idea of having their own Battalion had 'gripped' the hearts and minds of the people, as evidenced by the many mentions it generated in the Stratford Express. The council realised it had an obligation to those who had already enlisted and on the 23rd September 1914, Councillor Greaves wrote to all two-hundred men on behalf of the Mayor. His letter informed them that even though the formation of a battalion was refused, arrangements had been made *"for them to form a Company of one Regiment. If you are still willing to join Lord Kitchener's Army you should communicate immediately with the recruiting officer and produce this letter. The Mayor regrets, that owing to the exigencies of service, the West Ham Battalion cannot be formed..."*

These *"exigencies"* were primarily due to the huge flood of men volunteering for their own local battalions, all across the country. The numbers had taken the British Government and the War Office thoroughly by surprise and the logistical problems of dealing with so many men were enormous as there were only roughly one-hundred and seventy-five thousand barrack accommodations available in the whole of the United Kingdom. There was literally nowhere to put any newly raised battalions and they would equally need to be clothed, fed, and equipped. Most importantly of all, these civilians needed to be rapidly trained up for combat and the myriad of supporting services.

William Crow was not the type of man to be passed over easily. He immediately travelled across London and requested an interview at the War Office. Disappointingly, he came away with nothing more than a letter, hand written and personally handed to him by Lord Kitchener, on behalf of the Army Council. It expressed their thanks and appreciation of *"the patriotic spirit"*, but reiterated that *"the authority to raise a battalion"* could *"not be granted"*. Crow ended his term as Mayor a deeply disappointed man.

Meanwhile, the war continued with a shocking brutal fury and the casualty lists grew at an alarming rate. Within the space of a couple of months the British Expeditionary Force (BEF) sustained such losses that the Reserve, together with the Territorials and the Special Reserve, had been fully committed. It was painfully obvious to everyone that this war was not going to be like anything ever witnessed before.

When the aggressive German offensive was finally brought to a shuddering bloody halt by grim British determination in the freezing November mud, the War Cabinet reconvened. It was shaken to the core by the sheer volume of losses and the decision it faced was not difficult. The Army urgently needed all the men it could get, regardless of the incredible logistics nightmare it was bound to create. The national characteristic of improvisation took hold and once again the proclamation was sent out: "Your King and Country needs YOU!"

On a chilly, damp winter evening the newly elected Mayor of West Ham, Henry Dyer stood up, cleared his throat and addressed the hushed Council chamber. He informed them, and the Borough, that he had just received a communication from the War Office announcing the formation of another volunteer army and *"formal sanction"* for the raising of the 13th (*Service*) Battalion ("West Ham") of the Essex Regiment.

It was December 29th, 1914, and to the undoubted pride and personal satisfaction of Councillor Crow, the West Ham Battalion was born.

Chapter 2

The First Three Hundred

All across the United Kingdom, the training facilities of the Regular Army were overwhelmed by the sheer numbers of civilian volunteers answering Kitchener's appeal. In places like West Ham, that had never traditionally supported a large military contingent in its midst, it was particularly evident. Characteristic improvisation led to large public buildings such as schools, church halls and warehouses being taken over for recruitment and training. The West Ham Battalion's Orderly Room was swiftly set up at 'The Chestnuts' in Stratford Broadway while the Forest Gate skating rink in Woodgrange Road was secured on a temporary basis as a drill hall. Additional recruiting centres were set up at Grove Crescent Road in Stratford, the Public Hall in Canning Town and the Town Hall in East Ham. There was an office in East India Dock Road, Poplar and at 'Baltic House' in Walthamstow and travelling up and down the main thoroughfare, from Aldgate to Plaistow, there was also a bus staffed by loud Recruiting Sergeants, full of banter, offering round trips *"to Berlin and back..."*

The numbers and quality of the men enlisting was impressive, especially to the West Ham Council. Overall the volunteers were healthy and strong with many of them formerly employed at the Thames Ironworks. There were so many former employees that the Council quickly proposed to the War Office that the crossed riveter's hammers be adopted as the cap badge of the West Ham Battalion. It would not have been the first unit of Kitchener's Army to have its own unique badge but it was officially decided that the Essex Regiment's cap badge, depicting Gibraltar Castle (a battle honour from the 1780's), should be worn. However, the West Ham Battalion was officially given the nickname *"The Hammers"*. Naturally, friends and neighbours were joining up. Good examples are found in eight men from Tidal Basin, all living in the shadows of the Ironworks' world renowned shipyard. From enlistment papers we can see that Pte (Private) Charles Free lived on Kerry Street and enlisted alongside Pte TW Carlile who lived in Alice Street, which was just a few doors along from Pte Gladding, Pte Charlie Brown and Pte JT Hall. Pte Tomlin lived around the corner in Fenn Street, very close to Pte Freeman in Sidney Street and Pte Charlie Fox who was living on Crown Street with his large family. The majority of the men were married, with an average of three offspring, although one of the volunteers was noted as having twenty children.

With all these recruits in the sudden expansion of Kitchener's civilian 'new army' there was a patently obvious shortage of experienced Non-Commissioned Officers (NCO's) to keep the volunteers in order. Their need was critical and led to retired Sergeants being urgently recalled and appointed to supervise the recruits. One was Sgt Paul Barth, born in Leytonstone. He had worked as a train guard on the railways before enlisting with a militia battalion of the Essex Regiment, serving in South Africa during the last weeks of the Boer War. Leaving the army in 1909, he re-enlisted in August 1914 and quickly joined the Hammers serving up to its disbandment. He survived the war and transferred, once again, back to the reserve in 1919.

Sergeant WG Wood was another who had rejoined the Essex after a lifetime in the volunteer forces. Holder of the Volunteer Long Service Medal, he left his wife and home in Priory Street, Colchester and gave invaluable assistance during these early days. He eventually transferred to the Training Reserve and died aged sixty-two in 1917. Today, he lies buried in Garrison Cemetery, Colchester.

At the same time some of the volunteers, due to their civilian experience, were quickly appointed Corporal and then Sergeant in the Hammers despite having no previous military service. A fine example is good natured George White. He had been a tea trader at Balloch's in Fenchurch Street for most of his working life, but had left England for Canada, seeking better employment prospects in 1912. A true West Ham lad, George had grown up in the heart of the Borough close to West Ham United's early home, the Memorial Ground. His parents now lived in Castle Street, next to the recently built Boleyn Ground and his mother had functioned as one of the Club's earliest kit washers. Their old house is now the location of United's Supporters' Club. Like so many, George had given up a new life abroad to answer the call to war, steaming back to England from Montreal on the SS Missanabie in November. Described as *"thoroughly honest, steady, intelligent and industrious, accustomed to controlling men"*, George enlisted at East Ham Town Hall on January 11th, 1915 and quickly became a well respected Sergeant.

By January 12th, nearly one-hundred and twenty men had volunteered. This prompted the formation of a Council Committee to take responsibility not only for the organisation and administration of the West Ham Battalion but also to handle the number of local *"young gentlemen desirous of taking up a commission"*. In another stroke of innovative thinking, Lord Kitchener had introduced 'Temporary' ranks which created officers with commissions valid *"for the duration of the war only"*, making a distinction between them and the 'career' officers. Temporary commissions were equally intended to fast track the promotion of suitable serving 'Other Rank' soldiers, especially those with recent combat experience or particular knowledge). For young civilian men from *"good families"*, it was an unprecedented opportunity in troubled times. Despite no formal military training, the brothers Joseph and William Robinson were born and educated in the Borough and living locally with their widowed mother. The Council Committee thought it was *"only fitting that they hold a Commission in the West Ham Battalion"*. Joseph and William, just one of innumerable instances of brothers joining together, both served as 2/Lt's with the Hammers.

Their fellow officers were equally as diverse in age as they were in experience. Norman Lang was a forty year old insurance agent who had been born in Cornwall but was now living at 'The Chalet' in Balfour Road, Ilford with his wife and four children. He had enlisted in the Royal Fusiliers at the start of the war but almost immediately his superb organisational skills were revealed and on 26th January 1915 Norman was granted a 'Temporary' Commission. A week later, he was formally posted, on request, to the Hammers and worked very closely and efficiently with the Hammer's Quartermaster, Lt TE Brind.

Thomas Edward Brind had worked on the Thames long before his thirteenth birthday, as an apprentice lighterman, carrying goods between ships and wharves. Now, aged fifty-seven, he was the epitome of a weather beaten cockney river worker, still fit from years of oar stokes. He had been widowed ten years earlier but had raised eight children and several of them still lived with him in Canning Town. His eldest son, Percy, was his apprentice on the river, although he too had by now volunteered, in another battalion of the Essex Regiment.

Another notable volunteer in the Hammers was William Walter Busby from Sherrard Road, just a few streets up from West Ham United's Boleyn Ground which he had witnessed being constructed. Twenty-four years old and one of those considered to be from a *"good family"*, he worked as a chemical analyst at Stafford Allen & Sons in the City. He was studying hard in the evenings for his chemistry Bachelor of Science (B.Sc) final exams in between many other civic activities. His experience in uniform was as a member of the Officer Training Corps at the London University and as a founding member and scout leader with the 2nd West Ham Troop, eventually becoming District Scout Master for the entire Borough. His elder brother Charles was a Commander in the Salvation Army, already serving in France in a non-combat role. William Busby was highly thought of at the Forest Gate Congregational Church in Sebert Road and he turned out to be an excellent officer and extremely well regarded by the men he commanded. Busby also left a brief insight into the early days of training and service on the frontline in the form of a diary, a vital source of the personal recollections of life as an officer in Kitchener's Army.

Other officers had varying military experience, usually from the far flung corners of the Empire. Two friends swiftly returned by boat from the Malay States (modern Malaysia) and then enlisted together in the West Ham Battalion. John Donald Paterson, of the Jawie estate and Robert Swan from the Krian estate were both successful rubber planters. Paterson was thirty and had risen to the rank of Second Lieutenant (2/Lt) in the regular army, being regarded as *"much above average"* in intelligence and soldiering. Business interests had then lured him to the Malay States, but he maintained his military commitments and enlisted in the local volunteers where he met Robert Swan. Twenty-nine year old Swan had many years of military experience under his belt, having first joined the British Guiana Artillery in the Caribbean as a Trumpeter before spending 1903 to 1908 in Trinidad prior to moving to Malaya. Swan gave JD Paterson a glowing character reference and both their applications to the Hammers were personally signed off by the Mayor Henry Dyer. Such men typified the volunteer ethos. A grant of £50 and a starting salary of 7s 6d propelled most of them into another world. They smelt of freshly tailored khaki with their leather accoutrements creaking from newness. Many had a less than extensive military knowledge and some felt more comfortable wearing elements of their own working clothes than a uniform.

It was the age of the amateur soldier and the most unlikely companions suddenly found themselves comrades in arms. Businessmen and dockers, factory workers and farmers, foremen and labourers, craftsmen, sportsmen, sailors, professionals, clerks and barrow-boys all rubbed shoulders in fields of tents all over the country.

Chapter 3

On Wanstead Flats

To house the flood of volunteers to the West Ham Battalion, wooden huts were hastily constructed on Wanstead Park in the grounds of the 'Old House' which today forms part of the golf club. Some men naturally took the option of being billeted in their own home but taking up residency in one hut was a young Swiss national, Conradin Donatz. He was a professional waiter, working at the Stratford branch of the fashionable tearoom chain, J. Lyons. It was a popular spot, especially with young officers like William Busby and his friends. Conradin lived in Walthamstow and was so caught up in the excitement of the nationalistic outpourings that he popped in to the Recruiting Office at Baltic House and signed up. No record survives of any comments by the recruiters but as a German speaking 'foreigner' he will undoubtedly have attracted interest, particularly in light of the simmering anti-German feelings then bubbling in the east end. Whether he was proudly defending his adopted country and Europe or cajoled by snide comments and white feathers implying cowardice (which some had already received through the post), Donatz joined the army and found himself in someone else's war.

The days in Wanstead were taken up with acclimatisation to military routine and terminology and it was not too long before the free spirits of the cockney volunteers were sorely tested by 'the army way' of doing things. Their lives were to be transformed forever. It began with physical fitness, march discipline and some basic field craft. Then there was drill. Whether hated or enjoyed by soldiers since the beginning of organised warfare, it nevertheless taught the basic tenet of obedience to orders: performing and reacting as a group with an expectation, through repetition, of what was required of each man. As new phases of training were reached different skills and disciplines would be introduced into the schedule, all based on a form of drill. It was a common perception that it was purely intended to remove their spirit and initiative and, of course, the Hammers were made up of men who were fiercely independent. Its composition underlines an important point of the West Ham spirit and is the essence of the 'New Army' battalions. The Hammers volunteers were largely but not exclusively, from a very working class background with strong traditions of industrial militancy combined with an unusually wide understanding of the world through their experience at the London docks. They were not the products of a cowed deferential society. Totally without discipline in the conventional sense of the word and full of quick, sharp humour, they were a Drill Sergeant's worst nightmare. A good example is Pte David Stickley, a nineteen year old clerk from Aintree Avenue in East Ham. Stickley was keen to fight but did not take kindly to the individual attentions of the senior NCO's whose duties included maintaining discipline and, in consequence of being given seventy-two hours of 'Field Punishment' for a breach of King's Regulations, he went 'Absent Without Leave' (AWOL) for a few days. Nobody's fool, he knew the military Provosts and the local police would eventually find him if he returned home. His solution was to 'fraudulently' enlist in another unit, a Hampstead based howitzer brigade, but when this was discovered, he was court martialled.

He might have been sent to a dreaded civilian prison for punishment but, as was common during the early months of the war, Stickley was ordered to leave the Hammers and remain with the west London Howitzers, eventually serving with them throughout the conflict.

Towards the end of January 1915, spurred on by news of the first *"gas bag"* Zeppelin raids on Britain, the Council placed a front page advert in the Stratford Express, listing the names and addresses of the first three-hundred volunteers:

"County Borough of West Ham.
13th (Service) Battalion, Essex Regiment
(West Ham)

No gas-bag invasion can alarm us.
True manhood will win!

Join your friends in the West Ham Battalion
who have already enlisted
Men resident in the Borough
are being billeted at home.
Allowance 2s a day: immediate equipment.

Henry Dyer, Mayor."

The names included Pte James Fleming and Pte Frank Eade, living a few streets apart in Leyton. Listed side by side as civilians on the front page and with consecutive army service numbers on their official paperwork, it is difficult not to imagine that there was a friendship or bond between them. James was a twenty-two year old 'boy' on a delivery van, living a few doors away from his widowed father in Dawlish Road. Frank Eade, on the other hand, really was a boy living on Byron Road with his parents and only fifteen at enlistment.

Kit and clothing was always a problem. Large batches of rough 'Kitchener Blue' uniforms were being issued in place of khaki which was in critically short supply. These blue uniforms were deeply unpopular with the men because it made them look like *"bus drivers"* or postmen, with its *"ridiculous little forage cap"* and civilian overcoat. When the blue uniform supply ran out, they were given a half sovereign to provide themselves with boots, a greatcoat and suit. Soon there were more than five-hundred recruits and they now had an Adjutant, Captain SG Mullock, a Special Reserve officer who had seen service in the South African War. He went to France in 1914 before being wounded at the Battle of the Aisne and invalided home. On recovery he immediately received an appointment to the West Ham Battalion for this formation period, to organise the growing mountain of official paperwork and military administration that was being generated.

The Hammers also acquired their first 'hero'. Pte Frank Lawley was walking along Romford Road on a grey, chilly morning when two horses harnessed to a butcher's cart bolted. In the congested streets this was a dangerous situation but, as recorded in the Stratford Express, the young soldier showed courage in chasing and catching the pair and "*by his pluck and presence of mind he undoubtedly prevented serious injury as there were a great many school children about at the time...*" Pte Lawley had already been recognised as a potential candidate for promotion and was attending '*classes of instruction for the duties of a non-commissioned Officer*' and so, in recognition of his bravery, Captain Mullock authorised his immediate appointment to the rank of Lance Corporal. Lawley served with B Company throughout the war, reaching the rank of Sergeant before returning home in 1919.

Mayor Henry Dyer set up a West Ham Battalion Fund, inviting contributions from local businesses and private citizens. The money was for much needed equipment as "*the men are very keen and eager and anxious to learn their work quickly and get fit quickly. To ensure this, it is necessary to provide at once many articles of equipment for their training, such as bayonet fighting equipment, range finders, field glasses for Non-Commissioned Officers, band instruments, aiming rests, aim correctors, miniature rifles and targets, landscape targets and blackboards.*" The Mayor went on to point out that this would normally have been supplied by the War Office but, in extraordinary times, this was impossible. It was an indication of the almost heroic status to which the people had elevated 'their' battalion that he felt that such a demand could be made of them. Also requested were funds for "*the provision of sports equipment and for prizes for platoon and Company competitions in musketry and sports, for camp flags and similar objects...*"

The Hammers held their first social function, in the form of a 'smoking concert', popular since Victorian times as an event exclusively for men freely to discuss politics and issues of the day while enjoying cigars. It was hosted by the men of A Company at the Brickfields Congregational School off Devons' Road in Bromley (By Bow). By all accounts it was a great success with an excellent programme thoroughly organised by the former Malay rubber planter Robert Swan and hilariously chaired by Sgt Robert 'Reg' Rollings, a Walthamstow man from Jewel Road soon to transfer to the Royal Flying Corps. John Wilkinson of Cleves Road in East Ham gave a fine rendition of the very popular war song "Tipperary" whilst Sgt Major Shardlow of the Gymnastic Staff recited "The Day" by Henry Chappel. 2/Lt JD Paterson, the other Malay rubber planter, was no doubt reflecting wistfully on his Scottish heritage when he gave a rousing rendition of "I love a lassie". The Stringaloes, a popular local band from Goodmayes near Ilford, provided the musical background.

The Mayor and Mayoress were there too and, after announcing that the funds for the Battalion Bugle Band had almost reached the target, Mayor Dyer gathered them all around. "*My lads, I have come down here to bid you a hearty welcome to this club we have opened for you and I hope you will come here as often as you like. I am going to make myself as busy as I can in seeing you have amusement... Everyone in the Borough is proud of you men, especially as you belong to the West Ham Battalion. We don't know how long you will be here, it all depends how long it takes to raise the battalion, but we will be very sorry to lose you...*"

There was enthusiastic cheering as brand new khaki uniforms were proudly unveiled and distributed, followed by a hearty chorus of "*for he's a jolly good fellow!*"

Chapter 4

"Who Is Going To March On Berlin?"

The Hammers first parade was held at St Luke's Church, West Ham on February 7th 1915 where they were inspected by the proud figure of Lieutenant-Colonel (Lt-Col) Pelham Rawstorn Papillon, their freshly appointed Commanding Officer. Born in 1864, the son of an MP, he was raised at Lexden Manor on the outskirts of Colchester. With a sparkling pedigree, Pelham Papillon had lived a life of ease at the very upper end of society, unlike the men he now commanded. He had attended Winchester College before going up to University College, Cambridge gaining an MA in Law and becoming an excellent cricketer. He then joined the Militia. In 1899, when war flared in South Africa, the newly promoted Lt Papillon went off to fight the Boers and was 'Mentioned in Dispatches' by Kitchener. By 1901 the Boer War had degenerated into guerrilla warfare in which the now Captain Papillon was involved until the conclusion of hostilities. Returning home on the troopship Wakool, he considered his future and decided that he had 'done his bit'. In 1904 he retired from the Militia to his home in St Leonards before moving to the picturesque Catsfield Place in Sussex with his new wife, Constance. As their first two children grew up he served as a local Magistrate and maintained his inherited estates, including Crowhurst Park, and managed his many farms. When war loomed once again in 1914 he volunteered to the Colours and when the 'Temporary' promotions were offered to selected senior officers the now Lieutenant Colonel Papillon took command of the West Ham unit. Beside him was an old friend Major WF Hurst. He was another land owner of some considerable wealth in Sussex and held private estates in Oxfordshire. Major Hurst had served alongside Papillon in South Africa, continuing to serve under the Duke of Richmond until 1904. Patriotically rejoining at the outbreak of war in 1914, he joined the West Ham Battalion as second in command.

By the end of February the numbers of volunteers had risen to one-thousand and ten, no doubt encouraged by the popular children's cry of "We don't want to lose you, but we think you ought to go!" and the West Ham Battalion Fund showed a very healthy three-hundred pounds publicly subscribed. By early March they were getting close to full strength. Two weeks later, the Hammers held another parade, this time at St James Church in Forest Gate. A march followed around the local area led by the proud members of the Drum and Bugle Band, accompanied by the East Anglian Divisional Band. This prompted yet another influx of volunteers at the recruiting centres, including Ernie Kurtz, a thirty-seven year old trouser presser born in Bow, with no previous military experience. His German born father was a local tailor. Ernie had married Caroline Radden, a 'tailoress', in 1911 and they now lived with her parents in Bristol Road, Forest Gate. Walking into 'The Chestnuts' Recruiting Office, he signed on the line and was instantly posted to C Company.

As Ernie later revealed in a brief memoir, he had a hard time knowing who to salute as *"it was very strange to us when we started on our army routine. At that time I didn't know the different ranks among Officers, commissioned or non-commissioned!"*

Somewhere in the queue with Ernie Kurtz were the Lathangue brothers. Fred and Harry, joined later by Sid, all volunteered to the Hammers. They grew up in the Borough and were employed around the docks in various trades. Despite Fred Lathangue having a poor discipline record during initial training he was appointed Lance Corporal (L/Cpl). His brother Harry had previous military experience as a pre-war member of the Royal Artillery and their father was a Boer war veteran.

Attempts continued to entertain the large numbers of men proudly walking out in uniform. The staff of the Queen's cinema in Romford Road, Forest Gate opened their doors to the West Ham Battalion and eight-hundred and fifty of them attended to watch the latest films. There was an equally well attended variety show at the Stratford Empire where 2/Lt Alfred George Buxton was the Assistant Manager. Another of those from 'a good family', his father was a local magistrate. Buxton also organised a boxing competition at the East End National Athletics Club for which the overall winner was Pte Sims of A Company. While presenting the prizes, Major Hurst took the opportunity confidently to make a rousing morale boosting speech, reaching a crescendo with the question *"we might now have enough men to drive them back to the Rhine but who is going to march on Berlin?"* The answer came as one passionate voice, *"We are!"*

Less popular were route marches and these were becoming more regular as the training staff raised the level of military input now that the majority of the men were in some form of uniform. On Wednesday 10th, a typical route march took place, leaving Stratford Broadway and into the High Street. There they smartly passed The Alexandra Temperance Hotel, which was serving as the Officers' Mess (*"with palms and music"*). Epic battles were already taking place, on the billiards tables, between the 2/Lt's William Busby, his close friend Bernard Page and Leonard Holthusen. They were all from Forest Gate and Page's father was the proprietor of a very successful chain of florists throughout the Borough. Twenty-nine year old Leonard Holthusen, an engineering surveyor living in Claremont Road, became the Battalion's first Signals Officer. Len's elder brother was also a volunteer in the Hammers. As a local GP (with one surgery a few doors down from the church attended by William Busby), Alan Holthusen had quickly been appointed as the Medical Officer. Their father was a local 'ornamental confectioner' and Christmas cracker manufacturer. 'Reg' Norman was another local officer, previously running a fruit and vegetable stall in Stratford market on behalf of his father's long established company. Reg became good friends with twenty year old Frank Keeble who had left his father's successful farming estate in Brantham on the Suffolk/Essex border. Frank had taken up his commission in the West Ham Battalion in honour of his mother, who had been born in the Borough and was the daughter of a Council Alderman. Meanwhile another of the officers, Charles Carson, was from Congleton in Cheshire and had been a medical student at Manchester University. On getting his Commission he, like all of them, specifically requested a posting to the Hammers, although his reasons are as yet unknown.

As well as marching, football was being organised to raise the fitness levels. Some matches took place in West Ham Park and were well reported in the Stratford Express. One *"ended in a victory for 'C' Company by 3-2. Playing with a strong wind, 'C' Coy tried hard to score, but all their efforts were futile, largely through the fact that the ball was practically uncontrollable [because of] the violent wind. Half time arrived with no score. The second half opened with a smart attack on 'B' Company's goal, which was largely repulsed but eventually a nice opening was afford 2nd Lt Page who shot feebly, but sufficiently hard to register the first goal for 'C' Company...*

This seemed to serve as a stimulant to 'B' Company and from the kick off 'C' Company's back miss-kicked and Humphries fastened one on the leather and scored an equalising goal. Within five minutes of this success, a melee in front of goal provided an opportunity for Webb who gave 'B' Company the lead. Following this reverse, 'C' Company kept up a prolonged attack and the goalkeeper allowed a shot from Winter to pass through his hands. This success followed by another as Gillman, with a splendid drive, registered the winning goal for 'C' Company..."

Eventually, the remaining 'Kitchener Blue' uniforms were replaced by army khaki. With the necessary alterations and general wear and tear through continuous usage in training it was decided to establish a Battalion Tailor's Shop in the Headquarters Company. Ernie Kurtz, son of a seamstress and husband of a tailoress had found his niche in the army. *"Some of the boys thought I had a cushy job but I didn't! We got plenty of other jobs besides, too numerous at times to mention!"*

Finally, one thousand three-hundred strong, the West Ham Battalion mustered in a biting wind on Wanstead Flats. It was March 23rd 1915 and they were inspected by the keen eyes of Major General CL Woollcombe of Eastern Command as they paraded beneath their fluttering and unofficial hand-made copy of the King's Colour.

It had been collectively sewn and embroidered by the wives, girlfriends and ladies of the volunteers.

Chapter 5

"For The Honour of the Borough"

By the beginning of April 1915 the unit was complete and the question was asked in Council Chambers concerning the raising of a second West Ham Battalion. This manifested itself in another great civic effort which resulted in the formation of two West Ham Brigades for the Royal Field Artillery, stationed for training on the Memorial Ground, West Ham United's old home. Meanwhile, the management and staff of the former Thames Ironworks were equally busy, locally raising four gun batteries bearing their name and there was also an East Ham Brigade.

Infantry training continued and 2/Lt William Busby and L/Cpl's Smith and Goodchild were sent to Colchester for a trench construction course. Before he left however, Busby's diary entry for Monday April 5th briefly describes an unusual incident concerning Pte Jonathan Clifford who was appearing in the dock at the police court in Great Eastern Road accused of begging. Invited by Mr Trumble, the magistrate, to sit alongside him on the bench, the uniformed William Busby spoke up for the errant soldier who was subsequently 'let off' with a warning. There was no indication as to why he was begging but he was quickly ordered to move, from private accommodation at Winfield Road Stratford, into the huts at Wanstead. The lenient magistrate was the father of Frank Trumble, another local volunteer officer to the West Ham Battalion and billiards player at the Alexandra Mess. By requesting Busby to give a character reference for Clifford it offers a further indication of the close camaraderie blossoming throughout the unit. Following his time in court, William Busby met up with Smith and Goodchild at Stratford Station and the three made their way to Liverpool Street, caught the train to Colchester and arrived at 6.11pm. The L/Cpl's went straight to a tavern before hitting their army bunks. William Busby booked into the Shaftesbury Hotel, as did several officers from other regiments and after dinner he *"took a walk through town which was dark and very full of soldiers..."*

The entrenching course was run by Royal Engineers, recently returned from the front. Its purpose was quickly to impart enough knowledge to enable the students to pass on at least some of its mysteries to the rest of the Hammers. Early the next morning the course commenced at Plassey Barracks, with nineteen attending, only seven of whom were officers. With overtones of the situation in France the course instructor informed the class that it was *"likely to be over by Saturday as no explosives were available"*. Then, following a lecture, the class were issued *"canvas suits and a bag of tools"* before setting off to a field some fifteen minutes walk away where they *"dug a trench"*. This was a fairly typical 'basics' course for a recently raised New Army battalion. Over the following days they had further lectures on the scheme of trenches followed by more practical work digging communication trenches and building dugouts, loopholes, shelters, revetments and support trenches.

Busby learnt things which would have been commonplace to a military engineer like his Commanding Officer's direct ancestor David Papillon of the 17th century: fascines, hurdles, gabions and obstacles. These days, however, they were all adorned by that curse of the modern industrialised battlefield – barbed wire. The sessions were long, with work commencing at *"7am until tea at 5pm"*. William Busby did manage to have a *"pleasant and sociable"* lunch one afternoon, with the bonus of *"cider and cigars"* after watching a Scout display.

By the Saturday, the course finished with a lecture on mine warfare and trench sapping before they drew their travel warrants for the journey back to London. Busby returned to the Shaftesbury Hotel, *"settled up hotel bill (£2 -7/8d) and took cab to the station. Caught 4pm train and [...] on my arrival at Stratford I had tea at Lyons before home..."*

The newly promoted Lt Robert Swan was made Adjutant, replacing Captain Mullock, who was re-assigned elsewhere in the Essex Regiment. Swan was rapidly becoming a noticeably bad tempered officer, responsible for a near mutiny in Busby's No14 platoon of D Company after trying to rearrange the men with another platoon. D Company's commander, Captain Harford, was forced to step in and smooth things over, successfully so, and the pals in No14 platoon remained as they wished. Throughout training Busby was personally pulled up, at least twice, by Swan for some petty breach of the King's Regulations or another, in one case for wearing his slippers in the mess. Somewhat poignantly, Busby also had the sad task of digging a hole in the back garden at Sherrard Road to bury his dog Caesar. The old scruffy mongrel had become progressively unwell when Busby left for the entrenching course and he had found Caesar dead one early morning soon after his return. Promotions came through, with the rank of Lieutenant confirmed for Swan's good friend and fellow Malay rubber planter JD Paterson. The Mayor's son Leo Dyer had enlisted and was naturally quickly promoted along with the two Robinson brothers and Harry Handley Sharman, a well known and respected local man, regarded as something of a character in the Borough. He had seen active service in the Boer War as a Sergeant in the Essex with five clasps on his Queens South Africa Medal. In civilian life he was vice-president of the North West Ham Conservative Association and had been a member of the Executive Committee for the previous twelve years. His Commission in the Hammers was another personally sanctioned by the Mayor.

This period in April saw a major reorganisation of Kitcheners' New Armies and in the shake up the 33rd Division, with its double-three domino emblem, was created. It consisted almost entirely of newly formed units raised by public subscriptions and private initiatives. It was somewhat varied in the background of the citizen soldiers who formed its ranks. 'Public Schools' and 'Empire' battalions, together with 'Church Lads' and 'Footballers' were all London units drawn from the volunteers of the Royal Fusiliers and the Middlesex Regiments. This brave, but desperate, union of 'amateurs' did not fill the old regular soldiers of the BEF with much confidence. Meanwhile, on Saturday April 17th, while William Busby played billiards with Sharman and Buxton in the Mess at the Alexandra Hotel, the Stratford Express carried the following poem. It was signed JAD, who may well have been a member of the Dyer family

<u>To our West Ham Battalion</u>

*Men of West Ham's Battalion
you've answered your country's call.
You are ready and willing to do your bit
to hasten a tyrants fall.*

You heard the cry of the wounded,
you shed your tears for the dead.
God give you the strength to fight as well
when the final word is said.

Now is the time for action.
You've done a while with play.
We watch you march with hearts of pride,
in your soldierly array.

For the Honour of the Borough,
we know you'll do your best.
To prove you are men of mettle,
when your courage is put to the test.

Many there are amongst you,
who will play a Hero's part.
Leaving behind an honoured name
and a place in every heart.

Our hopes and thoughts are with you,
be upright, be brave, be true.
Men of the West Ham Battalion,
here's our "best respects to you".

Another route march took place on the 21st after some physical drill on Wanstead Flats. Their journey took them to Manor Park via High Street North to Barking. They then marched proudly along Green Street and passed West Ham Utd's Boleyn Ground before taking the Barking Road to Stratford and back to Wanstead Flats. This was followed by shooting (which William Busby noted was poor) and more physical drill which caused one of the recruits, Pte Pullen in C Company, to have an epileptic fit. He was a nineteen year old baker but for now his training was over.

Their transformation from civilians to soldiers continued as terrifying 'shop riots' broke out locally, with a large number of foreign owned businesses targeted, smashed and looted. Badly hit was John Hoebig's shop in Green Street as well as the family home of Otto Wiedecke and Karl Goebals shop in the Barking Road. People stole everything, from cash and commodities through to curtains and cutlery. Even a caged parrot was taken. Mr Schaumloffel had his bakery in Romford Road ransacked and all his flour stocks stolen by his neighbours. This was despite having two sons away fighting for England in the war, one of whom had just lost an arm. The following month he changed the family name by deed poll to Boreham. During the week of court appearances for the many looters who were rounded up by the police, the magistrate Mr Gillespie suggested that *"a West Ham Juvenile Battalion of Thieves should be raised"* owing to the number of defendants who claimed it was their children who had looted the properties all over the borough. The caged parrot appeared as evidence in one case, with its bad language causing loud laughter in the public gallery and from the bench.

Some of the volunteers were equally having second thoughts about just what exactly they had committed themselves to. The Police Gazette urged constables to be on the look out for *"C Baldwin, 38yrs, 5' 3¼", Born - Poplar. Complexion - Fresh. Hair – Brown. Eyes - Blue. Enlisted - 24/2/15, Canning Town. Deserted - 11/5/15, Stratford. Scar left knee."* John Buckley, a nineteen year old van guard from Bethnal Green (*"scar right hand and foot"*) and thirty-three year old WA Green, a tattooed sailor, were on the same wanted list for desertion from the West Ham Battalion.

Finally, the time came to leave the Borough. Sunday 16th May 1915 was a bright morning as the Hammers paraded beneath their home-made Colour on Wanstead Flats for the last time. Many thousands turned out to hear the service conducted by the Rt Rev Thomas Stevens. As Bishop of Barking he had been based at St Luke's Church since 1901 and over the years had married many of the men and christened their children. Also present were the West Ham Brigade of the Royal Artillery. A lesson was read by Mayor Henry Dyer and the hymns were accompanied by the combined bands of the East Anglian Artillery Brigade and of the former Thames Ironworks.

No doubt there were a few present who whispered dark humoured jokes about the Mayor, pointing out the irony of his longstanding business in Woodgrange Road. Since the end of the previous century Henry Dyer, the man who had called them to war, was a relatively successful undertaker with two of his four sons working as coffin and headstone makers.

Chapter 6

"Like A Joyous Crowd of Excursionists"

The next two days saw a flurry of activity as they packed stores and equipment, ready to move to the next phase of training. There was also the last minute tattooing of "*I love...*" on the arm, or a chest of Britannia. Some went for a simple "*mother*".

It was pouring with rain as each Company paraded at Brickfields with all personal equipment. William Busby was despatched to Stanford's in Covent Garden's Long Acre to purchase maps of the Brentwood area while Frank Keeble was sent with a personal guard, from leafy Stratford through Bow into the overcrowded and rough and noisy alleyways of Mile End, Stepney and Poplar. Although not part of the borough, many of the recruits came from these areas as well as Leyton, Walthamstow, Clapton and Hackney. Keeble's task was to pay off the rents on the billets some of the men had been staying at but up until now, he had only really known the open fields and slow paced villages of a country life on the farm in Brantham. It was natural for him to feel altogether nervous and rather vulnerable, being totally aware by sheer weight alone, of the value in the bag of gold sovereigns he was carrying.

On Wednesday 19th May 1915, the Hammers prepared to finally leave Stratford, having said their farewells to tearful loved ones. For many of them, assembled in their smart khaki outside the Grove at 9am, it was the start of a great adventure. For most came the awesome realisation that life would never be quite the same again. They had all been informed that there would be no leave throughout training and, on the balance of probabilities, none before going to war. With rifles slung and packs full of parcels from home, they formed up. A large bustling crowd of relatives and well wishers had gathered to see them off and, together with the soldiers, began a bit of a "knees up", singing and dancing. One Stratford Express reporter commented that *"they appeared more like a joyous crowd of excursionists than that of a Battalion of fighting men with such stern work before them..."* It was a glorious spring morning and their spirits were high at the thought of a thirteen mile march to their new HQ at Brentwood. At 10am, the Drum and Bugle Band burst forth with martial music as Henry Dyer, honorary Colonel of the West Ham Battalion proudly took his place alongside Papillon at the head of the column. Swinging round in front of the town hall the huge crowd gave them a tumultuous send off. Flags and handkerchiefs were waved amid unprecedented scenes of joy and sadness.

Thousands had lined the streets to say goodbye to 'their' boys. The men marched easily, almost strolling, as they puffed their pipes and cigarettes and joined in with the singing of the crowds gathered to watch them pass.

They were also accompanied for part of the way by the former mayor, now councillor, William Crow. As they reached the borough boundary the civic dignitaries stood aside and Henry Dyer took the salute as they marched past *"to take their place in history"*. For some time a few of the wives and sweethearts tried to keep up and one young son was even noted as carrying his father's rifle for a distance. Eventually the swinging crunching stride got too much and one by one the last of them fell behind. With a final tearful wave they watched the Hammers march smartly out of sight.

Following a brief halt just outside Romford they marched through without stopping. The men were still in good spirits and attracting large crowds as they sang and imitated the market cries, *"both human and bovine"* as a bystander was noted to remark. Oranges and *"liquid refreshment"* were handed to the troops, causing the NCO's to cover many extra miles up and down the column making sure the men remained sober.

Once at Brentwood they were housed by section, platoon and company in wooden huts hastily erected by the Royal Engineers. It seemed that every open space in the area was occupied by the army. With such a diversity of characters now living close together full-time, the structure and dynamics of groups quickly developed. Natural leaders, fast learners or incessant moaners emerged and, as they became intimate with each other's strengths and weaknesses, they became extremely jealous about the reputation of their particular hut. The Hammers settled down quickly to hard training, in Weald and Thorndon Parks, open spaces ideally suited for manoeuvres and the digging of dummy trenches. Larger scale exercises were then performed with these rudimentary trenches being attacked, defended and then re-dug. The trench warfare being seen in this war was not totally unknown, being widely practiced in the American Civil War and more recently in the Russo-Japanese War at the turn of the century. Field craft continued with particular attention paid to first aid training and there was great excitement when a few rifles arrived and weapons training commenced. There were open air lectures on various aspects of modern combat such as trench construction and wiring, the most popular from soldiers recently returned from France. The second Battle of Ypres had just been fought and a sinister facet of warfare had been introduced - poison gas. The basic principles of gas defence were explained in attentive silence.

Though known for its local beauty spots, it would seem that the toil and sweat of the military training left the men with little inclination to appreciate the finer points of country life. On May 29th a local reporter wrote that *"so far there seems every reason to expect that the men from West Ham will find Brentwood as an all round pleasant place to be quartered at. There is one fact that is somewhat puzzling, and that is that these "Londoners" do not seem to appreciate the country beauty of the district. Coming from a district like West Ham it would have seemed almost certain that the change from the dust and noise and the grim activity of the streets to the clean glowing beauty of the lanes and fields and leafy walks would have delighted the men but so far as can be judged from the way the soldiers amuse themselves off duty the appeal of the beauties of nature is limited to a comparatively few..."*

The reporter seems to have misjudged the nature of the men and certainly appears to have no concept of exactly what is required after rigorous military training in the hot summer sun. However, he goes on, with some increasing enlightenment, to remember that "*of course a large part of the day is taken up by drills or route marches which tire the body and do not leave a great deal of opportunity or inclination for walks in the country. The men are not on a holiday and perhaps are not in a holiday mood. They are separated from the conditions of their ordinary life and from their homes and families in most cases and no doubt their hearts are still in the main at West Ham...*"

Naturally, not everyone was entirely comfortable with this transition from the civilian to army way of doing things. Pte JJ Da Costa was found drunk on duty at 1.30pm on the 9th of June and placed on a charge. By the 12th June something had caused him to go AWOL for a couple of days and he was placed on a further charge. John Jacob Da Costa had enlisted at Stratford on March 4th, leaving his wife Leah and two very young children behind. Twenty-two year old Da Costa was one of a handful of Jewish members of the battalion, living in Calverly Street, Mile End. It was once a thriving Jewish area and today, after the slums were demolished, the location of the Ocean Estate. It was the same address given by his fellow recruit Pte Nathaniel Isaacs.

While dealing with petty incidents such as Da Costa's, Papillon took time to write to the editor of the Stratford Express to send *"our gratitude for the unfailing kindness and courtesy that has always been extended to us in the Borough... West Ham will always be the home of the Battalion, and in leaving it we feel that we are leaving a host of friends, old and new, behind us. Wherever we go or whatever may befall us it will be the earnest endeavour of one and all to show ourselves worthy of the kind and generous treatment which we have received."*

Papillon was pleased with his battalion and he liked his officers. They each had *something*. He could chat about the 'old days' with the Boer veterans, hear stories of fearless head-hunters in the Malay jungles or about new railways laid on the wild inhospitable frontiers of Canada. Some shared a passion for archaeology and enjoyed the story of how he dug up a carved ivory Roman gladiator, while living as a youth at his uncle's manor house in Lexden. Today the gladiator is on display at the British Museum after Papillon donated it to the nation in 1911. Meanwhile Frank Keeble, the farmer's son, shared a passion for history, especially English military. He was fascinated by the epics of Agincourt and the wars with France, battlefields of yesteryear being fought for again by Englishmen. Over cigars and drinks in the Mess, Papillon would naturally describe the first member of his persecuted Huguenot family to reach sanctuary in England: Thomas Papillon, the personal bodyguard to the French King Henri IV.

Training was still a dangerous process and thirty year old 2/Lt Alfred George Buxton, had a serious accident when he was thrown from the horse he was learning to ride and fractured the base of his skull. Buxton was formerly the assistant manager of the Stratford Empire and was good friends with his Alexandra Mess snooker partners William Busby and Frank Trumble (who was himself having continued trouble with his feet and about to get married). The three officers, all in D Company, had regularly billeted together but Buxton never went to France. He made a slow recovery, eventually moving to the newly created Royal Air Force with the rank of Captain, working as an administrator at the Air Ministry until the end of the war.

On Friday June 4th Busby took a car and drove with Dr Holthusen to Warley military hospital. There they visited the ten members of the Hammers who had become significantly ill after their inoculations and general fitness improvements. Naturally, the doctor took along a suitable comfort to aid their recovery: plenty of untipped cigarettes. Not uncommonly, two of the West Ham men actually died during this initial training period, from illness or disease, the first being Pte William Sarling from Brighton Road, buried in East Ham cemetery back in February. Now in June, Pte Harry James Newell from Barking died at the hospital and was buried close to the Essex Regiment church in Gt Warley. By September, Pte Stanley Steward had also died. He lies buried in Leyton St Mary churchyard.

Away from the rows of huts occupied by the 'other ranks', many of the officers were living at the surrounding farms. Frank Keeble, no doubt feeling very at home, had been billeted with some of the other officers from B Company at Sawyer's Farm. From here he wrote home to his parents relating one of the many practical jokes he was to become known for. Renting a donkey for the night from a local man he had met walking in the street, Keeble somehow coaxed it upstairs undetected to one of the bedrooms and tied it to the foot of a bed. He doesn't reveal who the joke was played on. He then retired to his own room and at about two in the morning the other officers returned, discovering in the darkness "*a fearful mess and the donkey started to kick. They had to leave it on the landing all night...*"

On the 1st July 1915 news came that the War Office had officially taken over the administration of the West Ham Battalion and that they were destined for a division assembling in the midlands. With the news came the rest of their weapons, Rifles no1 or more precisely the .303 calibre Short Magazine Lee Enfield ('SMLE'), with which the old British Expeditionary Force had wrought such a heavy toll on the advancing Germans last November. There were enough weapons for each individual soldier. There were also notifications of some well deserved promotions and JD Paterson was made Captain. A very popular officer, the news was well received by the men, in stark contrast to his friend Robert Swan. As Adjutant, Swan was annoying many of the men through his increasing irritability and short temper, brought on by his sudden change from a tropical climate in Malaya which resulted in insomnia and malaria attacks. 2/Lt's Carson, Trumble, Lang and Collier were all made full Lieutenants in the West Ham Battalion.

Reginald Howell, a new arrival from St Leonards in Sussex, had transferred in to the Hammers at that rank. He was the younger half-brother of D Company's commanding officer, Captain Harford and his father's construction company was responsible for most of the best buildings in Hastings. Another popular character, Reg quickly made friends with officers and men alike.

In the middle of this hot July, as JJ Da Costa went missing for the second time, the Hammers completed their first stage of infantry training and prepared to leave the 'leafy lanes' of Brentwood. Onboard two special troop trains they set off for the Midlands and the next phase of their preparations for France. There were emotional scenes as they made a slow deliberate diversion through Stratford.

The steam engines hissed as they halted for a few moments. At the trackside the Mayor and other notables said farewells, wished good lucks and gave more than three cheers. Families had made it there and were lining bridges, filling pavements and leaning from open windows, all waving hankies and flags. As the train whistles pierced the air with the shrill impatient signal of final departure, people pressed their noses harder through the railings. A thundercloud of black smoke and sparks ejected powerfully from the engine's stack and the great wheels began to turn in slow synchronisation. In the billows of gritty silver steam many had tear-filled eyes.

They now searched for a last glimpse of husbands, sons, fathers and brothers.

Chapter 7

Familiar Faces

On the 1st August 1915 the Hammers moved to Clipstone Camp outside Mansfield, one of the centres for advanced infantry training.

Clipstone was a massive army camp consisting of row upon row of stout wooden huts built three months earlier to house the New Army men. The previously peaceful Nottinghamshire countryside was alive with soldiers on route marches, digging trenches and practising on the many new rifle ranges. In common with army camps the world over, Clipstone also provided a purpose for those residents living nearby and the soldiers 'welfare' was looked after by local businesses keenly aware of the spending power of more than thirty-thousand men. At Clipstone, the Hammers were noted as being in *"fine physical condition"*. Their arrival completed the 100th Brigade of the 33rd Division. The three other battalions making up their Brigade had already arrived and were also raised by public subscription:

16th (Service) Battalion (*"Public Schools"*), Middlesex Regiment
16th (Service) Battalion (*"Church Lads Brigade"*), Kings Royal Rifle Corps
17th (Service) Battalion (*"1st Footballers"*), Middlesex Regiment

The "Footballers" and the West Ham men formed a natural affinity. In fact they knew each other *very* well. Many of the West Ham Battalion were regulars on the terraces of the Boleyn Ground and some of West Ham United's first generation of fiercely loyal supporters. The Footballers were formed from the volunteers of professional football, including the entire first team of Clapton (later, after relocation, Leyton) Orient. They knew just how intimidating the Hammers could be on match day but the two battalions were to be inseparable throughout the dark days to come, up to their eventual disbandment together in 1918. The divisional artillery meanwhile was raised in Camberwell and the engineers were volunteers from Tottenham - a London division in every sense of the word. The Hammers had also been followed north by a local man, JM Flatan of Ley Street in Ilford. He had been photographing the battalion since they were in initial training at Wanstead and the vast majority of the surviving images feature his name. With his cumbersome equipment and chemical powder 'flash', he set up numerous shots outside tents and huts as well as the barber's shop, and did a roaring trade.

It was here at Clipstone that one of the West Ham Battalion received frightening news which clearly underlined exactly what he and the others had volunteered to fight against. Thirty-eight year old Pte Henry William Banks was an insurance collector with the British Legal Assurance Company based in New Oxford Street. He had previously served before the war with the City of London artillery and lived with his wife and six children along Ashville Road in Leyton.

On the 17th August a German P-class Zeppelin, numbered L10 and commanded by Oberleutnant Friedrich Wenke, dropped a number of explosive and incendiary bombs on Leyton. From two miles high at about 22.40pm, he wrecked Ashville Road, killing two people, badly damaging thirty houses and blowing out the windows of nearly a hundred and thirty others in the street. Several roads on either side were equally terrorised, with four more Leyton civilians indiscriminately killed. In total that night, Wenke's attack on east London killed seven men, two women and a young child, seriously injured forty-eight and caused over £30,000 of damage. Henry Banks family, bombed out, were forced to relocate to a property in nearby Murchison Road. Wenke and his crew were themselves killed on another mission a couple of weeks later when lightning ignited leaking hydrogen above Cuxhaven.

Elsewhere, Pte JJ Da Costa had now gone missing a total of three times. Military life obviously wasn't suiting him. On his return (or capture) he was sent into the hands of the Mayor's son Captain Leo Dyer back at the Hammers depot who immediately sent him for a stricter punishment regime at the military prison in Colchester. From there, Da Costa was sent up to Paisley in Scotland to work for a couple of hazardous months at Doulton's & Co making TNT.

Following intensive infantry training the whole Division moved once more to Perham Down near Ludgershall on Salisbury Plain on 18th August for final divisional training. It was perched on the easternmost part of the Salisbury Plain training area amid the folds of the Wiltshire hills. They trained hard and this was primarily of 'musketry' practice. Not surprisingly, the standard of shooting was far below that of the regular army and it remained a problem throughout the war but every soldier had to pass through the three week firing course without exception. As winter approached, the weather-board huts of the camp let in draughts as the early snow flurries began and there were frequent windswept route marches along the ancient Packway. Their spirits were warmed by the news that West Ham Utd had beaten Millwall Athletic 2-1, in front of twelve-thousand spectators at the Boleyn Ground on October 30th.

At the beginning of a chilly November a letter was sent to Papillon regarding Pte Walter Stevens of C Company, a tea packer from Holme Road in East Ham who had enlisted back in April at Stratford. His mother Nellie, writing from the family home, informed Papillon that not only had Walter added a couple of years to his actual age but he was also *"blind after being hit with a bottle"* a few years before and *"I do not want him to go to the foreign service..."* On the 3rd November the medical officer, Alan Holthusen, confirmed to the newly appointed Adjutant Frank Trumble that *"Stevens is not fit for service overseas"* being *"blind in the left eye with only a perception of light"* and also *"obviously underage..."* To have come so far, it is likely that Stevens would have passionately pleaded his case. Despite small discrepancies like this, the Hammers had become a fine fighting force and Papillon sent a telegram to the West Ham Council expressing his feelings, which perhaps encapsulates the era: *"Please convey to the Mayor, Aldermen, and Burgesses the warmest thanks of all ranks of the West Ham Battalion for their good wishes. We shall all do our best to prove worthy of the great Borough from which we were raised and of the many kindnesses received from all classes in it..."*

With the conclusion of infantry training in mid-November, during which they had been joined by 2/Lt Hitch as a replacement for the hospitalised Buxton, they were at last considered fit for a role alongside the other Kitchener volunteer battalions in France. There were nine-hundred and ninety-three men with twenty-nine officers making up the fighting strength and, somehow *"on the decision of GR Aldridge"* from Eastern Command (and clearly against his mother's wishes) even included the one-eyed Walter Stevens, in another example of their close camaraderie.

The remainder, the Depot Company, were to stay behind, forming a nucleus who would initially be supplying local men as replacements to The Hammers as required. Their ranks included 2/Lt's William and Joseph Robinson and they were all under the command of Captain Leo Dyer. He wouldn't be going to France. No doubt his father, the Mayor, was deeply disappointed.

On the cold grey morning of November 15th 1915, at Clipstone Camp on Perham Down, Papillon read a despatch from the War Office informing him that the West Ham Battalion was ordered to France. He immediately summoned the officers to his quarters and informed them personally. No record remains of exactly what was said but Pelham Papillon was a man of some considerable style and, it is believed, produced a case of champagne that he had kept for precisely this occasion. The 'gentlemen' gave a toast: to the King, the Mayor, the Borough and loudest of all to the West Ham Battalion.

The 'great adventure' had begun.

Chapter 8

A Bad Omen

When any unit or battalion of the British army entered the theatre of war it was, and still is, required to keep a daily intelligence summary, commonly referred to as the war diary. This records the life of a battalion, its location, role, casualty numbers and anything else the author feels inclined to detail. For those of us looking at documents years later we are indebted to the battalion Adjutant, whose duties include 'signing off' this record. In this, the Hammers were well served. As the Adjutant, Captain Frank Trumble was responsible for the front line administration of the battalion. Growing up in Trumpington Road, Wanstead he married his sweetheart, Lottie Maher from St George's Avenue in Forest Gate, just after the Hammers left London for their initial training in May. Trumble was a precise and organised officer, a municipal clerk and the son of a local Magistrate.

However, in the case of the West Ham Battalion, we are particularly indebted to the Assistant Adjutant, who was *usually* sitting a distance from the trenches and for the Hammers this position was held by Corporal FA Jenns, an 'Other Rank, Clerk'. Although this highly important and deeply confidential role was always to be undertaken by an officer with a minimum rank of 2/Lt, Frank Arthur Jenns was somehow appointed as Assistant Adjutant. He was clearly 'officer material' but had enlisted late in the Hammers in June at Stratford (after the last of the 'Temporary' Commissions was filled by Reg Norman) and the initial training was well underway. Twenty-three year old Jenns was the son of a plasterer and had grown up surrounded by sisters in Toronto Avenue, Manor Park. When his father died, the family moved to Shelley Avenue. Now, since his enlistment, there was little income back home and his youngest sister was full time carer to his invalid mother who was barely surviving on her small widow pension. Frank Jenns worked as a clerk before joining the Hammers and, to unofficially hold the position of assistant Adjutant, he must have been exceptional. This is borne out in lengthy military reports showcasing his flawless typing. Whatever the reason for his appointment, Captain Trumble was quite happy to delegate a number of tasks which would usually be performed by him. Consequently, Jenns set the standards for the West Ham Battalion war diary. Hand written in waterproof pencil, often under artillery fire at least, occasionally in the front line action itself and sometimes days after the event, Jenns knew many of the men personally. If he was tasked with the mundane chore of double checking the letter censoring, he also knew them intimately.

This is reflected in the fact that for roughly the first year, virtually every soldier of the West Ham Battalion wounded or killed was individually named and numbered by Jenns in the war diary, sometimes including detail of the circumstances. This is a highly unusual and an extremely rare commitment in war diaries during the Great War. At the same time, just like the fact that Jenns was only a corporal, it was also *totally* contrary to army convention. However, it must be said that it was most likely approved by Captain Trumble and was perhaps even on the orders of Papillon.

On 16th November 1915, Frank Jenns commenced the war diary of the 13th (Service) Battalion (West Ham), the Essex Regiment. In it he, and at times others, recorded the excitement, tedium, the pride and sadness during the long, hard struggle 'for civilisation' ahead. On this day, the first departures for France were made by the advance party, consisting of four officers and one hundred and twenty-four other ranks, commanded by Captain Samuel 'Dick' Collier. Lately working at his father's brickworks in Marks Tey, Collier was chosen to ensure the Hammers had transport, supplies and billets on their arrival in France. It was his unenviable task to find accommodation and further transport for more than a thousand West Ham men.

This was no mean feat considering the transport officers for the rest of the entire Division were doing likewise. Captain Collier was accompanied by forty-six year old Lt Robert Shrapnel Biddulph-Pinchard, formerly a 'breaker' of the many thousands of 'remount' horses being taken from their regular roles and sent to the front. He was allegedly responsible for a nocturnal six-hundred head stampede of nags, mules and thoroughbreds through the streets of Southampton in the summer. After this incident he was appointed to the Hammers as a Lieutenant at the end of September. On the other horse drawn wagons was Lt Gilbert Simpson from Osbourne Road in Forest Gate and 2/Lt George Harry Ross from Sussex. They were joined at the last minute by the former Prudential agent Lt Norman Lang, whose organisational skills working alongside Lt Tom Brind, the Quartermaster, were proving to be invaluable.

In among the 'other ranks' of the party were carmen like thirty-eight year old Pte Joe Cooper from Limehouse, one of the innumerable older volunteers being commanded by twenty year olds. Joe was very experienced with his horse and cart in his usual job transporting cargos from the West India Docks and Regents Canal. Alongside Joe Cooper was the larger than life character of Company Sergeant Major George Cattermole. With many years service in the Royal Navy as a Chief Petty Officer, Cattermole had immediately volunteered in response to Henry Dyer's appeal. His previous experience, of keeping the navy 'matelots' in order, had resulted in his swift appointment as a Warrant Officer in the Hammers. Hugely popular with the men he would become an extremely effective leader in the field. There was a powdering of snow as the Advance Party left Ludgershall Station, en route for Southampton where they boarded a requisitioned ship and steamed through the cold squalls to the chaotically busy port of Havre on the coast of France. For Joe Cooper, it was his first ever time abroad. For Conradin Donatz, the J. Lyons tea waiter from Walthamstow, it was his first return to mainland Europe for several years. He was in the Advance Party due to his fluent French but it's hard not to wonder at his thoughts as he leant on the rail and watched his adopted country disappear in the sleet.

Back in Britain, at six in the morning on 17th November 1915, the rest of the West Ham Battalion paraded for war. In the freezing pre dawn light of Salisbury Plain, they formed up on the square. Ernie Kurtz, the battalion tailor, had been up since *"3.30am. The morning was dark and we had a heavy frost a few days previously. The ground had been beaten up by the* [horse drawn] *transports, so you can guess what we had to tramp over... I had a full pack, 120 rounds of ammunition, a greatcoat and a blanket... I can tell you honestly, when we were on parade that early morning, my thoughts were that I'd never return to old England again..."* Each man was individually inspected, had his hand firmly shaken and was wished good luck by Papillon. Many of the men had removed the wire stiffener from their caps in the style of the 'Old Contemptables' of the BEF, but this transgression was overlooked. It gave the caps a curiously rumpled look, but more importantly it also made them infinitely more comfortable. The steel 'shrapnel' helmet had not yet been introduced. Scrubbed and cherubic faces stood with weather worn older ones. Men who less than a year ago were strangers to each other, interspersed with numerous sets of brothers and in a few cases cousins too, underlining the all embracing nature of what it meant to be there.

Jenns records twenty-six officers and eight-hundred and sixty-nine 'other ranks' on parade that morning, volunteers in the truest sense. They were laughing and singing as they marched, rifles slung, out of the gates of Perham Down camp as the crisp and chilly dawn broke over the ancient barrows of Salisbury Plain. The steady crunch of boots, muffled slightly by fresh snow, echoed on the quiet walls of Ludgershall village. The men were hoping to march through the town receiving, as Ernie Kurtz put it, *"the adulation befitting heroes"* from the residents. This was, after all, still a great adventure for civilians too and the local people gave any front bound soldier's presents such as tobacco, pipes, socks and any other small items that could be easily stuffed in a pocket or a pouch. However, being, as Ernie thought, *"the unlucky thirteenth"*, they reached the little railway station uncelebrated and boarded a train bound for Folkestone, arriving at the harbour at midday. With the troop trains running up alongside the quay the West Ham boys were ushered straight to the waiting troopship.

Some chattered excitedly as they filed up the gangplanks to board the passenger steamship Princess Victoria, recently requisitioned from Canadian waters. Though still bitterly cold, the weather had brightened a little as the men lined the rails on deck to watch for submarines. For fifteen year old Frank Eade and his Leyton neighbourhood friend James Fleming, this was indeed part of the great adventure. A few had travelled halfway round the world just to be here at this moment. The escort of fast cruisers and Royal Navy craft standing off Folkestone harbour were kept busy countering the audacious German U-Boat fleet who, in their turn, were hunting the heavily laden and vulnerable troopships. Shortly before 12pm the signal was given for the crossing to start. The gang planks were hauled in and the Princess Victoria slowly pushed off.

She was soon delayed in her journey to allow the hospital ship Anglia to enter port. Commanded by Captain Lionel J Manning, the HS Anglia was returning from France full of evacuated wounded. In a sudden flash she struck a mine, laid earlier by the German submarine UC-5. Captain Manning was blown from the bridge to the deck below in the explosion but regained his senses long enough to order the lowering of lifeboats. The Anglia began to sink extremely quickly and bow first as one hundred and twenty-nine lives were lost. Ships and boats made frantic efforts to assist in the rescue. One was sunk by yet another mine, although without any further loss of life. With this unsettling welcome to the war for the Hammers, SS Princess Victoria resumed steaming her slow passage as a sea fog began to obscure the English coastline.

All eyes strained for their first glimpse of France as they steamed into Boulogne at 6pm. Ernie Kurtz would *"never forget the scene. The lights from the town as we came across the dark waters looked magnificent. As soon as we got off the boat we were surrounded by French girls. They were selling apples and when we heard their lingo, well you can guess what Tommies are!"* The disembarkation was hurriedly completed and the men formed up on the quay amid scenes of absolute chaos. The place was bustling and alive with uniformed men, both French and British. A roll call of sorts was attempted before the West Ham men marched up through the town past the grey and imposing old walls once besieged by English troops under Henry VIII, to Ostrohove Camp at the top of the hill. Any modern traveller will testify it is not an easy climb. With rifles, ammunition and personal equipment it was excruciating *"and well we knew it as we were going up! It nearly broke my heart. Our Officers were doing their best to cheer us"* but Ernie Kurtz was *"cussing the Froggies!"* Their destination was an immense staging area. Ostrohove Camp consisted of rows and rows of large white canvas bell tents, the kind that only the army can put up. Billeted by section, the West Ham men spent their first night on French soil.

At 6am on the 19th November they paraded and marched to Pont De Briques to meet the Advance Party and the battalion transports. Captain Dick Collier reported the next stage of their journey to Papillon, and the Hammers made their way to Thiennes station to travel by train to the Division assembly area just outside the little town of St Omer, on the Aa river. The town was a locally famous beauty spot before the war but had since been transformed into the busy central hub of organised chaos, acting as the main staging area for the BEF in France and Flanders. The Hammers journey to St Omer was typical but not very comfortable yet morale was still cheerfully high. No doubt Captain Collier and Lt Brind were relieved when they all finally arrived without incident.

New units fresh off the boat were commonly attached for instruction to Divisions already there and the West Ham Battalion would now begin to experience combat training in the most effective way possible, at the front and under fire. Among many other things, they lacked the ability to be 'handy', an army euphemism for being resourceful and determinedly innovative to improve their daily lives in the trenches. The atrocious condition of some sectors taken over from New Army units had been commented on by many old soldiers. Now the Hammers began re-learning trench construction & maintenance, but under field conditions. They were also brought up to speed in the use of trench mortars, together with the fighting essentials of sniping and 'bombing' - the term at the time for simple grenade throwing. Old Divisions of the regular British army were fast losing their original character altogether, a fact that was causing a simmering resentment amongst the regular soldiers. Battalions and even whole Brigades were being transferred over to the New Army Divisions, *'spreading the knowledge'*. On the 24th November 1915, the Hammer's 33rd veterans' Division was shuffled with one of the most famous of the original BEF divisions, the "Old Contemptibles". They had held the line at Mons and were in the thick of the subsequent fighting at Landrecies, the Marne, the Aisne, Ypres, Neuve Chapelle, Festubert and Loos. Now, the reorganisation of the army to incorporate the Kitchener 'civilian' men had seen the Hammers and the Footballers transferred in. Throughout the army, similar moves met with almost universal condemnation from the regular army men.

The West Ham Battalion moved from St Omer, via stops at billets in Boeseghein and La Pierriere. The journey to Bethune was completed on foot. William Busby flatly stated in his personal diary that the *"sound of the guns"* was reached but he was most likely exhibiting a certain degree of artistic licence. The guns would have been heard when they had landed at Boulogne. Busby had not been so far impressed with *"la belle France"*, regarding Bethune as *"the best I have seen but dirty compared with English towns..."*

Bethune was a large industrial town, the major railhead and staging area behind the lines for this sector of northern France. Billeted in the old tobacco factory, the men happily amused themselves, filling pipe pouches and chatting to those recently out of the line. The following day morale remained high as the Hammers marched out of the town en route for the support trenches at Essars and towards their first taste of life on the Western Front. The 'Front' at this point had by now settled into a four-hundred mile system of opposing trench lines stretching from the beaches of the North Sea coast to the Swiss border. It was far from simply being a fortified ditch. It was an elaborate defence in depth and the system developed by the British army was of three 'lines' and each was distinct in its role: the Reserve Line, the Support Line and then the actual Front Line with barbed wire facing out into No Man's Land. On the other side were the enemy trenches.

Sometimes less than twenty-five yards away, sometimes as much as half a mile, it was usually around two-hundred and fifty yards, roughly two football pitches, separating the combatants.

Chapter 9

Baptism

As they trudged towards the frontline for the first time the West Ham Battalion was officially transferred into the 2nd Division as part of 6th Brigade commanded by Boer War veteran Brigadier-General Arthur Daly. From now on, they were seldom out of the line. The Brigade consisted of:

13th Battalion, the Essex Regiment
17th Battalion, the Middlesex Regiment
1st Battalion, the Liverpool Regiment
2nd Battalion, the South Staffordshire Regiment

The Hammers were serving alongside their fellow Kitchener New Army Battalion of the Footballers while the two regular army 'Old Contemptible' battalions were the King's (Liverpool Regiment) and the South Staffords. An unlikely grouping on the face of it and what the French translators made of the accents is anyone's guess, but as a unit 6th Brigade worked superbly from the outset.

10th December 1915 was yet another day of icy rain in their visibly aging faces. Their march slowed as they neared Cambrin before the men were broken up into small groups *"to lessen the loss of life whilst being shelled"*. With every sudden explosion they were ducking their heads and shoulders instinctively during this introduction to light shelling. Ernie Kurtz *"passed through one village which was partly demolished and burned by fire. It made me think what war was..."* Through the rear area and lines of support they gingerly moved forward, up towards their waterlogged destination the "Brickstacks". Captain JD Paterson's C Company and Major Winthrop's B Company were the first to fully experience the reality of this war. The guides took Ernie and C Company *"through the communication trench until we got onto the front line - and well we knew it, up to our thighs in mud and water! I think my heart was in my boots..."* While getting used to their surroundings in the trench a few of them had their first sight of spilt blood when L/Cpl Charlie Swinnerton was wounded by shrapnel. Field dressings were applied by nervous hands and he was taken back to Dr Holthusen's aid post by stretcher-bearers.

The Hammers began to differentiate the various sounds around them and pick up the 'lingo' describing the angry flurries of artillery barrages with nicknames for every calibre. There were 'heavies', 'coal boxes' and a multitude of others. Then there were the spiteful rifle grenades, noiseless in flight and visible as they travelled over No Man's Land in large volleys or singly. Or else there were the snipers, in competition with others out man-hunting from well chosen spots. Yet another reason to keep your head down. Along with all that, they were getting used to being extremely cold and very wet. It was all set to become a mundane element of everyday life. *"Every four hours,"* Ernie Kurtz *"and a bomber had to do a one hour guard in a sap, which is like a short trench running out towards the enemy's line. We could hear the Germans talking, so you can bet we were not far apart. It makes you feel all nerves!"*

Some time after midnight, the warm welcome of artillery slackened off and finally quietened down. Then, one last lone shell suddenly screamed in from seemingly out of nowhere. It thoroughly obliterated the space occupied by Percy Victor Price of No7 Platoon in B Company. Writing up the war diary, Frank Jenns recorded the West Ham Battalion's first casualty of the Great War. A Hertfordshire lad, originally from the village of Boxmoor, Percy had been living in Manor Park when he enlisted at the East Ham recruiting office. He was seventeen years old. His shocked platoon comrades wrapped what remained in his waterproof sheet and quietly placed him to one side, silently absorbing the harsh reality and viewing their own lives in an entirely different way to an hour before.

The following day they handed over the trenches to D Company, under the temporary command of Captain Harry Sharman, and Captain Swan's A Company. With frequent malaria attacks to contend with Swan's tour didn't go too well. Equally, the absence of D Company's usual Commander, Captain Harford, was due to an accident twenty-four hours earlier when he was knocked into a ditch by a horse. The tough, grim looking forty year old Boer war veteran was taken to a casualty clearing station ('CCS') and it was during this tour in the trenches that D Company learned his injuries were worse than at first thought. Harford was taken to base hospital and eventually, after recovery, successfully requested a posting to Brigade HQ, in view of his age. The men of B Company meanwhile, carried away Percy Price's body and then buried him in the back area, with a service conducted by the Hammer's 'padre' the Reverend Westerdale. He would have given them words of reflection and justification but he couldn't have failed to notice the shock still lingering on their faces. The war had now become very personal to B Company, as it would soon become to the rest of the Hammers in time. Sadly, the efforts to make Percy Price's plot an adequate testimony to his sacrifice were in vain. In common with thousands by the end of the war the grave was lost, most likely through a few more years of all around shelling. Today, Percy Price is one of more than twenty-thousand names carved on the Loos Memorial to the Missing.

Three days before Christmas, they marched back to Bethune and a relatively comfortable period was spent at the old tobacco factory on the edge of town. It was the time to write those first postcards home, despite most of the men now being *"varminous"*. This was one of the many words the Tommy used to describe their never ending torment of being plagued by the itchy body lice breeding contentedly in the warm seams of their uniforms and armpits and crutch. The men sung traditional carols, accompanied by the many military bands in the area. Others learned the lyrics to some of the latest trench songs, huddled around a primitive open fire in the rubble of other people's shattered lives. Despite the impact of Price's death their spirits remained quite high and they still held a wry sense of east end humour. Shortly before Christmas, a letter was written to the Stratford Express by Pte W Latham and Pte GH Scales of the battalion transport section making a request for some mouth organs, tin whistles and other musical instruments to be sent out to the West Ham men. They'd only brought their bugles and not the drums because *"Kaiser Bill's Arabs hear them coming down the 8 inch deep muddy roads and it frightens them out of their dug outs..."*

Many letters were written on this first Christmas away from home and several were published in the Stratford Express. Pte Joe Hornsby, attached to the HQ Staff and a notable boxer, wrote requesting *"a football and a set of boxing gloves to while away the time while resting..."* He went on to describe that most of their relaxation time was spent singing or playing cards. He also said that *"at XXX [censored], where we were billeted before Christmas, the Huns bombarded and are now a wreck. What a bit of luck!"*

In a letter signed simply 'WAR' (which may have been Pte Walter Richmond, the only member with these initials), an unknown Hammer wrote to the Stratford Express with his story of "*The West Ham Battalion's Fish Supper*". Printed in the Christmas Day edition he suggested that "a*s it is somewhat unusual for the Germans to do a good turn for British soldiers and, as the latter were West Ham Boys, perhaps you can spare me a little space to recount an incident in which such was the case. It happened while the West Ham Battalion were in the trenches recently and three of the battalion signallers were in receipt of the Germans' favour. We were in the cellar of a ruined house situated practically on the banks of a now famous canal, and we were exchanging jokes with some boys from a certain Highland Regiment. Heavy shrapnel shells were bursting over our heads, but no notice was taken of these until one came directly over our heads followed by a loud splash. Immediately, two of the Highlanders rushed out and we followed them to the edge of the water where we found dozens of dead and dying fish. Evidently what had happened was that the shell had gone right into the water and the shock had killed or stunned the fish.*

Anyway, we picked up enough fish to satisfy the average angler in five hours fishing! Ten minutes later, an odour was issuing from our dug out that would have turned Sam Isaacs green with envy and we did full justice to the feed that followed. Just fancy - fried fish in the trenches! Needless to say we passed a vote of thanks to the German gunner who put that shell into the canal!"

Christmas Day was spent at relative ease, though there were the usual work details unloading stores at the railhead. Letters were written and received while officers toured their commands, handed out cigarettes and promised extra rum rations from the supplies being delivered. Military rum was sealed in ceramic jars (nicknamed 'grey hens' due to their squat shape) and marked with the letters SRD – Service Rum, Dilute - though the cynical Tommy often preferred the term 'Seldom Reaches Destination', alluding to the alleged habits of those engaged in its supply. Former district-scoutmaster William Busby was certainly witness to one instance of this, noting in his personal diary that the Christmas dinner was *"not altogether a success – the cooks were drunk..."* Finally, Lt Len Holthusen, the Hammers signals officer, brought the news that so many had been anxiously waiting to hear. West Ham United had massacred Arsenal at the Boleyn's Christmas Day Southern Combination League match 8-2, a score not to be equalled against the north London club for almost a century. Sid 'Puddy' Puddefoot thumped home five of the goals in true star-striker style.

On December 27th they marched ten miles to the rear to a village called Mannqueville and rested. Captain Trumble signed off Frank Jenns final entries in the war diary for 1915 while William Busby was in a reflective mood, quietly noting his hopes *"that the end of the year finds us back in England..."*

Chapter 10

"Itching for a Smack at the Germans..."

The New Year opened on the frozen fields around Mannqueville with the Hammers training hard, practising open warfare with skirmishing and attack formations. The theory of the 'spring breakthrough' was apparently still an option, for the die hard cavalry purists at least. There were frequent exchanges of officers for short periods, between the regular and the 'service' battalions in the Brigade. The Hammers exchanged with the South Staffords while the Footballers did likewise with the Kings. A Brigade field day was held, practising an attack from the trenches. The event was carried out in atrocious weather but the results drew approval from the divisional commander and Victoria Cross winner, Major General Walker. 'Musketry' training continued, with the instructors still struggling to bring some of them up to an adequate shooting standard. There was also frequent practice with grenades, under the guidance of 'bombing officer' William Busby. As the Grenadiers of the 18th century illustrate, it was not a new aspect of warfare, but the grenade had fallen into disuse through unreliability. Redesigned and mass produced, it was back as an ideal weapon for the static warfare of the trenches and fast became another regular feature of life. There were two types in use, the 'Mills' and the 'T&P' [Time and Percussion]. Both were as safe as possible, simple to use and effective in action.

In a quieter moment, Sgt William Wilder from Plaistow found time, on the 10th January, to write a letter to his old friend and neighbour Walter Wilson living on East Street in Portway "*for some of the news you have been asking for. Well, [...] it has been rather exciting here!*

The first day we were in the support trenches and could only work at night. During the day we had to make ourselves scarce and keep in the dug-outs, excepting the sentries. Whilst we were there, the Germans started sending over a few coal boxes [a shell burst causing a lot of black smoke] *on to our Stand To billets. I stood outside and saw several drop, but for every one the Germans sent over we sent back six or seven. The next time we were in the firing line it was much the same as in the support line only we did not have dug-outs to get into... During the night our officer, myself and three men went out between our front line and the German's front line. I took six bombs in case of accidents. We only intended to be out an hour... Well, we had not been out long before we heard a lot of shouting and whistles being blown. We did not know really who it was in front of us, but it wasn't long before we found out! They sent up lights and it was not long before the Germans started opening up with rifles and machine guns. You should have seen old bill crawling about in the mud! We would do a little run and, when the lights went up, down we would go again! Just before we got to our barbed wire, I fell head over heels into a shell hole. Bombs went one way and I the other. When I scrambled up, I saw that the bombs were at the bottom of the shell hole and so I let them stay!*

We all got back eventually without anyone getting hurt. That really was my first experience of being under fire and I must say I really quite enjoyed it! If all the Germans squeal and run like those we fell in with, I don't think we need worry very much! Yesterday our guns kept a terrific bombardment all day. Goodness alone knows how many shells they sent over. The Germans sent back very few, in comparison..."

No doubt Sgt Wilder's opinions were to change in the months to come, but he was soon to win the Military Medal, one of the first of the West Ham Battalion men to receive an award for bravery in the field. He was one of Henry Dyer's first three hundred volunteers and survived the war, returning to his family in Stratford Road. He was not, however, alone in his experiences. On the same day, a letter was sent to the Stratford Express by '*a well known and respected*' (though anonymous) West Ham resident currently serving with the battalion with D Company. It might well have been William Busby. The author described how "*Capt Sharman – "Nutty" to his friends - was in command during one of the 'exciting instances', when a shell whizzed close to them and he shouted 'Down'. They threw themselves in the mud and only one was wounded. The West Ham men behave very well under fire…*" It had been the Hammers' first exposure to gas, when a couple of chlorine shells had been sent over. Harry Sharman was briefly enveloped by wisps of the noxious cloud as he ushered the men away from the affected area and yelled at them to don their rudimentary gas masks. Typically he remained 'at duty', but it quickly began to have obvious repercussions on his health.

Brigade boxing competitions and football tournaments were also being arranged. William Busby watched one match as the West Ham Battalion took on the Footballers and he recorded that '*the play was good on both sides*'. Despite hard tackles against a team of very famous professional players, the Hammers held on to lose 9-0. Meanwhile, the Stratford Express still led the cause at home. Their offices were receiving a bundle of letters from the front every day, most referring to the general lack of items such as socks and scarves which friends and relatives were asked to send out. Many of the vociferous lads manning the battalion transport re-iterated their need for mouth organs and tin whistles "*to cheer them up sitting around the old camp fire because,*" they added with a classic touch of cockney humour, "*the only music we get is from the mules who enjoy the whizzing of shells as they move up towards the front…*" Pte Arthur Giess of No10 Platoon in C Company was another joker, noting "*one thing which surprised everybody was your statement* [in the Express] *that Capt Dyer* [the Mayor's son] *had been made Major. No one will credit it! Perhaps it was a mistake on your part!*" Arthur went on to explain that "*everyone is itching for a smack at the Germans. We consider they've been rooted here long enough and if anyone can shift them, it's us!*" His brother Alfred Giess was also serving, as a Sergeant in C Company.

It would be easy in today's cynical and 'diverse' society to forget the intensely local nature of Pals' Battalions such as the Hammers, and appreciate just how important local newspapers, football results, a tin whistle or a pair of socks become to lonely lads, some of them well under age and a few clearly overage, all probably feeling a very long way from home. Young men like Pte Walter Luck of No16 Platoon in D Company, who wanted a mouth organ to "*strafe the Kultur*" by playing ragtime tunes at the enemy. Evidently homesick, he reminded Express readers that these were the lads "*as were walking down the* [Stratford] *Broadway last summer…*" Lads like Cpl Fredrick Cansdale, also of D Company, who appealed for one of '*those new fangled wrist watches*' as his pocket watch was broken in the trenches. His main concern, like corporals everywhere, was that the sentries should be relieved on time. L/Cpl Charlie Watts just wanted a pair of hair clippers. A Company too, had its aspiring writers in Cpl David Young, L/Cpl Joseph Dunn and Pte William Sampson who appealed for writing wallets, while Pte John McGarva and Cpl Walter Shipp (from No 7 and No 8 Platoon respectively) were "*desperately in need of a concertina…*"

The Borough rose magnificently to the challenge and floods of parcels continued to arrive at the front for weeks. Cpl John Riley received his requested mouth organ and razor from Mr Thomas Hughes of Sprowston Villas in Sprowston Road, Forest Gate. Himself an old soldier, Hughes also enclosed a letter. John Riley replied and a very firm 'pen' friendship blossomed. Sgt George White meanwhile sent home a small postcard of a hand-stitched four leaf clover and the national flags of the allies. He complimented the well packed parcels he was receiving and signed off by saying that he was *"quite enjoying my rest..."*

There were letters being written elsewhere, however. Since arriving in France, Papillon's confidence had for some reason been lowered in regard to Captain Robert Swan, the former Malay rubber planter commanding A Company. Swan suffered frequent attacks of malaria and insomnia while they had been in the trenches. It tended to give him *"a cantankerous and unpleasant manner"* as well as *"a lack of initiative"* and he had become deeply unpopular with the men. At some point over this period an incident occurred which caused Papillon to inform Brigadier-General Arthur Daly that Captain Swan was no longer fit to command, especially *"in view of the very serious issues involved..."*
There is no specific mention of what had happened and, in the war diary it is obvious that the relevant detail written up by Cpl Jenns has been physically snipped out with scissors. Two thirds of the page is missing and effectively this time does not appear 'on the record'. Papillon's letter was joined by Major Winthrop, who agreed with the statement, reiterating that *"I do not consider that the Commanding Officer would be justified in sending this officer into the field in the command of a company..."*

Swan was outraged. He requested a meeting with Daly to present his case and even appears to have planned to call Papillon as a witness, reminding him in a letter that prior to this incident every sign was given that he was held in the highest confidence, having been not only appointed as the first Adjutant but also promoted to Captain by Papillon himself. Swan had by now realised the mistake in coming back from the tropics and straight into the army, but after nearly twelve years service in the colonial forces, seven of those as an officer, he deeply resented this blemish on a fine record. If Robert Swan believed it was simply down to his ill health, Arthur Daly held a different view. In response to whatever evidence of *"serious issues"* were verbally presented, he recommended Swan be sent back to England *"in some capacity which will not bring him into contact with troops..."*

Chapter 11

Desperate Actions

On January 11th, 1916 Frank Jenns proudly recorded (on the snipped out page in the war diary) that a regimental canteen was opened for the troops. It was organised by Lt's Norman Lang and Tom Brind in another demonstration of their superb organisational skills in adversity. The canteen was serving hot cocoa, and one suspects something stronger, to divert the troops focus of attention from the causes of Swan's dismissal. It was equally for those of the West Ham Battalion returning from the freezing fields of the training area and naturally it was a welcome distraction from the obviously dangerous yet somewhat monotonous daily routine. Newspapers were in plentiful supply, eventually ending up as toilet paper. The men were kept up to date with events back home, including a report that the Compulsion Bill (which required all fit men to enlist) was passed in the House of Commons by a large majority. This mass conscription was greeted with very mixed feelings amongst the volunteer 'New Army' battalions and caused much debate in the billets.

Snow was again silently falling as the West Ham men prepared for the move back to the front line. On the 16th reveille was sounded at 5.30am and the battalion paraded in full marching order, making last minute preparations for the day. At 8.15am, they left camp in column with Papillon on horseback at their head. Marching smartly to Berguette station, they boarded more cattle trucks and headed for Bethune. On arrival they were in range of the heavier guns of the German artillery so were swiftly moved on, trudging to the battered village of Les Chocquax. With sleet driving into their faces from the north the Hammers arrived around noon and moved straight into tents. The following day they marched to Les Quesnoy. It was, all in all, a difficult move as the weather and shelling had reduced the roads to mere muddy tracks. Despite the best efforts of the tireless Pioneer companies they were tortuous to march along in any sort of order. Reaching the support trenches, extra ammunition and trench supplies were taken on. After spending an uncomfortable night in flooded dugouts they moved up into the reserve trenches near the brickworks at Givenchy. As dusk fell on the 18th, the HQ Company, along with B & D Company, moved into the line. Papillon took personal command. A biting wind screamed and howled across the flat plain north of La Bassee canal, as the Hammers entered the reserve and support lines. They were shocked by the increased ferocity of the welcoming bombardments. It lasted all night and only slackened off in the early hours of the morning. They then endured it again when it resumed with an unabated fury at 10am. One shell blew in the side of the trench, wounding Pte F McAllister, Pte JC Picking and Cpl AG French. Cpl French was from Clarissa Road in Chadwell Heath and Picking lived on Sheringham Avenue in Manor Park. They recovered from these wounds and French was eventually appointed sergeant in the Hammers. A sinister trend then emerged. Not only had a senior officer been dismissed and a few men deserted but now a soldier was recorded by Frank Jenns as having a *"self inflicted injury"*. This phrase could mean many things and generally occurred for a variety of reasons. The act itself was militarily enormous in its risks and extremely painful in its reality.

Pte Samuel Ward in No8 Platoon of B Company, under the command of twenty year old Lt Frank Keeble, was a fairly typical member of the Hammers Battalion. A devoted family man, he was thirty-eight years old when he enlisted at the Stratford recruiting office on the 30th January 1915. He was a chair maker by profession, living in James Street off Globe Road in Mile End with his wife Louisa. She had lived two streets away from Samuel in Hadleigh Street before their marriage in 1896 at St Philips Church in Bethnal Green. Together they had four children, two girls and two boys. The youngest, Fred, was barely fourteen months old. Ward had no previous military experience and it would seem he was one of the thousands swept along by the patriotic fervour endemic at that time. That euphoria resulted in the birth of a fifth son, Ernest, in early October 1915 while the Hammers had been training on Perham Down. The medical examination of Samuel Ward revealed him to be of good physical stature. Though only 5'2" tall he had a chest measurement of 36" and was by all accounts a powerful man. He could also be somewhat brusque and undisciplined, revealed by an entry in the Company Conduct Sheet on 7th July while the Hammers were undergoing their initial training at Brentwood. The offence recorded was *"making an improper reply"* to his Company Commander, Lt Charles Carson the Mancunian medical student. The incident was witnessed by Company Sergeant Major White, a very experienced old soldier in B Company. Exactly what was said is not recorded but it was considered to be of sufficient gravity for Ward to be given five days 'confined to barracks'. Apparently rehabilitated, Ward sailed for France with the West Ham Battalion in November, serving without incident during their initiation to trench life. He had obviously not yet seen his newborn and now, just before Christmas, Samuel was told by letter that his son had influenza and was not expected to live. No papers survive in the public domain indicating any reaction or requests from him for leave, though it would be likely that these were made and duly turned down for very good reasons.

At 11am on 19th January 1916, Ward succumbed to his desperation and took the only option to get home as he saw it. He very literally shot himself in the foot. Sgt Pettey, L/Cpl Marsh, L/Cpl Bedford and Pte Weeden all described more or less the same scene: *"At Windy Corner, in reserve billets, on the morning of the 19th I was in a dugout seated about 6 yards from Pte S Ward. On hearing a report of a rifle I looked round and saw Pte S Ward sitting wounded through the left foot which on examination proved to be caused by a shot fired from his own rifle and fired by himself. Pte Ward made no statement in my hearing..."* Luckily for him, or more likely on advice, Ward deliberately pulled the trigger while in billets and not within the presence of the enemy. Immediately examined by the medical officer, Alan Holthusen, the wound was not found to be serious. Papillon immediately instituted a full enquiry as Ward was taken away for treatment at the Advanced Dressing Station, eventually ending up at an army hospital where they assessed that he would be fit for further service. Ward was subjected to a Field Court Martial and in the face of such overwhelming evidence was found guilty of causing a self inflicted wound and was sentenced to three months in a military prison at Rouen. It could have been worse for him. Upon release, he was returned back to Captain Leo Dyer at Base Depot and then transferred to the Labour Corps, where he served until demob in 1919. Perhaps he was lucky. At least he survived the Great War. Whatever we may think today with the luxury of hindsight, Samuel Ward never saw his son. Ernest had died at Christmas.

As dusk approached on January 20th, the Hammers moved into the front line taking over from the South Staffords. The Germans welcomed the West Ham lads with a heavy bombardment of rifle grenades and trench mortar fire. Sgt William Gilbert, of C Company, held no affection for this place, especially with the extra responsibilities his rank brought him. *"It was my job, every night, to dish out a small ration of rum."* This area was *"cold... and so flat and open, I couldn't even stand up to walk along, or kneel up... I had to crawl from one section of men, dish out the rum, crawl to the next lot and so on until the platoon had their rum... That was a nasty spot entirely, I didn't like it. It was in the open, pasted and pounded..."*

The sector at this point, officially known as 'B3' at Givenchy, had acquired the well earned nickname of 'Windy Corner'. There were a total of seven casualties during the handover, all members of D Company's Sapping Platoon.

Pte William King had been killed as he slipped over the parapet on a quest to find fresh snow to make a brew. King left a wife and six children (the last being born on the day the war began) at home in West Ham. Aged thirty-six, he was buried on the battlefield, at Windy Corner by his mates. Pte John Lincoln was also gravely wounded by the same flurry of shells. He was taken to the casualty clearing station in Bethune, but died later that evening. He was buried in the Bethune town cemetery alongside the CCS. Pte Billy Heighway had been evacuated, seriously injured, out of the immediate battle area to No2 General Hospital just outside Calais, but he too died of his wounds. One of the first to enlist, although underage, and from the Custom House area, he was eighteen years old when he was killed in action. He lies buried at the Calais Southern cemetery, again alongside the site of the old hospital. Also wounded in this barrage were Pte Charlie Mile, Pte Henry Holder, Pte Henry Greenwood and Pte Walter Charman. Mile and Holder survived the war as did Greenwood, who was from Morning Lane in Hackney. He eventually became a 2/Lt in the Essex Regiment in 1918. Walter Charman, a thirty-nine year old carman with previous military experience in the Boer war, had enlisted in April 1915. He also recovered and survived, returning home to his wife Ethel and their five children in Tower Hamlets Road, Forest Gate.

Chapter 12

To The Islands

The area around battalion HQ continued to be heavily shelled for the next twenty-four hours. On the morning of January 22nd, a huge mine was detonated by the Germans, just a few yards short of the line held by the Hammers Battalion. Naturally, they were all considerably shaken by the experience – and not just physically. Another member of No15 Section in Lt Frank Keeble's No8 Platoon was listed by Jenns as having a self inflicted wound. Pte Alex Wade from Suffolk Street in Poplar followed Samuel Ward's example and blew half his foot off to escape the local environment which was clearly sapping the spirits. The Division's history describes how in this area *"artillery and snipers are practically never silent, patrols are out in front of the line every night, and heavy bombardments by the artillery of one or both sides take place daily in various parts of the Line. Below ground there is continual mining and countermining, which, by the ever present threat of sudden explosion and the uncertainty of when and where it will take place, causes perhaps a more constant strain than any other form of warfare... In the air there is seldom a day, however bad the weather, when aircraft are not reconnoitring, photographing, and observing fire. All this is taking place constantly at any hour of the day or night, and in any part of the line. A steady and continuous fight has gone on, day and night above ground and below it..."*

On the 23rd January, Papillon led B & D Company out of the line. Replacing them were A & C Company with the HQ Company. This regular 'rotation' between the Front Line, Support and Reserve lines was a peculiarity of the British and colonial armies and a logistical nightmare for the battalion adjutants. It was also a constant headache for those responsible for finding suitable billets as most buildings were destroyed by shelling. But it did at least ensure each unit received equal time between the various duties – when the situation permitted. It would be fair to say that this diminished the local knowledge but it was very effectively countered by superb front line intelligence officers and supplemented by air observations and nightly patrols.

This rotation of men necessitated many more individual units to hold a given sector but it was better than being simply placed there and forgotten - as the troops of the other major combatants very often were. In this respect, and despite the drawbacks, the British soldier was far better off than his enemies *and* his allies. No matter how trying, tedious or downright awful each tour at the front, a British soldier always knew that within a few days he would be out of the danger area and into the comparative security of billets with the promise of slightly safer shelter, possibly warmer food and a chance to clean themselves and bury comrades.

This constant movement of troops all knowing that they would be looked after and would not be at the front for more than a few days (a 'tour' was normally between five and six days) resulted in the incredible strength of morale within the BEF.

The West Ham Battalion marched to billets in the village of Gorre, taking over in a support role. They resumed the dangerous soldier's routine of fetching and carrying equipment and ammunition to the front line, trench rebuilding and road maintenance as required while at the same time cleaning and repairing themselves, their kit and equipment: this was a series of occupations euphemistically known to the army as 'at rest'.

William Gilbert who had been quickly appointed Cpl while they were still in training and was now a well regarded Sgt in C Company remembered one incident around this time when "*we were out in the village in Support. Wherever it was possible men were forced to bathe, somehow or other. One particular morning it was my turn to take my platoon down there. We marched off and I happened to spot a couple of Officers coming down the road and I had an idea they were 'somebody', a bigwig. I could just see the colour of their headgear and that red band. I called the men to attention and smartened them up [...], it makes a difference!*

We marched down there like bloody Guardsmen and as [we] passed I gave him the 'eyes right', in beautiful order. We marched on, singing too by the way! A few yard up the road and I heard a bit of galloping. I turned round to see his Adjutant [Aide de Camp] come up, told me to stop. Name, Rank, Number... He wanted everything, where was the Company Headquarters and so on. That was that. We went on, done the job and returned home. We were back in the barn again when the Regimental Sgt Major collected me up to go before Colonel Papillon; you know quick march, left right left right. Well, I don't know what was happening here! "Ah, Sgt Gilbert, let me see. I've just received a good report about the soldierly bearing of your platoon on Wash Parade. I was very pleased and I'm to bear you in mind for future promotion!"

Although they were out of the front and reserve lines, there was always the danger of being shelled. On the evening of the 26th they were all put on 'stand to' in the expectation of a bombardment by the enemy. This was prompted by rumours of an unidentified mounted 'big wig' officer and his orderly moving around the area enquiring as to artillery positions, possibly the same encountered by Sgt Gilbert. Stood down in the early hours of the 27th January the men snatched what little sleep they could before moving up the following evening via the canal and 'Westminster Bridge', through 'Windy Corner' to relieve the trenches at the *"B2 subsection"* opposite the village of Givenchy. Here, the observers had a good view of the 'Brickstacks' and the Loos (mine shaft) Towers, which due to their similarity to the London landmark were known as 'Tower Bridge'.

Dawn broke over La Bassee canal on January 28th, the Kaiser's birthday. To celebrate, the Germans hoisted a national flag above the trenches opposite William Busby's D Company's position which his men swiftly "*removed by rifle grenades*". In response, the German artillery unleashed what Jenns describes as a "*terrific bombardment*", lasting for a nerve shattering seven and one quarter hours. Some damage was done to buildings in the vicinity of Windy Corner including the Regimental Aid Post, miraculously without inflicting any casualties. On the evening of Sunday 30th January, B & D Company were relieved from the trenches and marched back to billets at Gorre. As they left, D Company experienced the unwelcome attentions of German snipers. Cpl Therin and Pte Kunkel fell victim but luckily both were described as '*not serious*'. Busby moans to his personal diary about the lack of "*sniper-scopes*" with which to reply but the West Ham men were not yet ready for such advanced technical aids. As an illustration, Jenns records a basic error in the billets as Pte John Cochrane accidentally shot Pte Ernest Travers in the thigh. It reveals that the men were still green and understandably nervous beneath the incessant rain of shells. It was also why they were told not to keep a 'round up the spout' of their rifles when away from the line.

What subsequently happened to Cochrane is lost to history but it would have been likely that he received a field court martial and accepted punishment as handed down by Papillon. Cochrane was himself badly wounded in action six months later and never returned to the Hammers while Ernie Travers recovered from the accident and resumed his duties.

In Gorre, they waited for A & C Company still occupying a position at the Brickstacks but getting themselves together to move out. Perhaps the men with combat experience in the Boer War, like Pte Hugh Bannon, a former Grenadier Guardsman, reminded their comrades that attacks usually come when least expected. Something kept them alert and luckily too. Bannon, the late thirties dock worker living with a large family in Upton Park, and his friends in A & C Company became the subject of a small lacklustre trench raid by the Germans opposite. These men swarmed over the landscape around the Brickstacks and a period of hand to hand fighting quickly developed. It is a measure of the Hammers training that the attack was eventually repulsed. It is a measure of the West Ham men themselves that the violence lasted for some considerable time. All changeovers were suspended and they weren't relieved until Arthur Daly at Brigade was satisfied that it was merely a localised raid and that the immediate danger had passed. More local lads were wounded in this fight and the extra shelling accompanying them when they left the trenches, again listed contrary to army conventions by Jenns in the war diary: Pte James Calnan, Pte R Bull, Pte JW Smith, Pte AH Day, Pte R Cook and Pte SF Smith. On relief by their Brigade comrades the Kings, A & C Company under Major Brown were finally reunited with the rest of the battalion at Gorre. The following evening the entire battalion was relieved and they marched off to billets at Les Chocquax. During the march, Jenns noted that they *"stopped for tea at 8.30pm"* beside one of the little wooden huts run by the Women's Voluntary Service that were springing up along the routes to and from the front. It was *"much appreciated"*.

Attempts were constantly made for anything closely or even vaguely resembling 'home comforts' so no doubt L/Cpl ET Mills of C Company was pleased when his letter was published in the theatrical trade paper 'The Performer' on 3rd February 1916. Mills explained that he was *"very much in need of some old make-ups and piorette costumes for some concert work which I am undertaking out here. The boys look forward to enjoyment when coming out of the trenches, and I have a troupe of first class artistes, and the only thing I am needing is the make-up and costumes. Financial affairs are not over-bright here, so we cannot afford new stuff. I have written to one or two artistes, but have met with no success, and are now appealing to your generosity. I trust you will do your best for me, as an old artiste [...] I am anxious to do what I can for the enjoyment of the boys..."*

For such an accurately maintained record, as Jenns had ensured the West Ham Battalion war diary was, it seems odd that the death of Pte Wilton from 'wounds' on the 4th February would go unrecorded. No explanation can be given and Wilton now lies in Bethune Town Cemetery.

The Hammers were kept busy with platoon drill, route marches, lectures, seemingly endless working parties and then the inevitable drubbings by the Footballers in Brigade tournaments. For the officers, it was a chance to visit other units to gain information and ideas. It was equally an opportunity to relax, as guest in the mess of another battalion. Dining was the nearest thing possible to civilised living for officers and they clung to the illusion tenaciously. William Busby made the most of the situation and on February 5th describes how he hitched a ride on the mess cart and *"in the afternoon went with* [Reggie] *Howell to Bethune, had tea and saw 'The Shrapnels' at the Municipal Theatre"* followed by *"dinner at Le Salon d'Or..."* He and Howell had become good chums since they visited Reggie's family back in May when Busby was on another explosives course in Brighton. Now, two days later, they went riding together on borrowed horses with Busby mounted on Jess, Dr Holthusen's horse.

On their return they were greeted with the news that the Hammers were to return to the front line area. This time it would be for a total of sixteen nerve shattering days as their acclimatisation continued. Papillon outlined the next couple of weeks to his assembled officers: four days in a position known as the 'Village Lines' north of Festubert, followed by four days in the 'Islands', then four in reserve positions at Le Touret. Finally, the tour would end with four days back in the front line. The term 'islands' referred to fortified posts, usually little more than sandbagged shell holes in front of the main trench. This was a standard defensive measure and each island was large enough to uncomfortably hold sixteen men under the command of an NCO, with one man specifically tasked as a hand grenade 'bomber'. Heavily fortified positions placed behind the islands were known as 'keeps' and usually housed the Company HQ. Major Brown took over when Papillon left for England on leave a couple of days later. During a driving rainstorm, the Hammers entered the trenches on the 11th February. The scene of fierce fighting in 1915, the evidence was still alarmingly apparent to William Busby who *"found Festubert in ruins, but not so bad as Givenchy... many bullet holes bear witness to street fighting... Festubert church in ruins but reorganised for defence, shell holes in churchyard... bones visible..."*

On Valentine's Day, 1916, an order came for the entire West Ham Battalion to prepare to move along the line, to their left, into what was officially termed "subsection C2". William Busby made many notes, as usual extraordinarily detailed and strictly against regulations, describing how he *"visited Keep at stand to. [Lieutenant Bernard] Page called. Time in trenches altered, 4 days in then 5 days rest at Vermelles. Howell went with CO to see line we occupy tomorrow. Brigadier [Arthur Daly] visited Keep..."*

Tues. Feb 15th.
Requisitioned for sandbags and trench boards for Keep. Took out patrol... had difficulty in finding way back. About 11.30 went with Howell to visit A+B [Coys]. Along Pioneer Rd to Le Quirque Rue. L for 200 yds to C Lines, another 200 to Waggon + R to 'D' Coy. Went L behind old trench with [Lieutenant Eric] Bunting. Tour B held islands. Returned without mishap...

Wed. Feb 16th.
"Raining hard. Fatigue party on OBL [Old British Line]. Remainder at work improving trench and conveying fatigues. In afternoon explored Indian Village. Found 8" shell could scarcely lift..."

A & B Company were first into the trenches and Islands but later, as Busby *"went up to B to arrange about tomorrows relief"*, he witnessed a *"small bombing raid on No30 Island..."* Frank Keeble's men of No8 Platoon had a lively engagement, during which they suffered six wounded when a rifle grenade landed among them. Busby then watched as the German activity on Keeble was *"driven off by rifle fire and bombs..."* With field dressings applied Keeble's men were finally relieved thirty-six hours later by Busby's No11 Platoon from D Company and a platoon from C. A handful of men of A Company remained behind working as a Sapping Platoon. *"Saw Major Brown at B. Returned safely. [Papillon] returned from leave tonight..."*

During this handover two more men from B Company were wounded, with Sgt Willis Burden hit by shellfire while Pte Arthur Ley Davies was yet another recorded by Jenns as being *"accidentally shot by a comrade"*. Born in Saffron Walden in rural Essex, Arthur Davies had moved with his parents to Studley Road in Forest Gate. He enlisted at Stratford in January 1915 and was one of the first three hundred volunteers. Badly wounded, he was shipped home to recover slowly.

The hours of darkness gave just enough cover for D Company to continue the dangerous work of repairing the trenches destroyed by the occasional flurry of shells. At 1.45am on Thursday 17th February, Pte Frank Cowell from Upton Park was carefully and quietly sandbagging his bit of trench when he was spotted and shot in the stomach by a very keen eyed or audacious sniper. Dragged down into the trench and quickly given morphine by Busby he was evacuated out to the casualty clearing station at Bethune but died two days later, twenty-three years old. That evening, D Company sent out a six man patrol, on the lookout for any changes to the landscape. They slipped through the sandbags and wire during a violent thunderstorm. The patrol quickly exploded into a lightning disaster when they met a superior force of determined Germans happy to fight in No Mans Land. Everyone was wounded. Pte L Garner, L/Cpl HF Cook and Pte GE Gardner somehow struggled back bleeding to the Hammers lines dragging their three unconscious comrades. Two were dead by the time the password was whispered. Pte Henry Ralph Beazley was a twenty-three year old from Mile End and Pte Roy Broom, sixth son of Edward Broom, was from Blytheswood Road in Ilford. A twenty-nine year old warehouseman, Broom had enlisted at Stratford and, following training, joined the Hammers in France as a replacement for the early wounded only four weeks earlier. They now lie side by side in Le Touret Military Cemetery, Richebourg-L'Avoue. Pte Alfred Sekles was still breathing when he was taken to the Bethune casualty clearing station but he died of his wounds on 27th February. Aged thirty-five, he was another of the older volunteers to answer the country's call in 1914. Originating from Forest Gate, he lived with his wife in Church Road, Manor Park but was buried in the Bethune Town Cemetery.

Captain Trumble, the battalion Adjutant, went on leave to England passing responsibility for signing off the war diary over to 2/Lt Fountain. Frank Jenns notes on the 19th February how the Hammers left the trenches in good order and marched back towards billets, halting at the roadside at 10pm for hot soup served up at another WVS wagon. It was a bright, crisp night and an excited murmur quickly spread through the ranks. High ahead of them, the huge grey hulk of an airship, engines droning and bearing the Imperial German Cross, hung aloft in the sky with crewmen dropping bombs by hand. Through binoculars, some of the Hammers could just make out the intended target. No doubt with a groan, they realised it was their own billets at Les Chocqaux. As they struggled to their feet the ponderous 'gas bag' turned, humming back toward the German lines. The following days witnessed heavier snowfalls as the Hammers moved on to more billets at Les Harisoires and Mont Bermenchon, before reaching Gonnehem on the 22nd.

On arrival they attended a gas demonstration parade. It was no doubt influenced by the fact that Captain Harry 'Nutty' Sharman had seriously deteriorated following his earlier 'whiff' of gas and needed to be urgently evacuated back to England. His place was taken by the newly promoted Captain Charles Carson, who moved from commanding Frank Keeble and B Company to command William Busby and D Company.

Chapter 13

Artois Tragedy

At British High Command it had become clear that the French were being stretched to breaking point fighting the Germans around the fortress city of Verdun. In response to Marshal Foch's request for the BEF to take over more responsibility in the area the British Front was extended south by some 20 miles and the Division, including the Hammers, was sent to the new section running from Loos down to Ransart, north east of Hannescamps. The area included Vimy Ridge. The Brigade eventually centred on the small town of Souchez.

Before the war Souchez had been a prosperous little town, nestling in a green hollow of the Artois hills. In the spring and summer of 1915 it was at the centre of the French offensive in the Artois, the scene of heavy fighting made all the more obvious by the fact that this picturesque spot now lay in charred piles of rubble and churned earth. It was captured and recaptured a dozen times with various ruins being fortified and the French had eventually won the bitter fight. The Germans merely retired to the top of Vimy Ridge. Assaults on the new German positions up the hill proved too much and the French casualties were truly horrendous. Eventually both sides paused, exhausted. The Germans remained brooding over the valley while below the French dead lay rotting in No Man's Land. Many of them were eventually removed under a flag of truce, piled on hand carts and tipped, with little ceremony, into the mass graves of the huge Cabaret Rouge French Cemetery. Many more could not be removed at all.

When the British took over this sector from the French they were stunned by the almost Napoleonic appearance of the dead, in their bright red trousers and blue tunics, incongruous in the crater strewn sea of mud that the area had become. The defences handed over were dire indeed. Poorly dug and maintained, they were filthy trenches with pitifully few strong points or dugouts. They also contained still more unburied and decaying bodies – mostly French – which were in turn feeding a seemingly undefeatable immense army of carefree, bloated rats. Even if the trenches had been in good condition, the Vimy Ridge sector was a difficult one for the allied defenders, with the enemy having height advantage and looking westwards. The Germans had a clear view down that long unbroken gentle slope from the summit of the ridge, over the allied front lines and across the approach routes and artillery positions. For the French and now British observers the opposite was true. Looking upwards, they were unable to see the German artillery and supply routes on the far side of the summit as the reverse slope drops steeply towards the Douai Plain. This disadvantage hadn't actually mattered much, as this was a rather quiet sector since the horrendous fighting of September and October 1915. Here the French and Germans had for the last few months both operated a 'live and let live' approach to the war. Taking over the lines, the British immediately implemented an altogether more aggressive policy of disruptive artillery fire and trench raiding.

On the 25th February the Hammers marched for six and a half hours trudging through the whipping cold of another heavy driving snowstorm to Petit Sains in the Lens area only thirteen miles away. All the roads were thoroughly frozen, dangerously slippery and the men, more especially the horses and mules, had the greatest difficulty in moving. The following day they arrived at Bully-Grenay, taking over from French troops and facing an enemy up the hill on Vimy Ridge with a reputation for hard and daring fighting. The Hammers settled down and took in their new surroundings. The Artois was similar to the great coal mining areas of Britain, naturally beautiful but blighted by working mines with high wheel towers and slag heaps along the horizon like dark pyramids.

There had been some minor attempts at mine warfare between the Germans and French. Now the British arrived and doubled the efforts, much to the consternation of the Germans who up until now had had things their own way underground. From a military viewpoint it would have made sense for the British to actually withdraw some four-thousand yards, create a stronger defensive line and avoid the German tunnels running under the first and second trench lines. This option was seriously considered and recommended as the way ahead to the Commander-in-Chief, Sir Douglas Haig who in all fairness tacitly agreed. However, to do so was a *political* impossibility as the French lost many thousands of men in crawling up these slopes in 1915. The army deployed a number of Royal Engineer Tunnelling Companies in response to the German mining nuisance. This underground clash developed into a desperate struggle, with both sides blowing mines to destroy enemy infantry positions, and camouflet charges to disrupt the opposition's tunnels. There was just as much combat above ground, with each side attempting to gain control of the resultant huge craters. The engineers and tunnellers excelled in improvisation and the British quickly gained the upper hand.

Frank Jenns had left on leave on the 15th but had returned by the 22nd as February ended in another blinding snowstorm. 2/Lt Fountain, the acting Adjutant while Captain Trumble was on leave, had himself been taken to hospital having fallen ill from the general trench life so 2/Lt George Harry Ross, from Hove in Sussex, now took over the duties of acting Adjutant with a view to learning the administrative role more fully. In other changes, Capt Dick Collier had taken charge of A Company after Captain Swan was dismissed from duty and forty-six year old Lt Robert Biddulph-Pinchard replaced Collier as the Hammers transport officer. Sgt William Gilbert remembered how at this time some of these older men were painfully *"stiff with rheumatism"* from the freezing damp conditions.

The Hammer's billets were still being constantly shelled and two men from B Company, Pte W Douglas and Pte SC Hall, were wounded by shrapnel. As ever, the stretcher bearers were out in the thick of it. On March 1st, as one of the stretcher bearers, Pte Thomas Sparrow, arrived to assist a badly wounded Pte Relland, both men were killed outright by another shell. The nineteen year old Sparrow was from Sperling Road in Tottenham and another scrubbed off the list of the first three hundred volunteers. Thirty-four year old John Relland (who was Lt Bernard Page's batman) left a wife and child at Beech Hall Road in Highams Park. Both men were buried in an extension to the French Cemetery at Bully Grenay.

The freezing weather was having painful consequences elsewhere. Sgt Gilbert was forced to escape the incessant shelling by jumping in a shell hole, *"which I think had been iced up because it was freezing then and fractured my left leg..."* Although not considered a 'Blighty' wound, he was quickly transferred back to England for recovery, with the addition of an unexpected invitation. *"At this time they were clearing every* [Casualty Clearing] *station they could, all hospitals, everything was cleared empty. Everybody down there was going to be pushed home straight away. I came home, pushed onto a boat...*

While I was at hospital I was running about in a chair, one of these with wheels, with my leg stuck up front. They came and told me I was going with a party to Buckingham Palace Mews to see the Queen. I felt such a bloody fraud! There was me, with me leg stuck on a board, and the other poor sods with crutches, and blind and so on..."

The Hammers remained at Bully-Grenay and L/Cpl Samuel Mayo, a married man living at Grove Crescent Road in Stratford and another member of Frank Keeble's No8 Platoon in B Company was killed while preparing to move out. After dark on the 5th March 1916 they handed over their billets to their old friends the Footballers and quickly marched back through the snow into the support trenches around Calonne. The smashed houses there faced the German occupied town of Lens. Heavy snow fell quietly on a bitterly cold and windless night as C Company was 'stood down'. The various sections probably thought themselves lucky not to be required at their posts until the morning. Crowding into the cellars of the wrecked town of Calonne, they were desperate to find any smashed building still offering a little warmth and some shelter from the elements. One section led by L/Cpl Ryan crammed thankfully into an inviting cellar beneath one empty wreck within a street of shell smashed houses sitting along Rue Brunel. It was relatively dry, with some battered pieces of furniture still lying about. There was even proper warmth from a coke brazier, lit by the recent occupants who were by now trudging north through the snow to 'God knows where'. One member of the section dragged the brazier into the cellar doorway, presumably in an attempt to cut down the drafts from the smashed door and brickwork. They settled down to sleep, happy with their good fortune.

By the morning all but one were dead, suffocated in their sleep by carbon monoxide poisoning from the brazier. Eddie Ryan was twenty-eight years old and lived with his wife in Affleck Street in Kings Cross. Pte Billy Loynes was barely nineteen and from Cambridgeshire. He had joined, along with so many others underage, for excitement a year before. Pte Ernest Barber was twenty-one and from Stepney. Buried with them in Loos British Military Cemetery are Pte James Carter along with the great friends Pte Henry Chaplin and Pte Arthur Busby, who had stood together in the recruiting office as their service numbers indicate. Henry Chaplin, a carpenter by trade, left a wife and seven children. Pte Ernest Parker was barely alive when the sentry desperately tried to wake the group. He was immediately rushed to a casualty clearing station at Fosse 10 but was dead on arrival. As happened so often in 'Pals' battalions, the tragedy was doubled for two families. Nineteen year old Parker was the brother in law of Henry Chaplin. It was his sister who had persuaded her husband Henry to enlist 'for adventure' and, more importantly, to look after her young brother. Ernie was buried by his friends in the cemetery alongside the CCS, just outside Sains en Gohelle. Pte Charlie Payne, sleeping closest to the door, was still breathing when the sentry found them all and Alan Holthusen, the West Ham Battalion Medical Officer, made every effort to save him. Charlie Payne had lived with his wife in Grafton Street, Plaistow but was buried in the Bully-Grenay Communal Cemetery alongside the CCS where he died without regaining consciousness.

Despite the war raging around them, the sheer sadness of this tragedy cast a gloom over everyone. As the story had unfolded overnight, L/Cpl Ernest Willie Crisp somehow got drunk, perhaps by several illicit and large doses of military rum. Crisp was a thirty-seven year old carman living at Buckingham Road in Stratford and in his alcohol fuelled anger he sought out and severely assaulted the unnamed sentry who, he no doubt believed, should have kept a closer eye on his dead friends. As the Regimental Police arrived, he resisted arrest and beat them too before finally being overpowered and shackled. At his court martial, Crisp was sentenced to one year hard labour by Brigadier-General Arthur Daly and lost his L/Cpl stripes. This punishment was soon reduced to six months.

Their deaths were recorded as 'died of wounds' by 2/Lt Ross, currently maintaining the war diary as part of his 'instruction' in the duties of Adjutant. The page listing this event is written in Ross's light neat script and stands out from Frank Jenns's usually hurried and heavy handwriting. On the 10th March the Reverend Westerdale, who had conducted all the funerals, left for a posting to another Division. The thirty-one year old was shattered by what had happened in the cellar but remained, as ever, outwardly cheerful. Westerdale had followed in his father's footsteps and was a Wesleyan Minister. He had seen combat in France the previous year, as a stretcher bearer before returning to England and completing his Ministerial training. By the time the West Ham Battalion was being raised he was First Minister at Stratford Wesleyan Church in the Grove, and became the Hammers 'Padre'. He was present at their first parade at St Luke's Church (where he was reminded not to wear his sword on parade) and had got to know many of the men very well since. He naturally shared each loss when one was killed. Not only was he conducting church services in rubble or on farmland but he was also fearlessly fulfilling his vocation on the battlefield. He firmly regarded himself very much *"as a Priest and as a Tommy"* and, as an illustration, William Busby showed no hint of surprise when he noted in his diary a month earlier about hearing believable (yet clearly misinformed) reports of Westerdale's death: vaporized by a shell while *"carrying a wounded man..."*

After Reverend Westerdale left the Hammers (and there is no record of another 'Padre' arriving), the next couple of weeks were spent in and out of the line in the Bully-Grenay area. It was here that they vented their energies and general frustrations by digging and constructing a very long communication trench, their first in France. Today, its line has become the Rue Emile Zola, but in 1916 it was proudly christened 'West Ham Lane'. On the 18th, they set off *"in glorious sunshine"* to Bruay. Somewhere on this relatively 'safe' journey Pte Asser and Pte Shuttleworth strangely went missing. George Asser was forty and lived with his wife Matilda in Gurley Street, Bromley (by Bow) while twenty-seven year old Alex Shuttleworth grew up in Patriot Square in Bethnal Green but, for whatever reason, 2/Lt Harry Ross doesn't record their names nor mention the deaths *at all* in the usually detailed war diary. Equally as strange is the fact that the diary month of March is merely two pages, rather than the more usual four or five. Frank Jenns had by now been back from leave for a number of weeks and resumed his assistant Adjutant duties so would be most likely guiding what 2/Lt Ross entered.

However, no explanation can be given for George Asser or Alex Shuttleworth's deaths because another three consecutive days are mysteriously missing from the battalion record. But, as seen just two months before, it wasn't unknown for the record to be tampered with or altered. Neither mans body was ever found and the death certificates simply state "missing, presumed dead". They are today both remembered by name on the memorial at Arras.

When the battalion finally reached Bruay, they learnt that West Ham United had again beaten rivals Millwall Athletic, 2-1, at the Boleyn in front of twelve-thousand supporters.

With this happy news, some of the lucky ones commenced their first leave since arriving in France.

Chapter 14

Leave!

In the orderly room, Jenns pinned up the leave roster. Most of the lads lucky enough to be first with passes for ten days back home packed up their trench warfare souvenirs and crammed themselves on horse carts to the station. There, they boarded trains to the coast and caught a steamer 'back to dear old Blighty'. A few stayed in France, booking into the numerous estaminets at the coast, seeking the considerable comforts of clean sheets and hot baths. Then of course, there were the Mademoiselles - with 'blue lamps' for officers and 'red lights' for the other ranks. Some of the officers begged, borrowed or rented motor cars and sought out the timeless delights of a carefree Paris.

Meanwhile 11,000 cigarettes (Craven A's and Woodbines) together with a huge consignment of socks and mufflers arrived, a gift from *"the people of West Ham"*. The remainder of the Hammers stayed in huts, as the Brigade carried out the usual 'at rest' routines. It was here that they welcomed back Pte JJ Da Costa, the serial absentee during initial training now returning to the West Ham Battalion after his few months punishment spent making TNT up in the far corners of a freezing Scotland. He evidently brought the weather with him as by the 24th the winter had returned with a vengeance in the form of yet more heavy snow, halting all but essential work. Parades and games were also cancelled and so letters were written, including thanks from Papillon and Captain Collier to the people of West Ham for the cigarettes and socks, with special mention going to The Women's Society, The Romford Road Congregational Church, The Nursery Staff at the West Ham Asylum and Mr W Morris of Plaistow Road, West Ham.

At the end of the month Papillon took on overall command of the Brigade during the home leave of Brigadier-General Arthur Daly. One of Papillon's first acts while in command was to commute the sentence of Pte Crisp, who had beaten the sentry and military police. He reduced the six months in prison doing hard labour down to ninety-one days of field punishment and allowed him to remain with the Hammers to serve it. In Papillon's absence, Major William Henry Winthrop took temporary command of the West Ham Battalion. He was thirty-seven and another experienced soldier, wounded in South Africa while serving with the Dragoon Guards. He had joined the Hammers in March 1915 after Papillon's army friend Major Hurst had moved elsewhere. Home leave also meant William Busby took over responsibility for command of D Company in the absence of Captain Carson.

By midday on 2nd April they all reassembled at Bruay, some feeling more refreshed than others and at 9.15pm they marched out of camp to the railway station. Boarding more cattle trucks they headed to Barlin and then Coupigny where they finally took over billets from the Highland Light Infantry at noon the following day. Another casualty occurred on the 6th, although this time not due to enemy action. Pte James Stuchfield, who lived with his parents at West Street in Mile End Old Town, died from appendicitis. He was twenty-four years old and now lies in Lillers Communal Cemetery.

A period of training followed until the 9th April 1916 when Papillon returned from commanding Brigade. A couple of days later Captain Frank Trumble, the Adjutant, was granted special leave back to his wife Lottie in England after the birth of his first child the day before. 2/Lt Martinson duly took over his duties and responsibility for signing off Jenns entries in the war diary. Working parties struggled to improve the defences in both Bully-Grenay and the shattered town of Souchez. It was an unenviably gruesome task for the men owing to the seemingly endless French and German corpses and smashed bits of body revealed hourly by their digging.

On the move once again, the 13th April saw the Hammers reach Calonne Ricouart where they boarded another steam train, bound for Aire Station. Once there, they marched to a training area outside Delettes, ten miles away and engaged on Brigade training around the villages of Rupigny and Greuppe. They practiced raiding, night patrols, bombing accuracy and various other trench warfare techniques. On the 15th a large scale Brigade field day exercise took place attacking a skeleton enemy. The Hammers led a central attack with the Kings making a flanking move. Both had the Footballers in support while the South Staffords formed an unemployed reserve. Papillon attended a Brigade conference in the evening where the West Ham men were complemented for their days work. The training period was completed on the 17th. They marched to Aire station, to begin the journey back to Bruay, but went into billets for an overnight stay. As they awoke the next day, the sky opened and a torrential rain accompanied them on their return journey to the frontline.

By 8pm the next evening they were back in the trenches of the northern subsector facing Lens and Lievin. The Hammers were immediately subjected to the usual warm welcome of heavy shelling which this time decided to continue non-stop for their entire tour of four nerve shattering days. Miraculously there wasn't a single casualty. On the 22nd they were relieved from the trenches by the Footballers. Moving straight back to their familiar billets in the support area around Cité Calonne they were promptly shelled, again heavily, for another four constant days and nights but again without any injuries. Jenns began to circulate the news that leave was being restarted. William Busby was no-doubt in a good mood when he wrote up his personal diary for Monday 24th April 1916. He was *"to go next..."*

Busby was by now the Hammers Bombing Officer and also temporarily deaf in one ear after he'd had an accident with a Newton rifle grenade a few days earlier. The sun was well up into a clear blue sky on Wednesday 26th as he was busy in the 'retaliation post' carefully setting another fourteen rifle grenades in position. He received the expected tap on the shoulder from a battalion signals runner with confirmation that his Leave had come. One of these runners was Pte George Greeno and just like the stretcher bearers they were often out under very intense shellfire, "in all weathers". Busby engaged on a whirlwind withdrawal, first sending "*Martin* [his servant/batman] *to* [Lt Robert] *Pinchard's billet to get kit - then back to Front Line to report to* [Papillon]... *left Calonne via Calonne nord. Some shrapnel. Reached Bully Grenay where found* [Brigade] *HQ and obtained warrant... Proceeded to Pinchard's billet, where changed and dined... Left Pinchard at 12.15*[pm] *to find that lorry had left Iron Gates at Fosse 10. Proceeded in mess cart at top speed to Bethune in ample time to catch the 2.19*[am] *train..."*

As Busby left, shelling of the support areas greeted the return of the Adjutant, Captain Frank Trumble. He was still beaming from fatherhood yet wincing from the painful feet he had been suffering ever since initial training. The shelling on the Hammers continued unabated overnight. With the first hints of dawn on April 27th, the damp early morning mist slowly drifted and thinned across No Man's Land. This twilight was where the dreaded German snipers, in carefully chosen hideaways, plied their cold calculating trade. Despite the risks, a working party commanded by 2/Lt Alfred Oscar Ollett was desperately trying to repair a blown in wall before daylight fully broke. Somehow enough of a man appeared briefly above the parapet and gave a sniper his target.

Ollett took a single shot straight through the head and was dead on the duckboards before his squad could react. In consequence, the twenty-one year old brewery clerk from High Garrett in Essex became the first officer of the West Ham Battalion killed in action. He had only been out at the front for four weeks. He was buried in the Bully Grenay Communal Cemetery and CSM Warr, who was a local teacher before the war, painted a delicate watercolour of the grave for Ollett's parents.

Later that day L/Cpl Wilkinson from East Ham, who had given the fine rendition of 'Tipperary' at the Hammer's first gathering in Devons' Road, became yet another listed by Jenns as *"accidently wounded"*. William Busby though was undertaking a *"very slow and tedious journey to Boulogne. Arrived at 9.30am and breakfasted at [officer's] club. Found that boat did not leave before 7pm [so] wandered along harbour, saw torpedoed Sussex and a supply vessel about 1 mile from shore plainly visible at low tide. From the latter trawlers were salving goods. Lunch at Hotel Maurice and thence to cinema..."*

Back at the mud, sandbags, damp and bloodshed the incessant shelling continued. The ever resourceful Quartermaster, Lt Norman Lang, was wounded as he sheltered in C Company's dugouts. Evacuated to a CCS, the deep cuts, bruises and concussion were not found to be life threatening and after a spell of convalescence he returned to full duty.

In the afternoon, as the German's fired some trench mortars, jagged pieces of shrapnel struck thirty-nine year old Pte Joseph Cooper and he crumpled in a heap. Joe was an experienced carman from Poplar who had enlisted early in 1915 and had travelled over as part of the advance party. As a family man he may have been one of the lucky ones who had recently enjoyed a period of home leave. As Joe lay bleeding, L/Cpl Norman Bellinger was immediately in attendance. He was one of the most experienced stretcher bearers and as the bombardment continued Bellinger was himself exposed to the unrelenting mortars. The shrapnel from one close call hit him in the right knee, chest and the fingers of his left hand. Despite these painful wounds he continued to give assistance as Cooper was brought in which earned a personal recommendation from Papillon that his bravery be recognised. Joe Cooper left a large family in Limehouse and on the Isle of Dogs to become another of the West Ham Battalion buried in the Loos British Cemetery at Grenay.

Norman William Bellinger had enlisted at the East Ham recruiting centre on 16th January 1915, one of the first three-hundred men listed on Mayor Henry Dyer's front page of the Stratford Express. Twenty-eight years old and a labourer, he lived in Howard Road, Barking with his wife Lillian and their four year old daughter. He was a fairly typical volunteer to the West Ham Battalion. His steady nerve and resourcefulness was recognised early on, almost as soon as the Hammers arrived in France and he was appointed L/Cpl on 20th December 1915. Although only 5'4" tall he was immensely strong and selected to be a stretcher bearer. He clearly took his role very seriously and there were to be many men who had cause to give thanks for this man's strength but more for his undoubted bravery.

Soon after, the Hammers left the support trenches and headed for billets while *"after tea at Club"* William Busby *"went on board second boat. Crossing very smooth and landed at Folkestone about 8.30pm"*. He *"just secured seat in Pullman"* and was *"very sleepy..."* Arriving home at Sherrard Road in the early hours and, after waking the family, he *"showed souvenirs and then to bed..."* The spiked helmet picklehaube was a very popular trophy to bring home to friends and family, as were German belt buckles, bayonets and sometimes even loaded handguns or live grenades.

Back in France in billets on May 2nd, L/Cpl James Gregory Farrington of C Company received some bitter news by letter from home. His youngest son Freddy, barely 18 months, had died of whooping cough and measles. From Castleton Street in Hackney, Farrington was a twenty-seven year old working at the LCC tram depot in Commercial Road before enlisting at Shoreditch. Somewhat poignantly, a few days before the letter had arrived, he is likely to have been one of the many family men of the Brigade who were invited to enjoy an Easter sports day organised by Arthur Daly. There were conjurers, egg hunts and gramophone music for the local French children who were still, incredibly, living within two thousand yards of the front line.

In England meanwhile, William Busby was enjoying his leave immensely, renewing old acquaintances from his days as District Scout Master for West Ham and catching up with friends from the area, in one man's attempt to regain a little bit of sanity before returning to the madness of war. He was equally taking time to solemnly visit the family of Roy Broom at Blythswood Road in Ilford, a member of D Company killed back in February. Next, the family of Sgt Clark in Kilchurn Road, Forest Gate, to check if all was well with them, just as he had promised to do.

Finally, he called on his old Company Commander, Harry 'Nutty' Sharman, whose health was broken by gas back in the early days in France. He found that 'HHS' was recuperating in Brighton, so wrote to arrange to meet before William returned to the front. In the meantime he went shopping armed with requests for goods from the men he had left behind. Busby also bought several volumes of Kipling for himself.

Harry Sharman duly replied and on May 3rd they met at Mansion House in the City, making their way to Simpson's in Piccadilly. It was over lunch that William learned of Ollett's death. The two friends then struggled through the crowds to Hatchett's where they *"had drinks"* before attending the Lyric Theatre to see the *"very good acting"* in Edward Sheldon's latest play 'Romance' starring the pin up girl of 1916, Doris Keane.

As the Hammers trudged back into the wet trenches at Bully Grenay, the inevitable shelling welcomed them. This time it was *"heavy"*, killing one of the early volunteer replacements, Pte GH Potter. He was there despite only being seventeen years old. He came from Romford and is another with a grave in the Loos British Cemetery. The indiscriminate shrapnel also found its way into four more men, with Pte AJ Skerritt, Pte WT Bonser, Pte D Divver and Pte GW Osborne all wounded. Divver remained patched up at duty while Skerritt and Bonser required a higher standard of medical attention but they both eventually returned to the Hammers. Most seriously hurt was Osborne. He died in hospital a few weeks later and is now buried in Abbeville cemetery.

At the end of his leave William Busby made a final call, as promised, on the family of his old friend and billiards opponent Bernard Page who he had left back in the trenches. William was invited to supper by Mr Page senior who was a successful florist with a clutch of shops in the borough. Page was naturally eager to know everything about life at the front. Then *"BRP's younger brother"* took William for a drive in the country, *"through Chigwell via Abridge to Theydon, then on to Loughton and Chingford before arriving home in time for tea..."*

His final evening at home was spent with his father, reflecting no doubt on what was ahead and what had been, in the age old manner of fathers and sons.

Fri May 5th
"Packed up things and left home. Train to L'pool St, taxi to Victoria. Just caught train. No seat in Pullman..."

Back at the front as dawn lit the sky at 4.55am, the gas alarm was sounded as a dirty yellow low lying cloud of chlorine floated slowly across No Man's Land towards the British lines. It bleached the grass as it came towards them. The cloud was trailed by lines of masked German troops, stumbling towards the left front of the West Ham men. The Hammers donned their recently issued new 'gas helmets' and stood to arms. The mild attack was easily beaten off by units on their left and the action was all over by 6.10am, with no casualties. This was followed by a *'harmless'* yet, no doubt, terrifying gas shell bombardment which fell directly on B Company's lines, without exploding or injuring any of the men.

William Busby was by now travelling from *"Folkestone 10.30am, Boulogne 2.30pm. Found train not until tomorrow, so booked room at the club... In evening went to cinema"* as a German patrol audaciously crept up to the wire in front of Lt Frank Keeble and his No8 Platoon of B Company, launching a ferocious and deadly rifle grenade attack. Before they were seen off by a flurry of close range retaliatory bombs, rifle and machine gun fire L/Cpl James Bedford was killed. Bedford was a twenty-eight year old from Islington and one of the witnesses when Samuel Ward had shot himself in the foot. Pte Fred Woolward was twenty one and from Goodliffe Street in Bromley (by Bow). Today they are two more buried in Loos British Cemetery at Grenay. Pte Preston was wounded in this attack, alongside Pte George Carter. The following day, a flurry of more trench mortar shells burst on the West Ham lines. Then another gas alert was declared, wounding Pte RB Pogson and Pte H Hawkins when they weren't quite quick enough with their gas masks.

Still returning, Busby *"left Boulogne about 2.30pm but did not arrive in Bethune until about 10.30pm. Went to club, became a member and slept there. While sitting in club this morning, Harford strolled in just off on leave. Exciting account of his tremendous responsibilities..."* On Sunday 7th May, Busby *"left by lorry at 8.30am for Pt Sains. Called at Pinchard's* [at the Transport lines] *and later in day walked to Calonne and reported at HQ. Told about the gas attack..."*

The *"tremendous responsibilities"* Busby mentions in his diary relate to Captain Harford, the Boer War veteran who had been thrown in a ditch by his horse back in December when he was D Company's first commander. On recovery he had been promoted to Major and tasked with forming a unit to look after (and, indeed, round up) the many young teenagers clearly visible in the ranks of the New Army. Harford would later describe how *"the young soldiers began to arrive in half-dozens from all parts of the line: English, Scots, Welsh, Irish and also some South African boys... Lance Corporals, Corporals, some with medal ribbons, tall boys, short boys, nondescript boys, many most indignant at being taken from their units..."*

On the Monday, the Hammers handed over their trenches to the Footballers who by now had lost a number of highly recognisable and notable players from their ranks. William Busby finally rejoined at the billets in Calonne and even here the German barrages still managed to claim more victims. Over the next couple of days Pte Desbury Clark and twenty-two year old Pte George Benjamin Noon from Wolverley Street in Bethnal Green, were wounded.

Re-entering the front line trenches three days later the Hammers sustained a further casualty to the galling shelling with 2/Lt AW Kaye wounded in the late afternoon of 13th May. That evening, just before 10pm, it was Pte JJ Da Costa's turn for sentry duty in the fire bay looking out from the front line. He was roused in his dugout by Cpl HH Gladwin, duty NCO with A Company. It was a wet night and Da Costa had a sandbag covering the barrel of his upright rifle which was leaning against the fire bay wall. As Cpl Gladwin went to wake another man, he heard a shot. The sandbag had apparently dropped as JJ Da Costa reached for his rifle, caught the trigger and blew off his middle finger and part of his palm on the right hand.

Papillon took the trouble to stress in his report to Arthur Daly at Brigade HQ that "*this man came with a recent draft and has had very little experience of the trenches. I do not think that he can be held to blame for what was apparently an accident...*" If it had been discovered to be a deliberate self inflicted wound, clearly in the face of the enemy, JJ Da Costa may well have been sentenced to death. Dr Alan Holthusen, checked the wound and declared him to be unfit for further frontline service on recovery. John Jacob Da Costa finally left the West Ham Battalion, but he didn't manage to leave France. He became a hard pressed waiter in an officer's Mess.

The next day, the continuous shelling wounded three more originals. Pte George Gibbs was from School House Lane off Ratcliffe Highway, while Pte Philip Windley had been a railway porter living in Kerbey Street beside Crisp Street market. But, along with Pte Arthur Edward Secker they recovered from their injuries and survived the war. During this period Frank Jenns still continued to record by name and service number most of the wounded and those killed. This really is fairly unique. The overwhelming majority of battalions and units rarely mentioned 'Other Ranks' with the exception of those displaying behaviour that resulted (or was likely to result) in medals being awarded. The actions, arrivals and departures of officers however always tended to be recorded. Yet again, here in the West Ham diary Jenns hardly ever gives them a mention, including the slight wounding in the left calf of Lt Keeble during that last tour of duty. However inaccurate, it remains a clear indication of the close camaraderie which was still prevalent in the Hammers at this time, especially when it is realised that the names of men like JJ Da Costa were deliberately left out of the record. However, as the number of dead and wounded 'originals' began to mount alarmingly, this feeling clearly became increasingly difficult to sustain.

By May 15th 1916, they had been under sustained shellfire for some ten days, visibly aging faces and stretching already taut nerves as they crouched in the funk holes and shell scrapes. The heroes of the hour were, of course, the stretcher bearers tirelessly putting themselves in mortal danger rescuing the wounded. L/Cpl Norman Bellinger had already been recommended for a bravery award after his actions trying to save Joe Cooper back in April. Bellinger was still recovering from shrapnel wounds to his chest, fingers and knee when he was once again seen to crawl out, under fierce hostile shelling. This time it was to try and rescue a badly wounded L/Cpl James Dutton. Having dressed Dutton's' wounds on the exposed ground, he assisted to bring him to Alan Holthusen's aid post. Bellinger's actions again caught the eye of Papillon but unfortunately James Dutton did not survive and he is yet another buried in the Loos British Military Cemetery. The Hammers were eventually relieved and marched back into familiar billets at Bully-Grenay. The transport sections remained at a point known as Fosse 10, forming working parties. Being well within the range of the German artillery, the drivers were inevitably subjected to the attentions and Pte Joseph Lygoe, a twenty year old from the Peabody Estate buildings in Herbrand Street, off Russell Square in Holborn was killed. Pte W Thorne and Pte E Gibbons were seriously wounded.

Many of the horses were also shredded by shrapnel or had to be shot.

Chapter 15

In Search Of Tranquillity

The British Expeditionary Force was by now coming under increasing pressure to mount a major offensive within their area of responsibility. The French were taking a savage mauling at Verdun and desperately needed a diversion from the German attentions. Haig favoured Flanders, to nip out the Ypres Salient, but once again was over-ruled by politicians in Whitehall. The army had to be seen to be co-operating with the French allies as no extra French troops were available. None could be moved and certainly none taken from Verdun, therefore any major joint offensive had to take place where the two army areas met and where the French divisions were already in place. In consequence, a total of five BEF divisions were ordered to move to add to the build up of strength assembling south of Arras on the Somme River. This meant some large scale troop movements and the shuffling of Divisions, with major adjustments to the areas under the various commands.

Although no-one could have known it, this all took place at an inopportune moment. Back in April, as the vagaries of war often dictate, Ernst von Ziethen, the German general in command of the IX Reserve Corps with an entire division centred on the Vimy area, had fallen ill. He was replaced by the little known Baron von Freytag-Loringhoven. A staff officer of the Supreme Command and serving under Falkenhayn himself, Freytag-Loringhoven was an expert in military logistics and had served as a staff liaison officer to the Austro-Hungarian Great Headquarters in the Balkans. His son would later perform a very similar role for Hitler (by contrast, his nephew attempted to assassinate the Nazi leader). A court socialite widely travelled and briefly the third husband of an infamous Dada-ist performer ten years his senior, the Baron carried a glittering army career under his belt. He had never, however, commanded troops in battle. Like so many he sought the undoubted 'glamour' brought by a combat field command.

Using his considerable influence he began to make representations to assume temporary command of von Ziethen's men. When this was granted on the 15th April he took over in the line opposite the British at Givenchy en Gohelle. His initial assessment was that he had arrived at a *'windy corner'* of the front. The severe damage being done by the British tunnellers, both physically and mentally, had to be stopped at all costs: *"If by attack we could throw the British over the position and so rob them of all their mine shafts and hold the position won, we should have tranquillity..."*

Freytag-Loringhoven's solution earned him high praise indeed from army commander Crown Prince Rupprecht himself. With such eminent backing, he was assured of *all* the men, material and heavy artillery his plan required.

On the evening of May 17th, The Hammers marched away from the unrelenting guns of the front line to Coupigny and the relatively safe billets there. Papillon left for the UK on a leave of absence. The constant nerve shattering shelling of the last few months were beginning to tell on not only him, but everyone. Major Winthrop took over command once again and the ever cheerful Captain JD Paterson became second in command.

On the night of the 19th/20th May 1916, the changes in the British army previously mentioned began to take place, resulting in a considerable movement of troops in all directions. The West Ham Battalion marched to Divion via Fresnicourt, as the whole division moved into reserve at Bruay on the 21st. Speculation was rife as to what exactly was going on. Since 5am that morning the German bombardment on the Berthonval sector had been very intensive and it had continued, unbroken, until 11am - and then it paused. At 3pm, an even heavier shell and mortar fire opened up on the already cratered front line occupied by the British. This bombardment was also deep, falling not only on the front trenches but all the way to the artillery positions too, some eight miles back. The shellfire also included tear gas and was without doubt the heaviest concentrated shelling of the war so far.

Freytag-Loringhoven had secretly arrayed eighty artillery batteries on an 1800 yard front, all out of sight on the reverse slope of Vimy Ridge. Seventy thousand shells fell in four hours, destroying trenches and cutting all communications. In the dry conditions, dust obscured all vision. The British artillery duly replied, but made little effect on slowing the relentless barrage. Events began to overtake the West Ham men as they jostled each other for the safest spots in their billets. They knew something was happening as they had all heard, and indeed felt, the staggering effects of a huge mine going off some distance to the north during their march. It was a German mine, blown directly under the British front line at 7.45pm. Simultaneously, the German artillery barrage on the British support lines was lifted and the pause heralded the start of a massive infantry attack. The Germans flooded across the smashed front line almost unhindered.

At 11pm, an urgent despatch from Brigade arrived at the West Ham HQ, immediately placing the battalion on orders to move within the hour to the area of Carency. On the 22nd May, a fleet of forty 'Old Bill' buses, including some originally from east London, and thirty-five motor lorries arrived to rush them to Maisnil Bouche. On arrival at the front the Hammers were immediately thrown into the fight to halt the German advance. It was being monitored at GHQ and General Henry Wilson was all for mounting local counter attacks, while von Loringhoven was still consolidating his advances.

Haig though decided full and thorough preparations were to be made for the defence of Arras, and that a defensible line should be gained and re-established. The counter attack, to be made on 23rd May, was to follow a short bombardment from hurriedly reinforced artillery. But Freytag-Loringhoven had planned his attack well and, at 8pm (twenty-five minutes before the British counter attack was due to start) the Germans again opened a heavy bombardment on the British assembly positions, killing a hundred men before the infantry assault even began. Confusion spread as the remainder of the men went 'over the top'. Signallers desperately flashed messages that they could not attack and runners were sent to halt the attacking troops. The message didn't get through to everyone and a Company of Royal Fusiliers advanced on its own. It was wiped out, along with the attached section of Royal Engineers. Elsewhere, other British units got to their objectives only to be fought straight back out of them again.

The Hammers were ordered up in support of this counter attack which eventually brought the German assault to a halt but with grievous losses for the British. A persistent rain and the never ending heavy artillery continued unabated as they relieved some badly mauled units in the new front line. A measure of the confusion and chaos is illustrated by this handover. The relief by the West Ham men commenced at 7pm on the 25th but was not completed until 3am on the 26th, when the shredded remnants of the London Regiment wearily struggled out of the line.

At dawn, Minenwerfer, (a sort of large German trench mortar which was noiseless in flight), began pounding the British lines and it was the Hammers first encounter with them, as recorded in the war diary. This particularly unpleasant experience was bought to a halt by the timely intervention of excellent shooting from artillery units recently arrived at this section of the front. As Jenns simply states, the Minenwerfer *"were not heard again for some time..."* Overnight, a patrol by the Hammers in No Man's Land didn't go particularly well, with 2/Lt Martinson, L/Cpl G Keer, Pte W Baker and Pte AC Giles all wounded. They managed to return and Baker and Giles remained at duty. Having captured their objectives in the mine craters, the enemy advance halted, dug in and began to consolidate their new line under continued bombardment. Reconnaissance aircraft showed that Freytag-Loringhoven's attack was merely local and not the full scale offensive to capture Arras initially feared at GHQ. As unsatisfactory as the situation was, it was by no means untenable and Haig determined to make the best of it. Besides, he didn't have the troops for any full scale offensive to retake the lost ground.

On the 27th another dreaded gas alert was sounded and more of the originals were struck off, with two killed while enduring heavy artillery bombardments. Pte Arthur Sidney Motton was twenty-one and lived in Hartland Road, Stratford. Pte Alfred Winsper Perceval was twenty-three and came from Woodville Grove in Mildmay Park, Islington. Both now lie buried in the Cabaret Rouge Military Cemetery. Also wounded were Pte W Waving, Pte F Branton (who remained, patched up, at duty), L/Cpl FW Gevaux and Pte George W Carter. Carter was taken to the Advanced Dressing Station just outside Souchez but was so badly wounded that he died two days later. He was forty and had left his wife Bessie with their three children at home in Chapel Street, Feltwell near Brandon in Norfolk. He too now lies in the Cabaret Rouge Military Cemetery.

Frederick Gevaux had his 'Blighty' wound, hit by shrapnel in the right shoulder, very close to the spine. A glassblower by trade, he was another Huguenot. The silk weaving Geveaux family originally came to England around 1685 from the Lot-et-Garonne region of south-west France. The shrapnel was never taken from Frederick's back but he lived until 1933, dying at home in Hornchurch aged fifty-three.

The shelling, described for the next two days as *"continuous"* wounded two more of D Company. Pte HG Weston also had a 'Blighty' and by August was discharged with a Silver War Badge for *"services rendered"*. 2/Lt Harry West meanwhile had only been with the Hammers for a few weeks, having completed his officer training course in the Spring. He had seen action at Loos the previous year as a sergeant and had a lot in common with William Busby as master of the Ingatestone Scout Troop.

While the German offensive gradually petered out on May 30th, Papillon arrived back from leave, bringing with him the battalion's relief, in the form of their old friends the Footballers. Due to the uncertainty of the situation the West Ham men were placed in support and formed into working parties. Beneath the bursts of shelling they set to the task of repairing the trenches and consolidating the new line while remaining ready for immediate action.

L/Cpl Henry Thomas, who had enlisted at Stratford, was killed outright and later buried in the Cabaret Rouge British Military Cemetery, while Pte J Tully, Pte AA Spurling and Pte PJ Llewellyn were wounded. Eventually the bombardment ceased and the line settled down into 'normality'. There was some anxiety that evening when a 'stand to' alert was ordered at 8pm after German troops were seen moving around behind their line but, as the Brigade war diary laconically states, "*nothing came of it...*"

Freytag-Loringhoven returned to his staff job a much lauded hero but the respite from the attentions of the detested British & Commonwealth tunnellers, hard won for the Germans, was only brief. As the new line settled down the Royal Engineers began opening new entrances and swiftly broke into their old galleries.

Within a few days they were right back under the German lines in the northern sector of Vimy Ridge.

(Newham Archive)

William Crow,
Mayor and Councillor of West Ham

(Essex Regt Museum)
L-R: (unknown), Alf Buxton, Harry Sharman and Frank Trumble, the Adjutant

(Essex Regt Museum)
Harry Handley Sharman

(Essex Regiment Museum)
Harry Sharman (R) leads men of D Company along Stratford Grove

(Newham Scouts) (Newham Scouts)

William Busby, District Scout Master of West Ham becomes 2/Lt WW Busby

(Michael Holden)

Lt-Col & Mrs PR Papillon and the Hammers Mess staff

(Keeble Family)

(Alston Collection)

Charles Carson stands to the right of a seated Frank Keeble. Behind are believed to be Robert Swan (L) and JD Patterson (R), the Malay rubber plantation owners

on left, Dr Alan Holthusen, Medical Officer of the West Ham Battalion

(Newham Archive)

The West Ham Battalion march along Stratford Grove, April, 1915

(Essex Regt Museum)

(L-R) Harry Sharman sits beside Alan Holthusen. An unknown Officer is sat beside the Robinson brothers
And on the right is believed to be Robert Page.

(Greeno Family)

Members of the HQ Company. On the far left stands George Greeno, a signals runner. Third from left in the front row sits Ernie Kurtz, the battalion tailor while in the centre sits Sgt William Gilbert. The Corporal sitting on the right may well possibly be the writer of the War Diary, Frank Jenns.

(Essex Regt Museum)

The West Ham Battalion Drum & Bugle Band

(Michael Holden)

On the left, Ernie Kurtz as the West Ham Battalion tailor

(Bannon Family)

(Greeno Family)

(Essex Regt Museum)

Members of A Company (top), C Company (middle) and D Company (bottom)

(Michael Harris)

Robert Shrapnel Biddulph-Pinchard,
Transport Officer for 6th Brigade

(Michael Holden)

Seated at the back, Paul Barth in
the West Ham Battalion Post Office

(Essex Regt Museum)

The West Ham Battalion barber shop

(Shillingford Family)

Tom Shillingford notes that this photo of his PT routine was taken at 5am

(Michael Holden)

The West Ham Battalion Police and their shackles. The Corporal on the left also appears with the dog in the photo of the barber shop. It is unknown if the dog travelled to France with the Hammers.

(Alston Collection)

Members of the Hammers Battalion do their laundry...

(Essex Regt Museum)

...and relax with bread and tea

(Alston Collection)

Photo entitled Kitchener's Kitchen

(Alston Collection)

"After Dinner"

(Karen Harvey)

Members of D Company including, second in from the right, William King with his arm in a sling and cap on knee

(Essex Regt Museum)

Harry Sharman seated centre with Dick Collier on the right. Other officers as yet unknown

Part 2

Reinforced

The Somme, 1916 – The Ancre, 1917

Chapter 16

"Your Loss is Ours Too"

June 1916 began with the West Ham Battalion still in support around Carency, centred on Souchez. As if to underline the 'business as usual' attitude of the tunnellers, three huge mines were exploded on the 1st under the Germans opposite. The Footballers then determinedly engaged in a vicious bayonet fight to capture and hold the resultant craters, the largest of which they christened 'Football Crater'. The Hammers were heavily shelled as they hurriedly assembled to be bought forward in immediate support. C Company formed into carrying parties bringing up ammunition, sandbags, tools and any other equipment the Footballers needed to strengthen the positions in the craters. It was a highly dangerous role especially when conducted beneath a violent artillery duel. From mid afternoon to 10pm the German artillery rained shells on the craters and the British front line as Busby and men of D Company commendably assisted the Kings in a raid on the German positions, with the Sapping Platoon ferrying supplies of grenades to them. Consolidating this new line added to the already long casualty list written up by Jenns: L/Sgt W Oughton, Cpl FW Cansdale, L/Cpl JR Knight, L/Cpl TC Day, Pte AE Stone, Pte A Lewin, Pte HJ Hemmings, Pte F Smith, Pte AJ Dowse, Pte J Baggott, Pte WJ Jeans, Pte MT Emmings, Pte A Robinson, Pte SG Tanner, Pte B Gormley, Pte HA Puckett, Pte JH Hassell and Pte J Ince were all local men wounded by shrapnel or snipers. The German heavy artillery then joined in, severely damaging the trenches in front of Papillon's HQ. Despite this, it remained in-situ for the time being practically becoming the Brigade HQ for all troops in the chaotic area.

This equally applied to the Regimental aid post where Alan Holthusen, the medical officer, was working feverishly in very confined and extremely dangerous conditions. Since joining, Dr Holthusen had refused to wear his service tunic, opting instead to wear his tweed jacket which had served him so well at his GP's surgery in Wanstead. He also wore a battered trilby for his time at the front until the initial introduction of steel 'shrapnel' helmets a month or so before. Altogether that night, Holthusen personally treated over ninety casualties from three different regiments, including those Hammers listed above who were brought in by the fearless stretcher bearers like Norman Bellinger. Unable to evacuate them because of the intensity of the shelling, Holthusen and his orderlies took on the status of an advanced dressing station (ADS). They finally managed to move the wounded to the rear by motor lorry between 6am and 11am.

Another casualty was Pte Ernie Crisp. He had lost his L/Cpl stripes after the incident when he assaulted the sentry involved with the tragic deaths of his friends in the cellar at Calonne back in March. Crisp was coming to the end of his ninety-one days Field Punishment No1 when he was hit in the right leg by shrapnel and eventually sent back to Blighty to recover in hospital. He was then posted to the Depot Company, under the command of the Mayor's son Leo Dyer. Having remained in England, Captain Dyer had not seen any action on the battlefield and it is natural to wonder just how well they got on with each other.

The next day, Pte Joseph Newman from Bromley (by Bow) and Pte John Williamson from Hackney Wick (at that time attached to the Brigade's trench mortar unit), were killed by the ever present attentions of the German artillery. Both lie buried in Cabaret Rouge Military Cemetery. Jenns wrote up yet another long list of wounded: Sgt Percy Cotton, L/Cpl H Clark, L/Cpl HE Archer, L/Cpl PE Wilson, Pte WL Cooper, Pte JW Cains, Pte S Ault, Pte AE Burley and Pte DC Baker. The roll of originals ran ever thinner.

The stretcher bearers were 'out in all weathers' bringing these wounded away from the firing line. Norman Bellinger was finally recognised when he was awarded the recently instituted Military Medal for carrying out *"his duties in a brave and efficient manner, in many instances under hostile fire, particularly on 15th May 1916, at Calonne, when though not yet recovered from a wound previously received* [when he had tried in vain to save Joe Cooper], *he dressed the wounds of Lance-Corporal Dutton and assisted to carry him down when under shell fire, and also at Carency, Northern Sub-Section, on the night 1/2nd June, when he assisted to bring down several wounded men during the consolidation of the three mines blown in that night. Similar actions have been performed by him on other occasions..."* Bellinger went on to be appointed Corporal on 11th July 1916, a popular promotion and a further personal mark of respect from Papillon.

One man not requiring a stretcher bearer was Pte Thomas Crispin, a labourer who lived with his wife Charlotte on Walton Road in Manor Park. He was trying to grab some brief sleep in a funk hole when he was fatally hit by a large chunk of shrapnel. Crispin's body was wrapped in his waterproof sheet and placed to one side. On the evening of the 3rd June their ordeal, if not at an end, was very much reduced. Relieved by the Footballers, they were spotted by the German artillery observers who shelled them as they moved out to the north of Carency and the area of the Quarries. Pte JH Sart was wounded by shrapnel, but he '*remained at duty*'. For the following two days, the West Ham Battalion provided working and wiring parties, doing the mundane everyday chores which typified the highly dangerous life of a soldier at the front. A shell landed amid one of these, adding four more to the casualty list: Pte E Langley, Pte J Cross, Pte JS Turner and Pte GH Waite. Thomas Crispin was finally buried and became yet another Hammer lying in Cabaret Rouge cemetery. At last, on the 6th June 1916, the Hammers were relieved and moved out of the area into billets in Villers au Bois, a short distance behind the reserve lines. They were exhausted. Four days of rest in the hot sunshine was a time to repair their equipment, clean themselves and their uniforms, to receive mail and the news from home. It was here that they learnt of the death of the man whose finger had pointed at them all as they signed their enlistment papers. The Secretary of State for War, Field Marshal the Lord Kitchener, had died en route to Russia when his ship HMS Hampshire had been sunk.

It was also a time to write letters and, for the officers, they were to the relatives of men who had not made it this far. William Busby was the D Company officer responsible for writing to the parents of Thomas Crispin. Its composition was difficult and made all the more poignant because Busby was aware that Thomas's younger brother had died from wounds received at Gallipoli only six months before.

"I am writing to you on behalf of the Officers and men of D Company to say how deeply we sympathise with you over the death of your son. We have just had a very trying time in the trenches and it was during this time he met his death. At the time, he was not actually in the front line but doing his work in a shelter made in the hillside. A piece of shell penetrated this shelter and so severely wounded him that he died shortly afterwards. Although anything I say will do little to heal the wound caused by your bereavement, it may be some small comfort to you to know that he has always proved himself a very able and efficient soldier carrying out orders with a cheerfulness which was an example to his comrades, so that your loss will be ours too..."

Reading the obituary in the Stratford Express, Capt Harry 'Nutty' Sharman (still recuperating from his gassing) was moved to write to the grieving family that he *"was his old Company Commander from the early days in Stratford until the end of January last and always found him a good soldier and to be relied upon…"* It was a measure of the man that he should do this and a measure too of the strong bond among the originals of the Hammers Battalion: a tangible sense of pride and belonging which only exists between men facing death on a daily basis. A true 'Pals Battalion' in every sense of the word.

On June 10th, the Hammers Battalion moved further out to Estree Cauchie, taking over huts where they speculated about rumours they were hearing of a Big Push. Replacements began arriving, still local volunteers at this stage and mostly from Captain Dyer's depot but still men new to the true horrors of this war. More importantly, there were also the combat experienced officers who continued to be spread, albeit thinly, throughout the New Army. Although Jenns doesn't mention it in the war diary, totally contrary to army practice, three such desperately needed officers arrived as the Hammers returned to the front line in mid June.

The newly promoted Captain James Murray Round was from Witham in Essex. He had already been wounded twice when hit simultaneously by two sniper bullets, one in each arm, later described as *"nothing serious…"* Captain Round brought much needed experience. Only twenty-two years old and looking even younger, James Round was nevertheless a hardened veteran in terms of the Great War. His younger brother Auriol was already dead from action while his elder brother serving elsewhere had been awarded the Military Cross. Arriving with James Round was twenty year old Lt Henry Blamaires Wilcock who had seen service in Egypt. He was living with his family at the rectory in the village of Tolleshunt Knights near Colchester when war broke out. After his elder brother volunteered Henry was one of the many 'young men of good families' who became an officer. The third arrival, Captain Edwin Milward Charrington, was twenty-five years old. He lived with his parents and sister at Eton Terrace, a few doors down from Papillon's London flat. Charrington had been about to move to China when war broke out but put his job with the Union Insurance Company of Canton on hold. He had been serving in France since February 1915 and was very badly wounded at Fortun a few months later. His left arm was shattered by shrapnel in an explosion which also tore off his nose completely and inflicted severe damage to his head. He recovered his health and confidence and by November, while the Hammers were on the troopship Princess Victoria entering France, he was working at the Army Signal Service in Bletchley before successfully requesting another combat posting. This was despite having to wear an aluminium prosthetic 'tin' nose, noticeably severe permanent scarring and being exempt from route marching due to difficult respiration. Arriving at the West Ham Battalion, he would eventually become A Company's commander and was a very popular officer. The initial resentment of the class ridden regular army officers was gradually dissipated as young men like these proved themselves time and again on the field of battle.

Captain Trumble meanwhile had finally succumbed to failing health and was admitted to base hospital in the rear. He wouldn't be returning to the Hammers, eventually moving to a job at Brigade HQ. Consequently, Jenns and the war diary were being signed off by another new 'acting' Adjutant, Cyril Lionel Bishop Lyne. Born in Stratford and raised in Castleton Road, Walthamstow he had sailed, like many, to Canada seeking his fortune or simple employment and was quick to spring to the defence of the mother country in August 1914. After officer training, 2/Lt Lyne joined C Company while they were undertaking initial training on Wanstead Flats. The twenty-three year old was a regular billiards partner to William Busby and the others back at the Alexandra Mess in Stratford.

The intensely hot days towards the middle of June 1916 saw the West Ham Battalion about to return to the front line, but into the now relatively quiet sector near Berthonval with Berthonval Wood immediately to the south. Officially their position was at the southern subsector of Vimy Ridge and they were taking over from the Highland Light Infantry. Papillon, along with his Company officers, carried out the usual inspection of the lines prior to taking over responsibility. Though not the 'hottest' area in terms of enemy activity, it had been subjected to the usual destructive attentions of the German artillery. The industrious Scottish battalion was hard at work repairing and improving the battered trenches and they were naturally reticent to leave this 'safe' sector, with its huge underground caverns equipped with bunk beds for those out of the line. Their destination, Mont St Eloi, was far less luxuriously equipped.

On taking over on the 18th June, the West Ham Battalion spent a quiet couple of days settling in. Jenns records the fact that *"desultory German shelling wounded one man..."* Papillon was impressed by the condition of the trenches and was moved to report to Arthur Daly at Brigade HQ praising *"the excellent work done by the battalion who handed over to us. My Company officers and I reconnoitred the line and the improvement in all the conditions was very marked when we took over. A great deal of hard work must have been done under none too favourable conditions..."* It would, however, appear that it was not only the Highlanders who had been industrious. The Germans opposite had also been very busy in the last few days. Intelligence officers had discovered a number of mysterious anomalies appearing on the German frontline. Alarm bells began ringing at Divisional level.

The Hammers immediately stepped up their night patrols, exploring No-Man's Land and collecting more information.

Chapter 17

Seeing Red

20th June 1916 blossomed into sunshine as Papillon, Lt William Busby and Lt Frank Keeble, marched sixty-two 'other ranks' off to Divisional HQ at the Chateau de la Haie, close to the village of Servins. The Hammers had been selected by Arthur Daly to mount a major raid on the German lines opposite Vincent Street trench which was a definite vote of confidence in the 'untried' New Army battalion. Trench raids were essentially intelligence gathering operations, collecting anything of value including, of course, prisoners. Sometimes trench mortar positions or machine gun posts were targeted if they had become too 'annoying' and, on the whole, the success or not of a raid had a direct effect on the morale of the units involved. No doubt some of the Hammers selected for this raiding party cautiously remembered just how well they had defended themselves against experienced German trench raiders at the Brickstacks back in the January frost. For others, perhaps that was an extra encouragement.

The sixty-two 'other ranks' had been hand picked by Busby and Keeble for their aggression and determination learnt the hard way: fighting bare knuckle on the quaysides and in the wharves and pubs around the London docks. Keeble himself was described as an officer with *"push"*, *"drive"* and *"the right spirit..."* With them was the Hammer's regular second in command, Captain Arthur Gracie Hayward. He was thirty-three years old and the son of Reverend Samuel Gracie Hayward, vicar of both Upton Cressett and nearby Monkhopton in Shropshire on land owned by relatives of Pelham Papillon. One farm in the diocese was coincidentally named Upton Park. Hayward had studied for his Masters Degree at Oxford where he was also a noted champion boxer, especially against Cambridge. After a spell as a private secretary, Arthur had left England, travelling to Fiji to become a civil administrator in the colonial service but, again like so many, had put his career on hold and returned at the outbreak of hostilities. He became a temporary Inspector for a local charity in Stratford while he applied to the Royal Flying Corps, but on finding that it would take some time to gain his wings and see action, he enlisted instead in the West Ham Battalion.

The woods and gardens surrounding the Chateau de la Haie were a veritable paradise after the conditions they had been enduring in the trenches. Four fine avenues laid out to the points of the compass led to the chateau which was huge enough to easily accommodate two full battalions. The grounds, covering fifty acres, featured a wide array of wooden huts built as messes, theatres, offices, assembly rooms and a myriad of outbuildings. The chateau was well within range of the enemy heavy artillery, yet it remained almost untouched and it was rumoured to belong to a German Count. It was here that on the 22nd the raiding party heard of the death at No30 Field Hospital of L/Cpl Edward Probyn of B Company. Only twenty years old, Edward lived with his parents at Hockley Avenue in East Ham and had been wounded a few weeks before. While he was buried in Quatre Vents Cemetery back at the trenches Pte E Hill and Pte EJ Godfrey were both wounded.

Twenty-five more soldiers, led by the popular acting Regimental Sergeant Major George Cattermole, arrived at the chateau to find that dummy trenches, resembling those of the intended area of operations, had been dug. The training continued through the hot summer days even when the West Ham raiders were visited by an excited group of French and Spanish journalists. They watched approvingly as the Hammers carried out their first full scale rehearsal. Then the heavens opened and a torrential downpour lasting for two days turned the ground into a quagmire.

Rehearsals continued despite the weather but on the final day of their training, an unfortunate accident marred the budding excitement. William Busby was conducting bombing practise with a group of raiders when a grenade suddenly exploded prematurely. Whether it was someone's personal mistake or a manufacturing flaw, Pte Albert Giles of Melbourne Road in Walthamstow took the brunt of the explosion and was killed instantly. He was to become another buried in Caberet Rouge Cemetery. Pte Arthur Ellis, an Islington man, was close enough to be badly hit by shrapnel, but he fought on for a further twenty-four hours. Today, he lies in Barlin Cemetery. Pte RP Pogson (who was still recovering after being hit during a trench mortar attack back in April), Pte E Baker and Cpl JJ Karkell were also wounded in the grenade accident but eventually all three returned to duty.

Back at the frontline trenches there had been some excitement when a German observation balloon was seen to be shot down in flames by British aircraft. These observers were used, among other things, to 'spot' the accuracy of the artillery. Despite the loss, the light German shelling remained constant and on-target for some days. Pte HJ Chace became a casualty as did Pte Albert Pluck, CSM Fred Bartley and Pte J Ward. While Pluck and Bartley remained patched up at duty, Ward died later that day and was buried close to Arthur Ellis in Barlin Cemetery. The shelling then increased in intensity, wounding Pte AW Stanton and L/Cpl CE Pears but killing Pte Jacks. George William Jacks was twenty-six years old and from Plaistow, where he lived with his parents in Corporation Street. He received a battlefield burial in a marked grave and now rests in the Canadian Cemetery No2 at Neuville St Vaast. L/Cpl Pears became yet another patched up by the efficient Dr Holthusen. Pte Fred Arnold was also wounded and evacuated but at the CCS this quickly turned into 'trench fever', a virus spread by the body lice and with symptoms similar to malaria. Arnold was from Acacia Avenue in Leytonstone, but unfortunately his illness also led to the discovery that he was underage and after recovery he didn't rejoin the Hammers.

Returning from the chateau, Captain Hayward's preparations began immediately. Of prime importance was the selection of replacements for those injured in the grenade accident. Despite his recent wounds, CSM Fred Bartley was chosen, along with several other violently capable men. The raiders were billeted in 'Zouave Valley', which was not much more than a shallow dip in the countryside. It was named after the gaudily dressed French soldiers, in their blue jackets and scarlet pantaloons, who had fought and died in their thousands at this spot in the bitter 1915 defence of their homeland. Zouave Valley now teemed with khaki clad British and Commonwealth men, from every arm of the service. They were sheltered from enemy observation balloons but were not immune to a speculative shell whizzing among them. Here, the raiders enjoyed a special meal together, organised by Lt's Norman Lang and Tom Brind. It was a real treat by the standards of the front. Soup was followed by beef and ham sandwiches and finally some cakes for desert. Cigars and the '*usual liqueurs*' were then shared out. Frank Keeble had ensured that this '*Zouave Buffet*' even had its own unique menu with a Hammers theme, somehow organising an excellent illustration in a very convincing imitation of the popular artist Bruce Bairnsfather, featuring a signpost pointing back to West Ham and a papillon/butterfly fluttering amid shellfire.

After the meal some quietly wrote those last letters home. They had all long ago filled out the Last Will and Testament page in their pay book. Discarding any item that might rattle or which contained anything of a personal nature, small groups chattered nervously as the tension began to take hold. Elsewhere, momentous and tragic events were unfolding as 1st July dawned and the Battle of the Somme began.

As dawn broke here on the Vimy sector, a final conference was held at the advanced Brigade HQ. Among the senior officers in attendance were Major General Walker VC commanding the Division, Brigadier's Daly and Saunders who was commanding the Divisional Artillery. Zero hour for the raid was fixed at 0039hrs that night and several signals and code words were approved. These were primarily in case of unforeseen problems which might cause the cancellation of the enterprise. It was planned that there was to be a whirlwind bombardment by six specially assigned Stokes mortars at zero hour for exactly one minute. They were manned by soldiers selected from within the ranks of 6th Brigade and included some original members of the Hammers, such as Pte Stan Kirvan, a 19 year old van boy from Bidder Street in Canning Town. The Stokes mortars were particularly nasty but highly effective, little more than a light trench mortar redesigned as an anti personnel weapon and strikingly similar in design to versions still used today.

The artillery would also place an accurate 'box barrage' around the target area from zero hour and maintain it until the raiding party had returned to the British frontline. Intended to reduce the danger from the German defenders themselves, the box barrage equally prevented both reinforcement and escape. The 'advanced bombing posts' in the 'sap' trenches edging out into No Man's Land were to be withdrawn prior to zero hour. The remainder of the West Ham Battalion would be placed in 'stand to' positions in case of any hostile counter attack. Finally, the system of signalling with coloured lights would be placed by the signallers out in No Man's Land. The lights would be facing the British front lines, denoting the area of attack and, more importantly, acting as a guide to the returning troops as they stumbled back in the inky blackness before dawn.

The conference lasted for about an hour. Papillon and Captain Hayward then returned directly to the men. Communications were, as now, considered absolutely vital. The use of coloured lights and bugle notes had their advantages in some circumstances but in the middle of No Man's Land during an artillery bombardment both were of very limited use. Between themselves Papillon and Hayward devised a system of communication as brilliantly effective as it was simple. Dubbed the 'four in hand', it consisted of the attacking raiding party being divided into four 'sticks' or columns of fifteen men, all controlled by Hayward. He would move forward slowly, assessing the lie of the land, before deciding which group to pull forward next. He was connected, by four long lengths of twine through the darkness to the officer (Busby and Keeble) or Warrant Officer (Cattermole and Bartley) in charge of the particular 'stick'. When it was safe to move quietly closer to the German trench, Captain Hayward would simply tug on the appropriate line and the stick would silently advance a few more yards. This had obvious advantages when silence was of supreme essence. In a war that had become horrendously wasteful with lives it was well received by the men who were about to trust their lives in the darkness of No Man's Land to this unusual innovation.

A final briefing took place in the warm sunset over the Zouave Valley. As evening darkened, the conversation turned to news filtering through of the massive attacks along the Somme front. Though not yet realised, it was to be the blackest day in the history of the British Army with sixty-thousand casualties, of whom more than eighteen-thousand were dead. The opening artillery barrages could be heard across Europe, even back home in Forest Gate, where one resident, Harry Smith of Henderson Road, wrote to the Stratford Express to describe how some of his neighbours *"feared it was an attempted invasion! I have never in all my life heard so persistent and continuous booming of guns..."*

Eventually, conversations and small talk tailed off as their last preparations were completed. Minds focused on the target for tonight in the German front line. A few days before, air observations had picked out what appeared to be previously unknown positions for Minenwerfer (a German version of a trench mortar), together with new machine gun emplacements. The purpose of this raid was to confirm or otherwise the existence of these anomalies and also to pick up any available intelligence about the general German positions. Prisoners were wanted for interrogation.

Straps were tightened. Weapons checked again and again. Faces and hands had been blackened with charcoal. The men wore balaclavas or their black woollen 'cap comforter' hats in place of their peaked caps and tin hats. Apart from revolvers, most of the weapons were almost medieval in nature. Razor sharp fighting knives, brutal knobkerries wrapped in barbed wire, heavy clubs bristling with rusty nails and crowned with gear cogs, long spiked knuckle dusters and other personal favourites were fingered with nervousness or confidence and adjusted into easily accessible positions around the body. These were essential items for the close quarter fighting anticipated. Some were keenly looking forward to it. Now really was *"the chance to get a good smack at the Germans..."* As the clock ticked down to zero hour the men were quietly assembled by Captain Hayward. Papillon spoke a few private words of encouragement and firmly shook the hand of each member of the raiding party as they filed into their 'jump off' positions in Vincent Street trench. Finally, a brief, whispered meeting between the officers took place. They shook hands, smoked a last cigarette and wished each other good luck. Papillon chose a spot on the fire-step to watch what he could of proceedings and remained there for the entire operation.

Captain Arthur Hayward, the controller, took his place ahead of the centre party. Behind him, RSM George Cattermole led the right centre party alongside CSM Fred Bartley on the left. Alongside was Lt William Busby's party on the right with Lt Frank Keeble leading on the left. These were the men who would be responsible, not only for holding the sections of trench captured for the duration of the raid but also detailed for various specific jobs such as Bartley bombing the dug outs, 'blocking' parties under William Busby holding off any reinforcements who might make it through, identification parties led by Cattermole and finally, six men under Frank Keeble specifically detailed to search for and retrieve the suspected machine guns. A further forty men were detailed as stretcher bearers, signallers and runners, to form a covering party. They would remain back in No Man's Land, under the command of another NCO.

Ten minutes to go. Hayward slipped over the lip of the front line trench and slithered out into No Man's Land followed after a few minutes by the other raiders as he tugged on their line. They crawled and crept silently, unobserved, to within sixty-five yards of the German wire, arriving in position on either flank of Hayward. There they waited and waited. Now the battalion runner set off, back to the artillery observers. Pte George Greeno was to return by the quickest route possible, silently. On arrival, he gave the thumbs up and reported that everything was ready.

At precisely 00.39hrs the Stokes guns opened up, intense rapid fire as planned, for exactly one minute. The Hammers out front lay hugging the ground as they watched the terrifyingly brilliant orange and blue flashes illuminate the German lines. Knuckles whitened. With each deafening explosion they heard the desperate screams of the enemy caught in this vicious and unexpected barrage cutting the wire. Captain Hayward checked his watch and as the last Stokes fired he tugged all four lines, stood up and raised his pistol. His raiding party was unleashed and flew past with a throaty terrifying roar of "Up the Hammers!" and "Up the Irons!" Both battle cries seem to have been initially used in the West Ham Battalion, another possible indicator of the number of former Thames Ironworkers within its ranks.

Lt Frank Keeble, the fit farmer, accelerated forward over the chopped up ground and led the charge by a couple of yards. Above them all, an intense artillery bombardment opened up, as planned. It screamed over their heads and accurately targeted the communication trenches to the rear. From here, the German defenders would normally expect instant reinforcements but they were now effectively blocked, as were the flanks of the frontline trench. This barrage would continue unabated throughout the raid, precisely defining the battlefield and adding to the sheer terror of those trapped, 'boxed in'. Before the Germans knew it, the Hammers were on top of them.

On the left Lt Frank Keeble, still sporting a sore three week old wound on his left calf, was the very first man of all the screaming trench raiders to leap down at speed into a mass of confused and terrified men still cowering from the bombardment. As he landed, he broke part of his left leg but immediately levelled his Webley pistol and shot dead the three Germans closest to him. Keeble was then wounded in the arm, shoulder and leg on the right hand side, by a grenade. It might possibly have been due to 'friendly fire', on account of just how quickly he had entered the trench.

The Stokes guns, for their part, had evidently done their work perfectly. As well as cutting apart the barbed wire very efficiently, one mortar fired a lucky shot. A German ration party had been feeding a squad who were engaged on reconstructing part of their frontline. All were killed outright precisely at the moment the first Stokes mortar shells struck. Captain Hayward, the keen pugilist, later recalled that he was *"aware of around ten to twelve enemy dead before the fight began..."* He was wounded in the arm soon after, by shrapnel or a bullet. Behind him, the Hammers dashed to the German front line and poured over the lip of the trench with only one casualty, possibly caused by the box barrage. In the murky gloom a fierce, violent fight instantly erupted. The specially chosen group of brawlers very pugnaciously gained the upper hand with pistol, knife, club, fist and boot. Now, in all parts of the congested trench, illuminated like a strobe by the constant flashes of the 'box barrage' and with screams muffled by the noise of explosions, the Hammers had "*seen red*". In fact, they were *"thoroughly enjoying themselves"*, as Arthur Daly later described it, *"killing Germans..."*

While this was happening, some of the enemy had initially fled along the narrow communications trench to the rear, fearing a full scale attack. The nimble ones who escaped quickest were the first to be chopped to pieces by the well defined box barrage of No9 Battery, Royal Field Artillery. Only wide enough for a couple of men, the long zigzag communication trench became a terrifying bottle neck when they were closely followed by William Busby's party and *"bombed"*. His men were pitching grenades with accuracy and following up with well practised unforgiving bayonet butchery. They worked their way along, stepping on the dead and ignoring those pleading for their lives. Twenty or so were reported by him as being *"definitely killed"* with more left wounded and bleeding out.

Over on the left, Frank Keeble was himself still bleeding in three places from the shrapnel of the grenade. With adrenaline proving to be the wonder of nature he then further ignored the pain of his broken leg and attacked his second objective. He had to deal with short 'sap' trenches which led towards the British frontline like fingers. Keeble's party destroyed them with accurate and intense bombing, killing at least five more Germans on the way. However, the suspected machine gun post was found to be empty so they moved on to the Minenwerfer position which was found to be a mineshaft. A number of grenades were quickly dropped down the entrance.

Meanwhile, a group of confused Germans were *"seen off"* by Captain Hayward's centre party. The left section, led by CSM Fred Bartley, had already encountered stiff resistance in the trench. One group of Germans re-entered a dugout but were personally dealt with by Bartley. Six of them were killed and scores more wounded. His group then engaged in a desperate hand to hand fight during a vicious melee in and around the dugout entrances. On the right, CSM Cattermole's section had enjoyed the element of perfect surprise as they dropped in from No Man's Land, screaming fiercely, on a huddling group of young Saxon recruits. In his report written later, Arthur Daly concisely describes it as nothing more than *"bayonet work..."* The West Ham men tore into the hapless enemy. Five Germans were killed before six more were run to ground in a shallow dugout. Here five of them were killed, including one by George Cattermole personally. That German was an officer, most likely the enthusiastic and well-liked Leutnant Hammerich. George alone then suddenly remembered the purpose of the raid and the last German still alive in the chaotic bloodlust was taken prisoner. The young conscript must have expected the very worst when Cattermole produced his cut throat razor, considering the nightmarish butchery still erupting around him. But George calmly bent down and cut one of the shoulder straps from a dead man, stuffing it in his tunic pocket. It bore the insignia of the Saxon 162nd Regiment. Searching the pockets of the dead Leutnant Hammerich George then found *"two books of military value"*, all vital intelligence. The conscript was taken as the sole prisoner from the raid and George also retrieved Hammerich's pistol, as a souvenir.

After these twenty minutes of furious brutality and carnage in the enemy front line, the bleeding Captain Hayward blew his whistle and gave the order to gather up the wounded and retire back to the West Ham lines. With a backward glance, George Cattermole was the very last man to leave the body strewn trench.

Now was the danger time, after the German artillery had recovered from their initial shock of the assault. As the raiders slowly picked their way back across No Man's Land, eventually meeting up with the covering party, the German battery commander correctly assessed exactly what was happening and began an extremely accurate and intense reply. Not out in No Man's Land, but directly in front of Vincent Street trench, the British front line. He knew the raiding party would naturally make their way back to safety by the shortest possible route and most of the casualties on the raid were received here, within spitting distance of the relative safety of their own trenches. George Cattermole and Fred Bartley, together with William Busby and a wounded Frank Keeble remained out in No Man's Land, guiding their men back through the wire into the waiting arms of their comrades and the relieved Papillon.

As dawn broke over the battlefield the four finally came in themselves, having brought back every man they could, alive or dead. There were in total forty-two wounded, including Captain Hayward and Lt. Keeble, and although hailed a great success the raid had made a casualty of nearly half of those involved. The dead were initially named as Pte W May, Pte EW Clark, Pte A Newton, Pte GH Moss, Pte HJ Edwards and Pte EH Turner. They had all been amongst the first to enlist, local lads buried together in the Zouave Valley Military Cemetery to the south of the town of Souchez. The wounded were immediately treated by Dr Holthusen, and then evacuated by Norman Bellinger and his stretcher bearers to aid posts nearby. Four died within hours of reaching safety. Pte Fredrick Argent was twenty-four years old when his life ended at the CCS outside Mont St Eloi. From Abbey Road in Barking he had enlisted at East Ham. He lies buried in Ecoivres Military Cemetery. Pte Tom Minahane was an Irish docker, living with his brother (who was also serving in the battalion) down East India Dock Road in Poplar when he enlisted and only twenty-one when he died. He is buried alongside his fellow Irishman Cpl Fredrick William in the Barlin Communal Cemetery.

Two more were posted as missing. L/Cpl Albert Bolton was only twenty years old, from Fern Street in Bow and considered to be one of the promising soldiers of Busby's D Company. Only his name is inscribed on the Arras Memorial.

Not much is known about twenty-eight year old Pte John Berney, other than he came originally from St George's in the East and was worthy of inclusion in the Roll of Honour compiled by theatrical trade paper The Stage. Berney was living on Hazlewood Road in Walthamstow when he enlisted early in 1915. He was most likely alive when captured, as the German 162nd Regiment's history notes the taking of a prisoner during this raid (which they also claimed to have "*beaten off*"). Berney didn't make it to a POW camp however and is "regarded to have died" somewhere later.

His is another name inscribed on the Arras Memorial to the Missing.

Chapter 18

Gongs

Early next morning, as the first light of dawn broke over the horizon, Pte Hockley dramatically reappeared from No Man's Land. He had become very lost in the shellfire during the return journey but, with a cheer, he was greeted as a hero by his Company. The angry retaliatory shelling continued for the next twenty-four hours during which Pte Fred Sage was killed. He was a twenty-one year old from Colchester who worked in a leather tannery. Despite being an orphan, he was no doubt mourned back at Brown's Yard, off Magdalen Street, by the seventy year old widow, Mrs Bareham, with whom he lived.

At 5am, Papillon sat down to dictate his report on the raid to Brigade HQ. He made particular note *"of the way in which Capt Hayward organised and trained the raiding party and the coolness and courage with which he carried out every detail as planned."* Later in the day Brigadier-General Arthur Daly made his report to Divisional HQ, informing them that *"it may be fairly claimed that the raid was a success. The effect of the one minute's bombardment by the Stokes guns (six were used for this purpose) was exactly what I had anticipated. The enemy were so bewildered and disorganized by the terrifying explosions that they were thinking only of their own safety and the raiding party was in on top of them before they had time to pull themselves together. I thoroughly endorse all that Lt Colonel Papillon says of Captain Hayward. Great credit is also due to Lt Colonel Papillon himself who took an infinite amount of trouble to ensure the success of the raid. He was in the front line himself all the time..."* Daly also included Frank Keeble's 'Bairnsfather' menu from the Zoave Buffet with his report.

The Hammers were relieved from the trenches and marched jubilantly to billets at Camblain d'Abbe for a well earned 'rest'. Two days later, they marched further away to take over billets at Estree Cauchie. On their arrival, freshly promoted L/Sgt Jenns notes that a congratulatory 'wire' was sent from General Munro and read to all ranks, praise indeed for the West Ham men. On the 8th, Pte George Greeno, one of the battalion runners, received a Commendation from Major General Watkins, the Division Commander, in recognition of his *"Conspicuous Bravery in the Field"*. And it did not end there. On the 10th July the Corps Commander arrived at Estree Cauchie to congratulate the NCOs and men who had been awarded the recently instituted Military Medal, for *"gallantry on the night of 1/2nd July"*. L/Sgt Charles Walter Daniel Browring MM continued to serve in the battalion until disbandment, when he was then offered a commission elsewhere in the Essex Regiment, ending the war as a 2/Lt.

Pte Alfred Therin MM was also eventually offered a Commission. He survived the war and finished with the rank of Captain. His brother Cpl George Therin was wounded for the second time early in 1917 and would be medically discharged from the Hammers. Both men were originals, enlisting at Stratford and arriving in France together on the Princess Victoria.

Pte George Leopold Brown MM lived with his parents on Newcomen Road in Leytonstone. Pte EM Wilding MM joined the Hammers on 8th February 1915 and had a family in Monega Road in Forest Gate. He was formally a tough Quartermaster in the Merchant Service and had steamed home from India on the outbreak of war. He was noted as having enlisted while thoroughly drunk.

Pte JM Miller and Pte EH Simonds were also awarded the MM for their part in the trench raid. Both were local men and although little is known about Miller he did at least survive the war. Ernest Hugh Simonds was another who went on to become an officer in another regiment but was killed in early 1918.

The West Ham Battalion was in a celebratory mood and the following morning the entire raiding party was marched back to Camblain d' Abbe. There, they were personally inspected by General Munro who then read aloud a message sent from Lt General Kiggell, Chief of the General Staff at HQ, about how *"the numerous successful raids carried out along our front during the last few days have undoubtedly been of considerable assistance to our main operations besides having added appreciably to the enemy casualties. The Commander in Chief desires that his appreciation of a good day's work done may be conveyed to all who planned and carried out the raids."*

Captain Arthur Hayward, Lt William Busby and CSM George Cattermole were then asked to step forward to receive a congratulatory handshake from General Munro in response to being awarded the Military Cross for "gallantry on the night of the 1st/2nd July". Later in the month CSM Fred Bartley was awarded the battalion's first Distinguished Conduct Medal for his part in the raid. He later became an officer in another regiment and won a Military Cross in 1918. Lt Frank Keeble had been immediately evacuated out by Dr Holthusen and so missed his handshake. He was by now back in Blighty, being treated at a hospital in Reading for thirteen days. Frank then spent the rest of his recuperation until September at the Atherton Road home of Lt Reg Norman, the grocer from Stratford market.

Meanwhile, Pte EE Ellis took the first opportunity to write and pay his condolences to the father of Pte Willie May who was killed on the raid. Instead, he ended up being the bearer of terrible news. By whatever administrative mishap, Mr May senior hadn't been informed of his son's death and had only just received a chirpy letter from Willie in France. He was completely devastated by what Ellis told him and took his deep sorrows to the bar of his local pub in Leytonstone. For more than a week after the death, No9 District Records Office at Warley still showed Willie May as being alive and serving in the trenches unwounded, but he'd already been buried in Zouave Valley Cemetery close to the others who died in the raid.

Lt Tom Brind, the Hammers Quartermaster, was another hit with bitter news when he discovered that his eldest son and apprentice on the Thames had been killed on the 'First Day of the Somme' with another battalion of the Essex Regiment. Percy, who he had taught so much about London's great river, was never found on the battlefield. He is remembered on the Thiepval Memorial.

These trench raids were held up as shining examples of military successes and were heavily reported in the newspapers back home. It was merely in an attempt to curb the effects on public (and military) morale of the horrendous losses being suffered.

The Somme was by now carving destruction along the entire front, as it swallowed men and ordnance at an appalling rate. The Adjutant of the local artillery battery took the trouble to inform Arthur Daly at Brigade that *"our allowance of ammunition has been reduced to three rounds per gun per day starting from today. Would you be kind enough to inform your battalions in the line of the present situation so as they will not expect much retaliation..."* With this not so comforting news, the West Ham Battalion prepared to go back to the north sub sector around Carency. The change over was complete by 8pm on the 13th July, 1916. A Company was assigned to the right flank whilst C Company occupied the centre, with the HQ Company. B Company provided the piquet while D Company was sent to occupy the Quarries at the edge of the town. There was the usual round of deadly trench life, with the 14th seeing a flurry of mortar shells falling on their lines at around 2pm. The only casualty recorded was Pte George Thomas Francker. He was from Canning Town but was buried in what is now the Canadian Cemetery No2 outside Neuville St Vaast. Heavy shelling followed over the course of the evening and Pte Robert Lee was killed outright by some of it. He was one of the recent local replacements and had lived in Forest Gate but was buried close to Francker. Sgt EJF Hawtin and L/Sgt CH Piddington were wounded, but both applied a field dressing and *"remained at duty"*.

At about 1am, the night patrol returned. Crawling about and flitting like ghosts beneath the flares fizzing eerily above No Man's Land, twenty-six year old 2/Lt George Harry Ross from Hove in Sussex and two 'other ranks' slipped through designed gaps in the barbed wire, whispered the password and tumbled over the lip of the trench. Ross then sat down in a damp dugout and wrote up his detailed report, describing events as he entered *"FOOTBALL CRATER and proceeded to the top of the enemy's lip to a point about 12 yards north of their barbed wire. From this point to the enemy's front line the distance must be well over 60 yards. There is no sign of any crater to the east of the point which I reached. The chalk slopes away for about 10 yards. The rest is grass.*

About 20 yards east of the ridge are two mounds some 5 yards apart. These were occupied and appeared to be small posts capable of holding about five men each. Bombs could be thrown from these posts into FOOTBALL CRATER, and in my opinion most of the bombs thrown from time to time into the crater come from these posts and not from the lip, as the majority fall short of our saphead..." After he had been on *"the enemy lip for about five minutes"* Ross got his chance to personally kill a German when *"one of the enemy stood up behind the wire about 12 yards to my south with a bomb in his hand. He did not see me and I threw a bomb at him which took effect. A number of bombs were thrown at me from the two posts above mentioned and I withdrew to our saphead, from which point we retaliated..."* Each night, the long row of huge craters on this sector of the front saw similar activity from both sides.

On the 16th the Hammers were relieved and marched to billets at Gouy-Servins for a couple of days before they moved to Bengin, in the Dieval area where the Division was massing. As each component unit arrived from the line, speculation was rife but by the evening, unwelcome news came through. The Division, and with it the West Ham Battalion, was being transferred to a new area.

They were joining the bloodbath on the Somme.

Chapter 19

The Devil's Wood

At 7am on July 20th the West Ham Battalion marched to Bryas Station seven miles away, to be herded into cattle trucks for the journey to a camp at Longeau. On arrival, *"packs were stacked"* before the men marched to an area close to the Corbie/Bray sector near the small town of Vaux sur Somme. This area was the assembly point for units arriving on the Somme and was known to the Tommy as 'Welcome Woods'. The valley was protected from the main ravages of the German artillery and consisted of huts and tents similar to those in Zouave Valley. This, together with plenty of hot food, made the woods a relatively popular place to be. A short march, about a mile or so, led downhill to the Somme canal. There the men could have a wash down.

Three days later they marched towards Bois de Tailles and then into tents, just back from the front line and on July 25th the Hammers moved up to the reserve trenches, known by troops as 'The Triangle'. Meanwhile the British launched a highly successful final attack on the remaining but heavily defended German positions in Delville Wood nearby. This wood had gained legendary infamy during three weeks of intense and bitter fighting. Originally it was a beautifully tranquil tract of woodland, approximately half a mile square with the western edge pushing into the sleepy village of Longueval, almost engulfing the houses there. To the east it marked the boundary of the commune of Ginchy. Delville Wood was now just tree stumps and all but taken by the early hours of the 27th July, earning the hearty congratulations of corps commanders. During the previous weeks, three entire German regiments were virtually annihilated, an indication of the desperate ferocity of the combat. The losses on both sides were tremendous. The following day the weary frontline units were relieved by the Hammers' comrades in the Brigade, the South Staffords and Footballers. They immediately faced heavy and determined counter attacks from fresh German troops. Despite ferocious fighting and casualties filling the aid-posts, the two battalions clung on desperately to the new line. At around midday on the 28th July, Papillon received hurried orders to rush the Hammers forward. The situation developed like an angry hurricane as they were pushed into the Breslau support trench and relieved the badly mauled and shocked Footballers.

Then, at 6.30pm, the West Ham Battalion went into action at Delville Wood. B & D Company were desperately needed to fill the widening gaps in the severely depleted ranks of the South Staffords. Throughout the night they assisted in repelling continuous, determined and heavy attacks from waves of German infantry on the northern fringes of the wood. Their westward facing defensive flank was equally mauled, by ever more aggressive enfilade fire.

The situation became confused as dawn broke on the 29th, with no pause in the indiscriminate shelling or the German assaults. It blossomed into a hot day, though few noticed the sunshine. A sultry afternoon passed into balmy evening with ferocious hand to hand fighting continuing unabated over possession of every freshly smoking crater created by the constant bombardments. This had been the situation for the last three weeks and no one knew where the frontline actually was at any given minute as shell after shell after shell came screaming in. Within a churned landscape of stumps and bodies, the trenches had ceased to exist in any recognisable form. Men were buried in this deluge of high explosive, only for their bodies to be unearthed in the same manner, before being ripped apart and flung into the faces of the living. Whole sections of trench were being blown in the air. This was truly hell on earth.

The West Ham Battalion somehow clung on to an ever changing series of smoking shell holes. William Busby was out in the thick of it, yelling encouragement over the noise of explosions to his 'boys' of No14 Platoon before being wounded by a bullet in the right knee. He somehow struggled back to an aid-post and was sent to No8 hospital in Rouen for twelve days of clean sheets. Not so lucky was Pte John Henry Hassell of Busby's D Company, one of the first early local replacements for the losses back in January and still recovering from wounds he'd received in the fight at the craters back in June. His body was never recovered from that dreadful battlefield. Hassell was married, living with his wife Annie on Willow Grove behind Plaistow tube station. The site is now a small unnamed community park, created by the Luftwaffe in the 1940's. That 'blitz' also buried his posthumous medals.

The Devil's Wood was by now shattered to matchwood by incessant artillery fire. It had certainly earned its nickname. Here and there fragments of 'crumped' trenches were visible with scrapes full of dead. In addition to the constant noise of explosions, the screams and moans of *"men bled white"*, there was the harsh ringing of steel betraying desperate and vicious fighting with bayonets, trench knives, entrenching spades – anything with the potential for a sharp edge which could kill. The smell of blood and cordite hung heavy in the summer haze. Then there were the bloated flies, another unwelcome distraction none would ever forget. As night fell the infantry attacks ebbed and finally tailed off. Both sides sat exhausted in the darkness, staring at one another. In some cases just a few yards apart. There was *"intense"* artillery and Minenwerfer activity on both sides during the lull, resulting in the wounding of Lt Reg Norman and 2/Lt HP Davis. Both men were removed to the rear where Reg, an original officer, was treated and sent down the line to a base hospital. He recovered from his wounds alongside Frank Keeble who was staying at the Norman's home on Atherton Road in Stratford. Reg eventually returned to the Hammers but twenty-six year old Herbert Pinder Davis had died soon after his arrival at the casualty station at Sailly le Sec. He was a classical scholar and had been on a walking holiday in Norway when war broke out. He returned to England immediately to enlist but was turned down three times due to poor eyesight and became a stretcher bearer before officer training. When the Hammers received orders to move to the Somme area Herbert had arrived, keen but not much else, with replacements a few weeks earlier. He is pretty typical of the extremely short life expectancy of inexperienced officers on the western front. Papillon wrote to his grieving parents at their home at Cavendish Road, Regents Park, telling them that "*your son had only been with us a short time, but he had already made friends with us all, and he was a most popular and promising young Officer, and we one and all deplore and mourn his loss."* He now lies in Dive Copse CWGC.

Night and day the stretcher-bearers braved the bullets and shrapnel as they scurried back and forth through the atrocious conditions bringing water, aid and hope to the dreadfully exposed West Ham men. One, above all others, stood out in the maelstrom – the squat yet reassuringly solid figure of Cpl Norman William Bellinger. Once again, his virtually suicidal actions earned the respect and admiration of both his peers and his officers. He was recommended again for a bravery award by Papillon and received the West Ham Battalion's second Distinguished Conduct Medal *"for conspicuous bravery and devotion in action in charge of stretcher-bearers. For several days he worked, without rest and under heavy fire, tending and bringing in wounded who otherwise could not have been brought in* [at] *Delville Wood."*

A new morning dawned as the Hammers held on through renewed aggressive and persistent German counter attacks. Casualties mounted steadily as they threw back assault after assault. Pelham Papillon, fifty-two years old and leading from the front, was blown off his feet by an explosive shell and then wounded by shrapnel from another. Yet he still shifted from shell hole to shell hole, constantly assessing the situation and keeping up the morale of his men despite sustaining a terrible gash over his eye.

By midday, the hot sun, buzzing flies and incessant shelling, together with the unceasing staccato rattle of the German machineguns was sapping the morale of even the bravest souls. The officers and NCOs were kept busy, directing fire and bolstering the spirits of the West Ham men. Captain James Round was running and jumping from shell hole to shell hole, gathering information the only way possible, in the frontline - such as it was. He was seen continually encouraging and supporting the weariest of the West Ham men with his quiet confidence and cool demeanour.

Within the chaos of that day, a group of German snipers very nearly succeeded in breaching the line in the afternoon. As effective as it was simple, the lead elements had got so close because they were disguised, wearing British steel helmets. The doubts and momentary indecision it caused was having dire consequences. Papillon issued a succinct order to Captain Round: *"return those helmets"*. Ably assisted by L/Sgt Charles Songhurst and a party of men, Round decided that rapid bayonet charges would be the most effective way to clear the infiltrators. Short sharp fights ensued, close personal battles fought face to face and knee to knee until finally *"they were seen off..."*

An unnamed *"cockney Private"* of a New Army battalion, later interviewed by Captain AJ Dawson for his 1916 bestseller "Somme Battle Stories" remarked *"you let me close in, same's we did in Devil's Wood and I'll back meself to serve you up Bosches fast as you can open oysters!"* His personal 'pub landlord' war-cry in this *"pretty hot shop"* was *"time gentlemen, please!"* The conduct of the West Ham Battalion throughout was remarkable and Charlie Songhurst and Pte Frederick Albert James were both awarded the Military Medal for 'Bravery in the Field'. Captain Round was wounded, yet again, but still led his party of skilled bayonet men in exemplary fashion and with great success. For his actions over this three day period, and a few weeks later at Guillemont, Captain Round was awarded the Military Cross *"for Conspicuous Gallantry in action. He carried out a daring reconnaissance and obtained valuable information. Later although wounded he remained at his post..."* At dusk, the Germans launched yet another assault on the Hammers' positions, including those of Captain JD Paterson of C Company, the former Malay rubber planter. An immensely popular officer with a steady voice and a renowned sense of humour, his effort was recognised with a Military Cross *"for conspicuous gallantry during operations. After his trench had been under constant shellfire and his men had suffered many casualties, besides having been without rations and water for twenty four hours, he repulsed an enemy attack. By his fine example under trying conditions he kept up the spirits of his men throughout..."* L/Cpl Fred Lathangue was equally in the thick of it fighting alongside his brothers Harry and Sid. Fred was hit in the face and hand but could only get roughly patched up in the chaos as another dawn broke on the 31st.

The artillery duel that had continued non-stop throughout the previous days and nights had comprehensively destroyed all semblance of a recognisable frontline system. There was little cover, no escape. All but the deepest dugouts were gone. Somehow, the West Ham men were tenaciously holding their ground. Then, disaster struck. Battalion HQ was located a short distance back from the action but it was still close enough. It took a direct hit from a shell which landed at the dugout entrance. The force of the explosion instantly collapsed the roof. Inside, Papillon was blown clean off his feet and flung against the crumbling wall before being buried in the blast which had instantly burst his eardrum. Also buried was his temporary second in command, Major Alexander Phayre Churchill, as well as the acting Adjutant 2/Lt Cyril Lyne and Lt Len Holthusen, the Signals Officer. Outside, the men of the HQ Company began frantically digging with shovels, helmets and their bare hands at the earth, sandbags, wood and corrugated iron sheeting still smoking from the impact. Frantically, they released the trapped and dreadfully shocked men.

Dr Holthusen was immediately in attendance and found that his younger brother Len as well as Major Churchill were both so seriously injured that they required immediate evacuation. Papillon was in severe distress but remained *"at duty"*, as did 2/Lt Cyril Lyne. With his head wrapped in a blood soaked field dressing, the wounded and clearly shaken Papillon continued to move around the battalion area. Undaunted by his injuries he continued directing operations and for his actions over these two days Pelham Rawstorn Papillon, first Colonel of the West Ham Battalion, was awarded the Distinguished Service Order. But for Len Holthusen, the Hammers snooker champion at the 'Alexandra Mess' back in Stratford High Street, the war was over. Evacuated to England his initial recovery took seven months. Even then he never truly returned to full health and the engineering surveyor from Forest Gate reluctantly left the army, a broken man.

At last, towards evening, the attacking courage and resolve of the young German infantrymen began to falter as casualties mounted horrendously. Their suicidal thrusts slowly ebbed. The British defences were now being bolstered by Lewis guns and the heavy Vickers machine guns. The Lewis gun was a portable light machine gun weighing about 12Kg with a top loading drum magazine, while the Vickers was a far more cumbersome, belt fed machine gun on a tripod. Both required two men to use and put down an excellent rate of fire.

Despite the fact that there were now twelve Lewis and eight Vickers firing at the Germans, two more of the officers had fallen victim to the unceasing bullet, grenade and shell storm. Captain Charles Graham Carson had been hit in the knee and left hand but had held out, fighting and bleeding until the late evening when during this lull he was evacuated. Carson was promptly awarded the Military Cross, *"for conspicuous gallantry in action. He handled his Company, under intense fire and most trying conditions, with great courage and determination. Later, though wounded, he remained at his post, setting a splendid example to his men..."* Charles Carson, the medical student from Manchester, would recover and return to the Hammers in October. Alongside him at the CCS was Lt Frank Tyhurst Folkard of C Company who had also been wounded. Folkard, previously an ironmonger, had enlisted in the Hammers alongside his Essex friends and near neighbours Captain Dick Collier and Lt Eric Bunting.

Relieved on 1st August, the weary blood soaked West Ham men returned to their positions in Back Trench at Breslau Support. During the relief, as was customary, the German artillery kept up a relentless bombardment of the support areas, together with the lines of communication. As the men began dusting themselves down and held their roll calls the fighting in the wood continued without respite. The Hammers suffered heavily in their tour with two hundred and twenty-one of the men gone, including nine of the officers. One quarter of the West Ham Battalion. Twenty of them were literally sent mad by shellshock. A terrible price, especially when it is remembered that they had not initially been in the front of the attack.

Counted as missing was the solid dependable figure of CSM James Wicks Valentine, Military Medal winner and scourge of the new recruits. Originally from Grimston in Norfolk, he had lived for some years in Upperton Road in Plaistow with his wife. As an old soldier he had immediately re-enlisted at Stratford at the outbreak of war. He was killed, leading his squad in a screaming bayonet charge, on the 30th. His body was never recovered and only his name remains, on the Thiepval Memorial to the Missing. Some of the Hammers had become separated and attached themselves to other units; some were simply lost in the dread confusion. A few were found wounded or mentally exhausted and were fortunate to be evacuated by a passing stretcher-bearer. Most, though, were never found at all. Blown apart or buried alive as they crouched terrified in their shell holes, waiting for the brief pause in the shelling which usually heralded another German infantry attack. The huge memorial at Thiepval bears the names of those West Ham men who fell in Deville Wood, and on the Somme, who today have no known graves. Among them is Pte John Riley of Busby's D Company. Twenty-five years old, he was married to Annie and together they lived along Coopersale Road in Homerton. He also had his 'pen' friend in Mr Thomas Hughes of Sprowston Road in Forest Gate. Riley had remained in regular contact with Hughes, the 'old soldier' who had first sent a mouth organ and razor out to him, via the Stratford Express appeal, last Christmas. The letters Hughes wrote would now lie unanswered.

Others named on Thiepval Memorial include Pte Samuel Doo of C Company, thirty-three years old and husband of Ellen Doo of Bow. Pte Harry Raven was just twenty years old and lived with his proud parents in Hockley Avenue, East Ham. Pte Eddie Humphries, one of the Mayor's first three hundred volunteers. He was twenty-nine years old and came from Third Avenue in Manor Park. Just some of those killed in action at Delville Wood. Also gone was Pte George Tranter, another member of the first three hundred, twenty-one years old and living with his parents in York Street off Abbey Road in Barking. Pte Hubert Ayers lived on South Esk Road in Forest Gate with his wife Alice and together they ran a small coffee shop in the local area. Pte Horace Stoneman, twenty-six years old, lived with his wife in Eversleigh Road in East Ham. Pte Tom Shillingford of D Company, an enthusiastic volunteer aged twenty-three years old. His last known photograph was taken by Mr Flatan during the initial training and was posted home with a moan about engaging in physical exercise at 5am. Then there were Ernie Kurtz's great friends, Sgt Charles Waterman of Enkell Street in Holloway and Pte Joseph Sait of Katherine Street in Forest Gate. Both listed among the first three hundred and both winners of the Military Medal. Neither of them lived long enough to receive this recognition of their bravery.

Also gone was Pte Conradin Donatz, native of Coire in Switzerland who had got involved in someone else's war and given up his life as a J. Lyons tearoom waiter. He was one of the many Hammers killed in action at Delville Wood during July 31st, 1916.

Out of the line and in reserve trenches, the ordeal continued at the Breslau Support trench. They underwent a heavy and concentrated artillery fire, which systematically destroyed the trenches there, so the Hammers began pulling back to shallow freshly dug positions a short distance behind. Many, including the senior officers and Papillon, were still in varying degrees of severe shock from the horrific pounding of the last few days. As they slowly limped back, they were passed on the road by a Machine Gun Company transport section, making their way towards Montauban. Directly in front of the numb West Ham men it was caught by the German artillery as a shrapnel shell screamed in, instantly shredding the horses and killing a number of the MGC men.

From there, the Hammers kept their heads down and patched themselves up for the next few days until the 5th August when, towards evening, they were again sent forward. This time it was to take over the frontline to the south of Delville Wood at Waterlot Farm. It wasn't actually a farm at all, having originally been a sugar refinery. However any architectural description was rendered unnecessary, as it had long since been reduced to scrappy piles of red brick dust and plaster. They remained there for twenty-four hours until relieved by their friends the Footballers.

The West Ham Battalion returned to the trenches at Mine Alley for another day of non-stop heavy shelling. It became *"intense"* towards late evening before they were ordered at very short notice up to the trenches at Trones Wood.

Somehow they were to prepare themselves for an immediate night assault.

Chapter 20

Hell at High Holborn

Monday 7th August was spent in nervous silence, with senses still numb from shock, sheltering in the deep dugouts beneath the trenches of Trones Wood. Overnight, even the hardiest found it impossible to snatch anything resembling sleep, especially as they listened to the attack being mounted, and failing, on the fortified village of Guillemont a short distance to the south. Brigade received orders to join the assault and attack to the north of the village. It was launched at 4.30am on the 8th, led by the Footballers and Kings. They attacked the 'ZZ' Trench and Guillemont Station but the secure positions, with a thicket of barbed wire and well placed machine guns, were held by tough, experienced Bavarians. The inevitable butchery followed the desperate attempt to capture the line. Although several strong-points were taken by individual platoons, as dawn broke it became dreadfully apparent that the other attacking elements had not achieved their objectives: they lay dead and dying, caught up in the uncut German wire. Reluctantly, the order was given to relinquish the hard won gains and the attack withdrew in confusion. Once again, the vicious sweep of the Maxim guns accompanied the men as they retreated back across No Man's Land. As some of the West Ham men watched this chaos it filled them with dread. They knew they'd be next.

During the early evening they were moved, up through Trones Wood to the trenches ringing its east side. At 8.30pm, Papillon was handed *"Operational Order 190, 8th August 1916"*. It required the battered and depleted Hammers to take a section of the German front line. On the right, they had to attack a position called "Deep Dugouts" and a trench called Brompton Road to capture the heavily defended rubble of Guillemont Station. Their boundary would be a trench they named Green Street. In the centre of the attack, they had to capture a position called High Holborn including the vicious citadel of 'Machine Gun House'. Then, on the left was the requirement to capture the southern stretch of 'ZZ' trench and also the two forks running from it. Although it was a formidable list of objectives Papillon had been assured that the artillery had obliterated the German trenches and that the wire was *"non-existent"*. But, it should be remembered that up to twelve officers were so far out of action including the experienced Charles Carson, William Busby and Frank Keeble, all currently in hospital recovering from combat. Equally, most of the best NCO's had been killed at Delville Wood. Papillon gathered his remaining Company commanders and broke the news. Responsibility naturally fell on the young shoulders of the remaining and 'untried' original junior officers of the West Ham Battalion. Men like 2/Lt's Bernard Robert Page and George Harry Ross. Equally called upon were fresh arrivals like 2/Lt Arnold Hone. Although only recently commissioned Hone, from Forest Gate, was already a combat veteran having seen infantry action in early 1915. There was no time available for any sort of preparation, no time for the crucial task of assessing the battlefield terrain. No time to explain to the NCO's what was required, no time for them to pass on to the men what they were all potentially about to die fighting for. No time even to evaluate why the last attack failed. They were simply to attack the same objective and in the same way. Grimly, Page and Ross assembled the troops.

The British trenches were already very congested: wounded; dying; reinforcements. Men pulling out or, like the Hammers, moving up to attack. Zero Hour had already been set as 4.10am but the trench guides they had been told to meet, to show them the way through the mazes and rat runs to the jump off positions, didn't turn up at all. It took until 3.30am on the 9th for the West Ham Battalion to be finally cajoled into position in the forward trenches.

As the men made their own personal efforts to gear themselves up for the attack there was less than ten minutes to go. In the pitch black of a warm night Page and C Company slipped over the lip of their trench and crept towards a long white tape which had been laid exactly parallel to the German trenches. As the British artillery bombardment opened up on the enemy wire and trenches, they crept forward in unhappy silence. The British artillery was firing a mix of high explosive, shrapnel, even smoke. As was the practice, the technique required C Company to remain close, a hundred yards or less, to the creeping barrage as it moved forward smashing obstacles. That was the theory. Behind, at about 4.20am and acting as the 'second wave', Ross and D Company took their place in No Man's Land and waited their turn.

Page and C Company remained so incredibly close to the creeping artillery barrage that when it finally lifted, they were up to the line of the German wire almost at the same moment. They rose from the darkness with a united roar of "Up the Hammers!" and charged into the smoke. They saw it too late. The barbed wire was practically uncut. Their speed and aggression took them into the mesh which then did the job to trap and hold them. From within the "Deep Dugouts", and at least five other positions, machine guns were brought up after the artillery barrage stopped. They were placed in position and opened up a vicious cross fire, with the ominously named 'Machine Gun House' at the centre of the defence. As Jenns baldly describes it, C Company was *"mown down..."*

After the failed attacks earlier, the Germans had clearly been extremely industrious repairing and improving their positions in the space of a few short hours. Equally, their trenches were still packed with troops and they were now engaging any survivors. When George Ross and D Company charged forward as the second wave a few minutes later, they were met by the horrific and confusing sight of the bloody, bullet riddled remains of Page's C Company. Ross and his men were then caught in the same trap, this time with an added barrage of many well aimed grenades. Lobbed from innumerable carefully chosen positions the grenades forcefully herded the survivors into the machine gun killing zone. Although *"a few men on the left flank succeeded in entering the enemy's trench"*, they were *"overpowered by superior numbers..."* As these terrible events began to be communicated back to Papillon by signallers and runners he could see precisely what was happening. The awful carnage was a *"needless and useless sacrifice of men..."* It threatened the very end of his West Ham Battalion. Captain Round, out again in the thick of it, began sending back reports that the expected support on the right of the Hammers attack hadn't materialised at all while on the left the Lewis gun fire was having little effect on the enemy's rebuilt trenches. Added to all that 'Machine Gun House' still stood, held by the enemy. Its fire was devastating. This was a futile waste. Papillon didn't hesitate to think of the personal consequences. Taking full responsibility for the decision he immediately ordered the unauthorised cancelling of the attack. Captain Round and Lt Brown-Paterson, the new Signals Officer, were promptly out in No Man's Land, bringing in who or what they could. With his wealth of experience, Round then *"re-organised two companies and rescued six men under fire..."* Both officers then quickly strengthened the Hammers defences in case of a counter attack, secured the lines and, by 10am, Round was reporting to Papillon that so far the estimates were of over ninety killed, wounded, or simply missing. C Company had taken the brunt of the losses, with over sixty of them massacred in the *"formidable obstacle"* of uncut wire.

As the morning wore on, it generally became *"quieter"*. The Germans patched up their defences along the frontline and looked out at the West Ham men hung up on their wire, new companions to the dead Footballers and Kings. It was a place no man present would ever forget. When darkness fell, the Hammers stretcher bearers noiselessly searched No Man's Land for any of the wounded who hadn't yet made it back. They found George Ross's body, brought it in and eventually buried him in the Delville Wood Military Cemetery. He was an original volunteer, his parent's only child, and was regarded as a very capable officer who had also been acting Adjutant 'in charge' of Jenns for a while. The Hammers had also lost yet another valuable senior NCO. Acting Company Sergeant Major Charles Dean was a resident of South Woodford and a former Reservist. He had returned to the Colours, at Walthamstow, immediately on the outbreak of war. He too lies buried in the Military Cemetery at Delville Wood. The stretcher bearers weren't able to get to Bernard Page, former West Ham Territorial. The body of William Busby's great friend and billiards partner was never found. A West Ham lad through and through, his proud father Robert was devastated when he received the telegram from the War Office. In common with so many families, his grief did not end there. Bernard's older brother Wilfred was also killed in action in March 1918. Today, 'BRP' is another commemorated on the Thiepval Memorial to the Missing.

Out of the gloom of No Man's Land not many were struggling back. Pte William Bone, bookbinder by trade, somehow managed it. From Eldred Road in Barking, he was so severely shocked by the attack that, back home in England, he never spoke of the war ever again. Pte James Mellish, a fancy cord maker from Bow, was another who scrambled back, bloodied. He was driven nearly mad by the carnage he had witnessed that morning and was sent to hospital. Finally, 2/Lt Hone returned, exhausted, dehydrated and wounded. Overnight, the recent events were written up by Jenns. There isn't his usual concise list of the dead and wounded, carefully recording their rank and service number. There were, tonight, simply too many to name.

The West Ham Battalion moved out of the line the next morning and marched wearily back to the reserve area at 'Happy Valley', north-west of Bray. This small village in its sheltered valley was a melting pot of lost and broken soldiery, a meeting place of the army. Bloodied units coming out of the line paused here a while, before being sent back to quieter sectors to patch up their wounds. They would meet freshly arrived men, camped on the parched and baked brown earth on either side of the valley. These men, new to France, would nervously watch the wide range of horrendously wounded carried into the casualty clearing station before being swathed in bandages and loaded on wagons or lorries to whatever private nightmare awaited them. The slopes of the valley were covered in canvas tents and crude huts. Surgeons vied for space with blacksmiths and other craftsmen providing the army with its vital services. The area teemed with life as humans, horses, mules, cattle and machinery of all kinds passed on their way to heaven knows where. As various units intermingled they swapped news, cigarettes and food but there was no water supply here. It all had to be transported up from the river Somme at Bray by seemingly endless convoys of water carts. For now, the Hammers occupied their own little piece of relative safety for a couple of days. They slept there on the open hillside before being marched four miles to Meaulte and into billets. Another short march then took them to Mericourt L'Abbe railway station from where, the following evening, they headed to Saleux. Arriving a little after midnight they transferred from the train to a column of 'Old Bill' buses, some of which had last worked the East End routes from Aldgate to Romford. These out of place, almost surreal reminders of home took the shattered Hammers in relays to La Chausee. They spent the next two days resting, cleaning their kit and writing letters.

Most of them were simply trying to fathom what had just happened in the last few weeks.

Chapter 21

"Anywhere sooner than France..."

On 16th August, the depleted West Ham Battalion set off once more, this time on a two-day route march to the northern sector of the Somme battlefield via Vignacourt and Bernaville to the Bois de Warnimont. In total, it was a distance of thirty-five hard miles under the draining August sunshine. Now wearing sergeant's stripes, Frank Jenns notes that during the march they passed the General Headquarters of the Commander in Chief at Beauquesne. Sadly, he does not record what expressive cockney opinions were no doubt heard coming from the ranks. The Hammers then relieved the Irish Guards in the right subsector in front of Serre on August 19th. This area was known as the Ancre Sector, named after the nearby river. In the flurry of shelling which invariably accompanied changeovers on the front line, three of the Hammers were wounded. Jenns doesn't list them, but they were immediately evacuated to a CCS where it was quickly discovered that one, Cpl Charles Poynter, was very seriously injured. He was sent over to base hospital in Rouen but died five days later. He was twenty-three. Charlie came from Colchester Road in Leyton and had enlisted early in 1915 at Baltic House in Hoe Street. He now lies in the CWGC Cemetery just outside St Sever. The Hammers left the trenches three days later but were soon back by August 24th, this time in the left subsector.

On this tour they were subjected to the usual *"heavy shelling"* which wounded six more men and killed three, including thirty-eight year old Pte Eddie Grubb. He was considered seriously enough wounded by Alan Holthusen, the medical officer, to be immediately evacuated to a base hospital in Rouen. He did not survive the journey and is another buried in St Sever Military Cemetery. It was a long way from his family in Digby Road, Homerton. Despite being older than most recruits Eddie Grubb had been amongst the first to answer Henry Dyer's appeal. Pte William Diaper was also killed. He was twenty-three and had only been with the West Ham Battalion a couple of weeks. Killed alongside him was another new replacement, Pte Eric Page from Clapton. Both men were taken to the rear and subsequently buried in the Military Cemetery at Euston Road.

On August 28th they trudged away from the front line, back into billets at Courcelles for three days 'rest'. It was here that Pte Charles Gladding, another of the West Ham Battalion stretcher bearers, finally broke down. The war, especially these last few months, had simply shattered the twenty-two year old. First wounded back in January, Charlie was one of a large group of volunteers from Tidal Basin. He had been especially encouraged to join up by his friend, neighbour and fellow Hammer, Pte JJ Yellop. Gladding had only been married, like so many of them, at St Luke's Church in January 1915. His son had been born two months later. Now Charlie was being shipped home with very severe shell shock, where his wife Annie was barely out of her teens.

'Divisional Order 202' arrived at HQ, listing those who had displayed immense bravery at Delville Wood and Guillemont: Sgt Percy Cotton, Sgt Fredrick Todd, L/Sgt Songhurst, Pte Fred James, Pte William Smith, Pte Harry Roscoe and Pte Walter Sampson were all rewarded with the Military Medal. There was little celebration. Promotions also came through, with William Busby, patched up from his wounded knee, made Captain on the 31st. Also 'Commended for Gallantry', though not in face of the enemy, was Pte Charlie Beck for *"stopping two runaway mules in limber"*. On the Western Front this was no mean feat and possibly relates to the incident with the machine gun transport company who were shredded by shrapnel as the Hammers were leaving Delville Wood.

Pelham Papillon was really beginning to show signs of combat stress now. Since the satisfaction of the first trench raid at the start of July, it had been a particularly intense and constant period of artillery bombardment and unforgettable Somme bloodshed. The majority of his officers were gone. Men he had known since the Hammers Battalion had first paraded at St Luke's Church and began training together. Papillon had, so far, been blown up in the shell holes of No Man's Land and later buried alive in his 'crumped' Delville Wood dugout. He was scarred for life from the deep gash over the right eye. This was combined with the intense, maddening ringing in his ear proclaiming his deafness. He had leg twitches which were getting worse with every hour of shelling. Somehow, he still found time to write back to the council reminding them that "*West Ham is constantly in our thoughts and our one wish is to be a credit to the great Borough from which we sprang…*" Yet the burden of command hung heavy around his neck and he needed a rest. Whether he applied for it or was ordered away by Dr Holthusen he left on Special Leave, back to his wife in Sussex. No such possibilities for the battle weary Hammers. Captain Dick Collier took charge with James Round as his second in command. Three days rest wasn't ever going to be enough but, nevertheless, after the short break they picked themselves up and marched smartly out of Courcelles.

The last light of September 1st faded, at the end of what had been a fine late summer's day, as Captain Collier led the Hammers back to the lunar terrain of the Serre sector at 6pm. A & B Company went straight into the frontline beneath relatively light shelling, taking over the right and left fronts respectively. The badly mauled and still reeling C & D Company stayed in the support lines. Everyone was reported to be in position two hours later. As the officers of A Company peered through trench periscopes across No Man's Land in the gathering gloom, they could see the smashed village of Serre, sitting at the top of a long gentle rise in the distance. It was menacing and, as yet, unconquered. The chalk excavations thrown up when the Germans had built three defensive lines were still gleaming white in the fading light. The enemy trenches were deep and solidly built, but that was to be expected after two years spent occupying the site. The barbed wire was very evident, extremely dense in places and piled six feet high at some spots.

To the Hammer's right front lay the long gentle slope of Redan Ridge, with its horrific detritus from July 1st, the first day of the Somme battles. Bits and pieces of human remains lay like a disintegrating carpet of inhumanity. In places, huge craters were fifty feet wide and just as deep. These were the results of huge mines laid by British tunnellers and they dwarfed the surrounding shell-holes. Each was filled with a toxic liquid mush. Around lay thousands of bodies, ripped up and mashed into the moonscape by the never ending artillery. The dead had equally been used as sandbags in front of some desperately held positions. Time and again, week after bloody week, that ridge proved impossible to capture. Until it was taken, things would remain a death dealing stalemate.

One way to break the stalemate was underground and overnight on the 2nd/3rd of September a bombing party under the command of Pte CW Gladdy began a silent guard duty. They were responsible for the security of the entrance to a subterranean sap called 'Mark Tunnel', running deep beneath the right front of the Hammer's lines and pushing on towards the Germans. The barricade they manned was designed to stall and, with grenades, block any possible German incursion. Gladdy first posted Pte A Branton down the tunnel, and tasked him to ensure that some guide candles remained lit. Branton had only recently returned to duty after recuperation from being badly gassed during an attack back in May. Here, moving forward in the claustrophobic gloom he could just make out a couple of men from the Royal Engineers at the far end. They were silently playing their deadly game of cat and mouse with the German tunnellers. At about 11.30pm, the two engineers came down the tunnel and left without saying a word as they passed Pte Gladdy and Pte William Wake at the barricade. An hour later, as they changed guard, Branton told Wake that he had been hearing a quiet drilling noise, *"a machine of some sort at work..."* Unknown to any of them, the Royal Engineers had been listening to it all afternoon and knew *"a blow"* from the Germans was imminent.

As Branton returned to Gladdy at the barricade, the tunnel was plunged into darkness by a sudden explosion, the result of a small charge placed on the other side of the wall in a parallel enemy tunnel. As Pte Wake, closest to the explosion, recovered from the shock he wouldn't have seen the hole but he would have smelt the gas now being pumped out. He stumbled for the exit but was overwhelmed before he could reach for his mask. The gas swamped him and flooded along Mark Tunnel. At the barricade, Branton and Gladdy were desperately fumbling to take off their helmets and put on their gas masks but both quickly collapsed unconscious. On hearing the explosion, the two engineers immediately arrived on the scene. In the company of other West Ham men and beneath a *"heavy bombardment"* of minenwerfers, they carried the three bodies out and into the care of the stretcher bearers, but William Wake was clearly dead on arrival at the casualty station, killed by the method most feared by soldiers of both sides. It could be a truly horrific way to go. Another of Henry Dyer's original three hundred, Wake was only nineteen when he enlisted and lived with his parents in Canal Road, Mile End. He was later given a battlefield burial by his mates and, after the war, his body was relocated to Euston Road CWGC Cemetery.

Above the tunnels, most activity occurred after dark. Regular nocturnal patrols in No Man's Land probed each others defences, to find gaps in the wire, to build up or hunt down new possibilities useful to snipers or as listening posts. Mostly, it was simply to see what changes had occurred in the lie of the land, as the constant shelling, tunnelling and mining could dramatically alter the terrain in a matter of seconds. These patrols, rarely comprising more than ten men, operated in pitch darkness and silent communication was of the essence. Their armoury was blackened knives and grenades, with pistols only as a back up. No lengthy bayonets or other clumsy and rattling equipment was allowed. Their faces and hands were also blackened to help them blend into the surreal landscape. As the light finally faded on the evening of September 4th, a day of constant heavy shelling, Captain Collier wished 'Good Luck' to the night patrol of the West Ham Battalion. They slipped very silently over the parapet of their trench and slowly disappeared into the inky blackness. They crawled like panthers through the wire and out into No Man's Land. Off in the distance they could hear the big guns continuing their deadly work and the horizon flashed like lightning. Every so often, a flare would shoot up, forcing them to drop and freeze like statues - the only way to stay safe and unnoticed by the lookouts and snipers during the slow, luminous descent.

One hundred yards away from them, in the German trenches, a Feldwebel (NCO) and eight men of the Jaeger ('Rifles') slipped out of their lines and began an intelligence gathering mission. This evening's patrol was to ascertain the extent of the damage inflicted by their artillery bombardment and whether there had been any effect to the ground from the charge they blew in the Mark Tunnel which had killed Pte Wake. They made their way, carefully silent, towards the British lines. By now, both parties were well beyond their wire. Contact was inevitable. They were each trying to decipher what they were seeing on the battlefield. Craters, fifty foot deep, full of decaying bodies, water, wreckage. The recently killed lay in the open, unnaturally twisted and mentally disturbing, feeding the carefree rats while others gnawed on the thousands of skeletal remains. Barbed wire, tree stumps, a discarded helmet or rifle might lie in such a way as to suggest to a scared or scarred mind the impression of safety or danger. Within all this visual chaos, one of them picked out the other. It wasn't quite close enough for knives, and so a "*brisk bombing fight*" began. Almost simultaneously, a batch of German stick grenades passed a bunch of British Mills bombs in midair. In such close proximity the effect on both sides was catastrophic.

Whether by luck or judgement, the German NCO was killed immediately alongside his second in command. Unfortunately, the exchange also killed Cpl Hunt, L/Cpl Miller, Pte Lee and Pte Evans. Frederick Hunt lived in Forest Gate before the war and had enthusiastically enlisted in March 1915 whilst James Lee from Canning Town had been one of the first drafts of replacements to the Hammers battalion nine months before. Herbert Evans and Henry Miller were both Colchester men and had only very recently arrived in France. Their bodies were never recovered from the quagmire of No Man's Land. All four are commemorated by name on the Thiepval Memorial to the Missing.

The remaining members of the night patrol had followed up their hail of grenades with an aggressive charge. One German was grabbed, wrestled down to the mud and taken prisoner, while the rest quickly fled into the darkness, melting within the landscape and back towards the German lines. The Hammers quickly checked each other over and found that they had all, to some varying degree, been wounded by the grenade fight.

Pte George Moore, who had unavoidably become the veteran of the patrol, decided they needed to return with the prisoner urgently. He knew that as soon as the surviving Jaegers returned to their lines the machine guns would immediately open up, sweeping the field. The others decided to trust Moore's judgement and sense of direction and followed him, making their way back and finally slipping into the West Ham trench lines to relative safety. George Moore was a member of the advance party which had entered France with Captain Collier a day before the rest of the Hammers battalion back in November 1915. He survived the war, but also forfeited two of his three Great War medals, only being entitled to the 1915 Star, due to having deserted for a while back in February 1916 around the time Samuel Ward and Alex Wade had shot themselves in the foot.

The next day, the West Ham Battalion left the trenches and went back into billets in Courcelles. One death recorded in this period was Sgt John Raymond Vautier. Another original who had enlisted in March 1915, he had been severely wounded at Delville Wood back in July. This wound was a 'Blighty' and he was sent home to his parents in Woodhouse Road, Leytonstone. On 5th September 1916, he died of pneumonia aged twenty-one and was buried in the City of London cemetery.

Coming to the end of a short home leave was Sgt William Gilbert, who had accidently broken his leg jumping in an icy shell hole back in March at Grenay. Whilst at home in Walthamstow he, like so many thousands of Londoners, had witnessed the downing of the 'Zeppelin' SL11, on the night of 2nd/3rd. Captained by Hauptmann Wilhelm Schramm, it had bombed north London before being engaged by the guns at Finsbury Park, Victoria Park, Clapton and West Ham and was finally brought down over Cuffley in Hertfordshire by a BE2c fighter piloted by 2/Lt William Leefe Robinson. There were no survivors and Robinson was awarded the Victoria Cross. The triumphant, merciless 'football crowd' roar which erupted as one voice across London as the 'gas bag' fell in flames is well documented. Gilbert, a furrier before the war, was now returning to the Hammers and after making his way to Felixstowe was kept hanging around at the port for five days. Returning from leave was always a 'dangerous' time for some men, as it was quite possible to be drafted into a hastily cobbled together group of reinforcements, assigned to another regiment and shipped off, never to return to your original unit or your mates. There were some soldiers though who were perfectly happy to see the back of the trenches. In this way Sgt Gilbert was drafted into the Connaught Rangers, to reinforce the Irish Regiment in the Middle East. It didn't seem a difficult choice. "*Well I thought to myself, anywhere sooner than France. Whatever happened, anywhere sooner than France...*"

September 5th was also the day Papillon returned from his special leave. Just over a week spent away from the trenches which were by now carving a deep scar inside him. The short respite hadn't had much beneficial effect on him. He was still twitchy but was masking it well. On the 9th, he led the Hammers back to the frontline trenches. Writing up the war diary, Jenns records that Pte Davies was slightly wounded the next day. 2/Lt PG Fountain also rejoined and resumed the duties of acting Adjutant. At 1.30am on the 11th, the Germans detonated a huge mine just short of the line, cracking more nerves and causing annoying tinnitus and temporary deafness. The Hammers watched as the chunky muddy tons of lifted soil and various pieces of decaying bodies rose to a great height before stalling and dropping back to earth just as a heavy artillery duel opened up. Beneath this, three men were wounded, including another of the originals, Pte J Clark.

In England, Frank Keeble had just about recovered from the shrapnel wounds he'd received in the first trench raid back in July. He was about to move out of Reg Norman's house in Stratford where he had been recuperating but, before he left to rejoin the Hammers, he arranged to meet the popular Reggie Howell, the former shipping clerk from Hastings who was just starting his home leave. The two had become firm friends since training together and now spent the day in London, managing to share a meal on the 17th at the popular Trocadero Restaurant in Piccadilly. Howell told Keeble all about the action and losses of the last few months and of how he was looking forward to a move over to the 'heavy branch' of the Brigade's machine guns. From there he would eventually move into the new aspect of warfare, tanks. Both men signed their copies of the Trocadero menu as a memento of the day.

Back in France the West Ham Battalion was in and out of the line, with its usual shelling and Minenwerfer, and at 9pm on the 18th, another terrifying shaking by an even larger German mine. The next day they gratefully left the trenches and marched to the Bois de Warnimont and the relative comforts of the huts and tents. Although out of the line, it was no rest. For the remainder of September they were set to training for the next offensive, probably the last before winter bogged down both armies.

Particular attention was given to aircraft co-operation and, ominously, assaults on trenches. Speculation amongst the troops was rife but the month passed without major incident for the Hammers. They were happy enough to hear of West Ham United's continued good run in the Southern Combination League, where they had beaten Arsenal 2-1 at the Boleyn at the start of the month and won at Millwall Athletic by four goals to one in front of 7,000 on the 23rd. Awards were still being announced in the London Gazette, with the Military Medal going to Sgt Burleigh, Sgt TW White, Pte FH Plato and Pte JM Smith for their bravery in the killing fields of Delville Wood and Guillemont.

Sunday, October 1st was spent preparing to go back to the Front and at dusk, they left for the trenches of the Sailly au Bois sector. The march proceeded as normal, until they began moving into the line. As they shuffled along cramped communications trenches, the artillery grew stronger and the battlefield detritus more gruesome. Word was suddenly and urgently sent back to Alan Holthusen, the medical officer: Papillon was in the midst of having a very severe nervous breakdown and had collapsed. He needed only a very brief examination before Holthusen saw the seriousness of the case. Placing him in the care of his most trusted medical orderlies, including Cpl Norman Bellinger DCM MM, Dr Holthusen had Papillon taken back to the transport lines of Capt Dick Collier. With the considerable assistance of Captain Robert Shrapnel Biddulph-Pinchard, by now the Brigade's transport officer, Papillon was taken by Bellinger to a base hospital on the coast, just outside Boulogne. He was immediately placed back on special leave and went aboard a hospital ship home, still in the care of Bellinger. That same evening they arrived at Folkestone and returned to the tranquillity of Catsfield Place. Late into the night Papillon fell into the arms of his wife, Constance Lauretta, a hospital matron. Norman Bellinger stayed in England too. He only shows up on the record again at the base depot in November. It's not surprising that he would have needed a long rest back home in Barking. By now he was classed as fifty percent disabled and had been rewarded with the Distinguished Conduct Medal and the Military Medal in his time with the Hammers.

As the news on Papillon spread through the ranks changes had to be made and made fast. Urgent messages flashed from Brigade to Divisional HQ. Orders were sent to Major (acting Lieut-Col) Harry Carter, DSO, MC, originally of the South Staffords. He was recently in charge of the Footballers and was immediately placed in temporary command of The Hammers, taking them in to the front line. His first order to the West Ham Battalion, no doubt to maintain their focus, was for the construction of a 'kicking off' trench, in the middle of No Man's Land in front of their sector. It was completed successfully and without losing a man. He officially took over command as the Hammers marched out of the line and back to Puchvillers via Bertrancourt on 7th October 1916.

Carter was to steer them through some difficult times ahead.

Chapter 22

A New Broom

Harry Carter was as different a man from his predecessor Pelham Papillon as it was possible to get. A no-nonsense fighting man with little room for sentimentality, he was already highly decorated having won the Distinguished Service Order and the Military Cross. He would go on to win both for a second time, receiving a 'Bar' to each medal, in a glittering and meteoric rise through the ranks. Born far from the officer's mess, Harry Carter was the son of a factory worker and his illiterate wife from Wolverhampton. Determined not to lead a humdrum life in the smoke of the industrial Midlands, in 1899 he took the Queen's shilling and enlisted as a private in the Army and saw action in South Africa. The life evidently suited him and he stayed in. When war was declared in 1914, signals sergeant Carter was every inch the professional soldier, a typical 'Old Contemptible'. Landing in France with the British Expeditionary Force, he fought before being commissioned in the field at the start of 1915. He then began a ride on the wave of 'temporary' promotions caused by the heavy losses among officers in the opening months of the war. By the time he was appointed to the West Ham Battalion he had reached the 'Temporary' rank of acting Lieutenant Colonel.

For most of October 1916 the Hammers provided men to supplement the 'working parties': carrying stores to forward supply dumps, repairing roads and restoring trenches. It gave, to a few, the idea that a major offensive was imminent. By now, some men were becoming seriously ill from the various effects of the last year spent living a trench life, including Pte Walter Richmond from Shoreditch, the possible author of the "Fish Supper" story in last Christmas's Stratford Express. His body could no longer take the chronic bronchitis from the damp surroundings and he was sent home. With him went Pte William Banks (whose family had been bombed out by a Zeppelin raid over Leyton in 1915) with 'trench fever', which was spread by the body lice inhabiting every soldier. On 21st October the West Ham Battalion moved once again, into the support trenches, east of Mailley Wood, and in their turn into the frontline. On the 26th the Germans unleashed a ferocious artillery and Minenwerfer bombardment on the British lines, during which L/Cpl Fred Lathangue, still recovering from his second set of wounds received at Delville Wood, was caught gambling and immediately lost his stripes. Others weren't so lucky. 2nd Lt Sidney William Hunt lost his life outright by heavy shelling and what remained of the twenty-three year old's body was taken to the rear at the end of the tour and given a battlefield burial. He now lies in the Sucerie Military Cemetery near Colincamps on the Somme. Three other men were seriously wounded but the war diary now falls in with army convention from this time onward. Sgt Frank Jenns, still the unofficial assistant Adjutant, was no longer detailing the names of those soldiers wounded as he had done religiously for the previous year. Only the comings and goings of officers would be mentioned by name, something Jenns, again contrary to convention, had hardly ever bothered to do. Perhaps it was on the direction of Carter or caused by mental exhaustion but anyone killed now would be referred to merely as an 'Other Rank'.

On the night of the 26/27th October, patrols were sent out to take a closer look at the heavily fortified German position opposite, known as the Quadrilateral, with a view to a possible future attack. Two pairs of patrols were sent out; firstly at midnight and then just before dawn. The first pair were led by 2/Lt JD Robinson and the recently arrived 2/Lt Finn. In early 1915 Mayor Henry Dyer had thought *"it only fitting"* that Robinson should be an officer in the West Ham Battalion. Yet he had only entered France, from the comforts of Capt Leo Dyer's depot in England a month or so ago. He had little combat experience, but was in command of the patrols.

At twenty past midnight, Robinson ordered 2/Lt Finn and the two combined patrols forward through the mud of No Man's Land to reconnoitre the German wire. Robinson stayed low in a shell hole peering at the inky blackness but for the advancing patrol it soon became that familiar eerie backdrop of carnage and industrialised warfare hiding many mortal dangers. They headed east and got as close as possible, eventually becoming blocked by the *"formidable obstacle"* of wire. Behind it, in the distance, they could hear the slow, rhythmic scrapes of a solitary German digging with a shovel. They then split up, with one party looking over the northern flank while the other scouted the southern side. This was equally covered in a dense, *"confused heap"* of wire. The patrol crawled about, probing for gaps and entrances or likely spots where entire sections might be moved if a man could *"drag it away with a rope..."* Finn then relocated to give a situation report to Robinson in the shell hole but the activity must have *"put the wind up"* the German sentries on the west side of the Quadrilateral as they suddenly discharged a ferocious three minute volley of sustained rifle fire. Then, from the left rear Robinson and Finn began taking machine gun fire causing them both to dive for cover. Meanwhile, the two groups who had been surveying the flanks of the position came under a rain of grenades. All fell thankfully short. As they withdrew beneath the unwelcome artificial sunbursts from parachute flares it quickly became obvious that Sgt Harold Joseph Morrison had been badly hit by the initial rifle fire and had just about bled to death. Sgt Brooks from Stratford and another soldier were equally bleeding heavily and were swiftly covered by practised hands with not enough field dressings. Now began the perilous journey back to the British wire before they died. Although it wasn't much of a distance, knowing that the Germans were on high alert caused them to take their time. Or perhaps it was the ever difficult problem of reading a compass bearing at night while under fire. Whatever the reason, it was over two hours later that they finally returned. Harold Morrison was a Forest Gate man from Field Road and became another struck from the list of Henry Dyer's original three-hundred volunteers. He lies in the Sucerie Military Cemetery. Thirty-four year old Sgt Brooks was taken away by field ambulance but couldn't be saved and today he lies in Couin British cemetery.

In the deep dark before dawn, Capt Charrington, the badly disfigured but cheerful and popular commander of A Company, sent his patrol out. It was 3.50am and damp. Sgt TW White, recently awarded the Military Medal for his hard work in Delville Wood, led six men across No Man's Land towards the western corner of the Quadrilateral. Silently, they moved fifty yards along the flank. They heard more digging, this time by a number of Germans and one man was *"seen to disappear through the wire"* however *"no shots"*, which might give away their presence *"were exchanged..."* Meanwhile, Captain Charles Carson, in command of C Company, was using his patrol to examine a different but just as crucial aspect. He wanted to see *"the ground in front of our wire with a view to forming up the company in waves for an attack"*. Carson had only recently returned to the Hammers after being hit in the knee and right hand at Delville Wood where he won his Military Cross. His patrol discovered that due to the wire and the very many shell holes close to the British frontline trench, any waves of men would have to be formed up more than twenty yards in front of their wire, quite a distance inside No Man's Land. Carson also registered another important fact: *"the ground was very sodden"*. These later patrols, experienced soldiers sent out by experienced officers, took less than half an hour to complete, with no injuries or shots fired.

At 6am, Arthur Daly requested Carter to send a party to investigate the crash site in No Man's Land of a British aircraft. It had been shot down the day before. Patrols were sent out, grumbling and ungrateful for this dangerous task, especially as the wreckage was being intermittently and accurately shelled by the Germans. They no doubt thought it an ideal spot for a British sniper position. Carter later informed Daly that the *"aeroplane is completely smashed up"* and that *"parts of the Observer were found..."* The West Ham patrol returned unwounded and they had retrieved the *"observer's map"* and *"the Lewis gun was brought in"*, but it proved *"impossible to find any article or papers to identify the Observer..."*

By the end of the month the Hammers were back at Bertrancourt, to prepare for the coming offensive. It was designed to be the last all out assault before the true grip of the coming winter precluded further large scale troop movements over the almost impenetrable mud and filth. The work became more intensive as the trenches were consolidated and strengthened. Communications trenches were widened. Crucially, the tunnellers were still busy underground, burrowing ever closer to the ground under the Redan Ridge.

On the 7th November the West Ham Battalion moved forward to new billets in the devastated village of Mailly Maillet, passing its fine old medieval church. Or, at least where it once stood. All that remained was an ornate entrance, lucky to have been facing away from the German guns, now padded with sandbags. For a few, there was the chance to visit the WVS tea huts and discover that West Ham United had last week beaten Spurs at the Boleyn 5-1 in front of five thousand spectators. Next they would beat Crystal Palace 8-1 and continue their great season. Other men took time to wonder at the huge tanks trundling and clanking through the muddy town, heading to their 'form up' positions north of the Serre Road. On November 11th, the attack preparations were nearing completion and at 10.30am they moved up to the frontline. Together with the South Staffords, the Hammers had been chosen to be the spear point of the Divisional thrust. Redan Ridge to their front had seen almost continuous action since July 1st. Despite bitter fighting, the lines had not significantly moved from their original places and the dead from that ill fated attack still lay out in No Man's Land. In such a hotly contested area the niceties of a decent burial were a rarity. Any attempt would invite instant death, either from a sniper's bullet or shell. More bodies were now becoming exposed by the weather as a heavy, incessant, rain set in. It turned the already sticky clay soil into a putrid horrorsome soup. In common with other records from the time, Jenns details how *"the ground was in a very bad condition owing to the constant rain...the trenches were, in places, waist deep in mud or water and in all trenches the thick mud was at least knee deep..."*

At the summit of the ridge, immediately to the West Ham Battalion's front, was the redoubt that had wreaked such havoc and destruction on July 1st: the Quadrilateral. This was the main objective, together with the four lines of German trenches immediately to the south. Known to the troops defending it as 'Die Heidenkopf', the Quadrilateral consisted of heavily defended machinegun posts, each with overlapping fields of fire and firmly ensconced behind walls of heavy duty flint filled sand bags. As if this was not enough there was row upon row of murderous rusting barbed wire, woven like a thorny thicket and acting as a boundary to the open graves of the approaches in No Man's Land. This much they had discovered on the night patrols when Sgt Morrison was killed. But the Germans also had very deep dugouts, cut into the well drained chalk and used to protect their machine gunners from the attentions of the British artillery. It was a formidable position indeed. The German units opposing the British consisted of no less than five infantry regiments. Traditionally each German regiment was the size of a British Brigade, approximately three thousand men. The West Ham Battalion, facing this stiff 5-1 opposition, moved into the flooded and muddy trenches. From here they would launch the mass attack intended to brutally flush the Germans from the ridge and finally gain artillery and observation mastery of the Ancre Heights.

No1 and No2 Platoons of A Company, led by Captain Charrington, together with No5 and No6 Platoons of B Company under Captain Round MC, formed the first (and largest) wave. The rest of their men would follow up as a 'clearing party' with Lewis guns. It was the clearing party's job to consolidate the captured positions, mopping up any surviving enemy who might be left after the initial wave of assaulting troops had advanced on to the next objective following the artillery barrage at three pace intervals. The second wave consisted of a Platoon of C Company on the right, under Captain Carson MC, while on the left was No14 Platoon of D Company, led as always by Captain Busby MC. The balance of their men would follow them closely, to 'clear' the German third line with another pair of Lewis guns. There were also two teams with 'Bangalore' torpedoes who would hopefully not be needed. It was their task to deal with any barbed wire if the men became *"hung up"*, as the essence of this attack was speed. However the weapon, looking like a long length of pipe, took time to use. The main hope lay on the artillery barrage and the huge wire-cutters which had recently been issued to officers to maintain momentum. The third wave comprised a platoon from C & D Company, with Lewis guns on each flank. Finally the fourth wave would come up, this time in the rear centre, with two more Lewis guns. Leading this fourth wave was the 'baby faced' 2/Lt Arnold Charles Hone who, although only twenty-two years old, was an experienced combat soldier, first landing in France in January 1915. Following commission he was posted to the West Ham Battalion in early July, just after their successful first trench raid. He was another local lad, living in Romford Road, Forest Gate, just a short walk away from William Busby.

As usual in these attacks, the signallers would be following behind the four waves and Hone had the West Ham Battalion's signals officer attached to him. It was 2/Lt William Brown-Paterson's task to secure communications back to Colonel Carter and Frank Jenns in Battalion HQ. Brown-Paterson, who had taken over when Len Holthusen had been invalided home after Delville Wood, was also responsible for selecting suitable locations within the captured German trenches for the relocation of the West Ham HQ and for Alan Holthusen's aid-posts. When the Quadrilateral was taken it would be the responsibility of Edwin Charrington's A Company to provide a defensive flank on the right, using a platoon and a Lewis gun. James Round's B Company would do similar duty on the left flank. William Busby's D Company had responsibility of constructing strong-points against the inevitable counter attacks. Four special teams would assemble, each of two bayonet men and three bombers. They would work as a tight, cohesive unit, skilled at blocking the German communication trenches to the front, right and left and keeping German reinforcements at bay. Grenades would be thrown over traverses closely followed up by the bayonet men who would kill survivors. Timing and co-ordination was everything in this dangerous task.

While the rain continued unabated, all ranks were reminded at their briefings of the need for speed and warned of the importance of keeping close to the creeping artillery barrage. If the Germans were alert enough to put up a counter barrage on them, the troops were ordered to *"rush it"* on the very sensible pretext that to pause in front of the machine guns of the Quadrilateral would result in certain death. Colonel Carter instructed them all to keep the old proverb in mind: *"He who hesitates is lost..."*

Long after sunset, Carter called Edwin Charrington and James Round to his dugout. He needed to speak to them about tonight's attack, only hours away. The three men sat in a cramped, smoky and subterranean world, where not even its primitive flickering electric light or candles cut through the all pervasive feeling of damp. No doubt Edwin Charrington had long been suffering uncomfortably with his scars and respiratory problems from the general poor climate. Jenns was ordered to 'witness' this conversation, as noted in the war diary.

Carter was immediately blunt and to the point with his experienced Captains and told them of his serious misgivings, that *"it was impossible to take the Quadrilateral by a frontal assault"*, especially for Charrington and Round's first wave. Carter issued new orders: the attacking force should be split and attack the position from the flanks to minimise casualties. Both men considered Carter's order. Given the state of the ground to be covered they doubted that the Hammers would be able to keep on the line of attack. All direction and speed would be lost. Added to that, a divided attack would certainly receive enfilade (cross-fire) from both north and south because of the layout of the well defended Quadrilateral. The Captain's knew what to expect, they had studied the ground and, more importantly, they knew their West Ham men. While the basis of Carter's argument was sound they strongly disagreed. With the counter-points Charrington and Round had raised, Carter had to make a final decision.

After much internal deliberation he let his orders stand. The attack would go in divided, although he was *"still in doubt as to whether I had done right..."*

Chapter 23

The Quadrilateral

The clocks struck midnight on Monday 13th November 1916 as the rain actually eased slightly. The codeword "Smith" was sent to Divisional HQ from all units involved in the attack, indicating their preparations were complete and that every man was in his place. A mist began forming in the bottom of the Ancre Valley, thickening and rising up to envelop the high ground in front of the attacking formations. Here and there sporadic fits of nervous laughter was muffled, as a fart or funny quip broke the tension, earning the deliverer a rebuke from an equally taut NCO. The 'ten per cent men' had earlier departed with those letters to loved ones and other small tokens intended to be posted home if a soldier did not make it through the attack. By not taking part, they would ensure there was no possibility of an entire battalion being totally 'wiped out', the 10% being intended as the basis with which to rebuild the unit from replacements.

At 2.30am the cooks came down the line, each with two containers of steaming hot cocoa suspended from yokes round their neck. Everyone perked up a bit and became a bit more *"cheerful and confident"*, despite most of them being knee deep in the freezing muddy water. A silence slowly descended on the West Ham Battalion as each man collected his thoughts. Some had been through this many times before, but for others it was to be their 'baptism of fire'. Half hour later came the order to move out, into the mud pit beyond the trench. This was to save time when the whistle blew, and time was of the essence.

The mist began settling on the battlefield and quickly reduced visibility to less than thirty yards. Crucially this was to stay the case until noon the following day. The Hammers had difficulty maintaining contact with the units on their left and by the time they were in the correct positions it was already 4.15am. Late by quarter of an hour. They waited in the mud with adrenalin building and heart rates increasing. At exactly 5.45am all hell broke loose. The barrage was delivered, rapid fire, and the first shells exploded like a witch's cauldron within the thick barbed wire in front of the German lines. Immediately the barrage paused, the angles of hot barrels were raised by a notch and it began again, creeping forward in a repetitive rhythm. It carved a ponderous path of havoc and destruction in its wake. Simultaneously, the whistles blew and the waves of the West Ham Battalion went gently forward at a three pace interval toward the huge wall of fire ahead of them which was ploughing the ground. The first wave, led by Captains Charrington and Round, began picking up their pace slightly before they ran and finally charged with their men into the thickening mist, screaming personal war cries drowned by the artillery. They arrived at their primary objective and engaged the positions. Closely following the first wave was Captain William Busby, leading his left hand side of the second wave with a yell of "*Come on, boys!*" to D Company. After that, all contact was lost. Then, from within the foggy mist came the dreaded sound of the staccato rattling from German Maxim guns. The '*typewriters*' had opened up and clearly at a furious rate. They didn't let up. Listening to this, Carter was convinced that something had clearly gone badly wrong, but the third and finally fourth waves went over the top at the specified time and entered the fog.

Two hours later, Carter summoned 2/Lt's Lowings and Sherman, each with two men, and sent them out in a desperate attempt to investigate the situation. What little Sherman and Lowings could see in the early morning light was shocking. The ground covered by the attacking waves had been truly awful. Trenches and shell holes were waist deep in a filthy, clinging slime, peppered with the unwelcoming smiles and beckoning hand waving of skeletons.

The constant rain had created a clawing quagmire, even on the high ground. Everything subsequently written about conditions on the Somme was encapsulated here in every square foot. After expending most of their energy simply getting to the German barbed wire, it had then proved to be a calculated and designed life grabbing hindrance to the attacking men. The advice to advance with all haste had been lost early in this deranged cratered stew. Moving to the right, Sherman and Lowings could find no sign of Charrington, Carson and their men, if they disregarded the disconcerting sight of those fresh bullet riddled bodies dangling like puppets in the wire. Heavy, fierce fighting could be heard; combat going on somewhere beyond the German line, but the mist was too thick to see exactly what was happening. Shifting their position, Sherman and Lowings saw that the situation of James Round's group on the left was a different matter. Through clear patches in the mist, soldiers could be seen lying in front of the German wire. Most of them appeared dead and there was no sign of Captain Round or Busby but one hundred yards in front of the Quadrilateral there was a small group of fifty or so, sheltering behind a small bank, under an incessant hailstorm of rifle and machine gun fire. Their position was beyond fragile, with both flanks exposed to counter attacks, but they were doing their best to stay alive. They appeared to Sherman to be a decimated mixture of the B & D Company third wave.

At 8.45am, Sherman and Lowings reported back to Carter and both gave the same summary from which could be drawn only one conclusion: if this was the remainder of the waves then clearly the whole attack had totally stalled. That would leave the right flank assigned to Charrington exposed, especially if the mist lifted. Carter immediately sent a runner to the fifty beleaguered survivors of B & D Company, with orders to *"consolidate and await further instructions"* and, if at all possible, the machine guns of the Quadrilateral should be rushed. The state of the ground alone showed this to be an impossible, almost ironic, request. The ground was a prime reason for the attack's failure. Clearly for Captain Round, his left side wave had become stuck in the heavy mud and 'hung up' in the wire but then, crucially, left behind by the rolling artillery barrage. As the barrage moved forward, churning up the ground ahead for any that might continue the attack, Captain Busby's D Company caught them up in the thick fog. The Germans then emerged from their deep protective dugouts as the barrage passed over and took up their chosen positions. Machine gun crews opened up a murderous rate of fire down on the men struggling through the wire and mud, cutting to bits the remains of Round's B Company and Busby's D Company. The Hammers' clearing parties engaged the German's but the fire was overwhelming and progress was slow.

On the right side of the attack meanwhile, efforts had been most successful, reaching their part of the German 'first' line but quickly losing Captain Charrington to a fatal wound. His place was filled by Lt HB Wilcock who raised his revolver and led the survivors forward with a yell, into the morass just created by the rolling artillery barrage. The second and third waves, led by Captain Charles Carson MC, had followed behind, cleared up and successfully penetrated the German defences. Passing the dead body of Lt Wilcock and many West Ham men, they progressed in low visibility. Carson and C Company got to within feet of the enemy 'third line' but then began to take heavy small arms fire from the left, somewhere within the thick mist where Busby and Round should have been. In one shocking second, Charles Carson was very badly hit, full in the chest and he dropped. Confusion spread, casualties quickly mounted and the attack stalled.

Then, from out of the mist, the luck changed.

For the men of the fourth and final wave, led by 2/Lt Arnold Hone, the advance would have been disconcerting to say the least as they clawed a path in and out of the fog and cordite mist. Following the bloody trail of the previous three waves they were passing ever more fresh bodies lying on beds of old bones as they trudged forward through the near impassable mud. Arriving at the new front line trench, and not long since Captain Carson was hit, they found C Company's attack in the midst of stalling completely. The men were in disarray and unable to think of a solution to the vicious fire they were receiving. Hone was alongside the signals officer 2/Lt Brown-Paterson, both having survived the terrible failure of the Hammers' attack on Guillemont only a couple of months earlier. Now, in an instant to be remembered for a lifetime, Hone took command and swiftly assessed the dire tactical situation. Brown-Paterson gathered all but the badly wounded into a small fighting group and found less than sixty or so West Ham survivors. Hone placed them where he could see they were needed most and began hurriedly consolidating the tenuous position.

A small squad of Germans came up and attempted to bomb them out but they were coolly seen off by Hone's Lewis gunners. Following a brief consultation both officers realised that if, as it appeared, Busby and Round hadn't made it this far and there were no British troops on their left *at all* then they and the survivors of C Company were in great peril of being outflanked. The entire Brigade attack itself was in danger of becoming a disaster as the Germans could easily flood through this gap on the left and do immense damage. Suddenly, they began taking heavy small arms fire from more German troops probing the position. Again, the Lewis gunners dealt with this threat and advanced a few yards to find better firing positions. With this moment to think, Hone utilised clever tactical positioning of his limited troops. Using the Lewis guns on several key junctions of the captured trenches, he was *"closing the door..."* By swinging left and putting a 'cross-fire' on any prospective German reinforcements or counter attacks he had, without realising it, just saved the day. He then organised ammunition to be gathered from the dead and wounded, water and rations to be pooled and the bleeding to get patched up and given a rifle with a bayonet. The small group of *"men of stout heart"* then spent the next forty-eight hours defending this critical spot, even capturing around sixty-five Germans in the process overnight. By the time Brown-Paterson got back to report the situation to Carter, reinforcements were already in motion and the threat to the left flank was being secured. On the 15th, two clanking tanks were brought up to scare off any remaining German troops and for their courageous and decisive actions both Arnold Hone and William Brown-Paterson were both immediately awarded the Military Cross. Other men, like Pte AF Spicer were awarded the Military Medal for bravery. Spicer was another local who had arrived in France as an early replacement back in January.

A deep frost began to take hold but it was actually of some benefit. It held off the inevitable decomposition of prone and stiff comrades now wrapped up tight in waterproof sheets ready to be prepared for burial. Crouched beside them in the water logged trenches, what was left of the West Ham Battalion wearily shook aching bones and struggled to stand on painful feet. They trudged away without a backward glance for the positions they had taken in the Quadrilateral. Slipping into a marching rhythm they could all keep up pace with, even while sleeping, they arrived at the rear at 2.30am on the 16th November 1916. The Hammers' advance party had arrived in France exactly a year ago to the day.

As the survivors passed the devastated face of Harry Carter, he anxiously searched for familiar sergeants and corporals. He was already aware that most of the officers were gone. Carter was aghast at the sheer scale of the casualties.

Each Company had been reduced to nothing more than composite Platoons, yet remarkably each had clung grimly to their gains. The Hammers had successfully taken the German "Minor" Trench, "Wolf" Trench and two platoons were still manning the top portion of "Egg" Trench waiting to be relieved. Thanks largely to Arnold Hone's *"splendid example"* of a cool head under fire there were also four Lewis gun posts on the new front line in the best positions. But the losses had been horrendous; nearly half of those involved had become casualties. Vickers machine-gunner Fred Lathangue had been wounded yet again, this time shot in the wrist. Some of the original volunteers, like Upton Park docker Pte Hugh Bannon of A Company, were the sole survivors of their section or even of their Platoon. In the confusion following the battle, nothing was actually clear. At this stage the most obvious effect was the lack of officers able to rally the survivors. No less than ten were immediately listed as missing. All the Company commanders had been seen killed. The huge numbers of wounded filling the trenches, RAP's and CCS's who had been pouring back for two days bore witness to the withering nature of the machine gun fire and the vicious desperate hand to hand fighting.

Sergeants finally managed to get the shocked remnants into some sort of order. They marched away, following the Serre road. It was merely a ghostly line in the cratered terrain taking them to temporary billets in Mailly Maillet, itself badly knocked about by the German artillery. The surviving NCO's attempted to take a roll call and Frank Jenns most likely gave a hand. Section by section, platoon by platoon, Company by Company, the awful truth became dreadfully evident. At this stage there were only six confirmed dead, probably those struck by the first hail of machine gun bullets a few days ago and carried out by the brave stretcher bearers. Their deaths were already recorded, the telegrams sent, tears shed. As more and more names went unanswered in the shadow of the heavily sandbagged medieval façade of the little town's once beautiful church, junior officers quietly attempted to form some sort of cohesive fighting unit out of the survivors.

Over three-hundred men were not present at that roll call, close to half of those who had stepped out into the mud of No Man's Land three rainy foggy days earlier. They included Henry Gladwin, the corporal who had been first on the scene back when JJ Da Costa had blown half his hand off while on sentry duty. Gladwin was from Maidman's Street in Mile End and before the war was a clerk in a sweet factory. Thirty-two years old and married to Lucy, his body was never found. Also gone was Pte James Fleming from Dawlish Road in Leyton, aged just twenty-two. His underage neighbour Pte Frank Eade with whom he had enlisted would now face the rest of 'the great adventure' without his friend. Pte Henry Pleasant was another. The Stepney born family man was the oldest volunteer in the ranks so far discovered, killed aged forty-seven.

One hundred and thirty-seven of the Hammers attacking the Quadrilateral had been very badly wounded, like nineteen year old 2/Lt Charles Clive Nafarfer Marshall, who had only arrived in France in October. He was captured, badly wounded, on the battlefield by the Germans and evacuated back to one of their casualty stations. Ultimately, Marshall returned from his POW camp to England as part of a severely wounded prisoner exchange but never fully recovered from his injuries and was discharged from the army. Back in the UK, Sgt James Barlex awaited news on the military grapevine of how his two cousins had fared in the attack. What he heard wasn't good. Before being captured, Pte Rupert Barlex had seen his twenty-seven year old brother Company Sergeant Major George Barlex killed in front of him. All three were from Barking and their fathers had worked their whole lives side by side in a local rubber factory. James hadn't gone to France, despite enlisting early in the Hammers and beginning the initial training with them. As a rough handed rubber worker himself, military wisdom had instead made him an instructor at the army school of cookery.

The survivors of the West Ham Battalion remained in varying degrees of undisguised shock. At 11am, they silently boarded motor lorries which took them in bone shaking discomfort to the comparative safety of the village of Vauchelles les Authies. They flopped in tents for a couple of days and were re-united with the 'ten per cent men' who disbelievingly absorbed the awful price of the "butchers bill" paid by the Hammers in the Battle of the Ancre. In addition to the officers, one hundred and sixty-five 'other ranks' had been posted as missing, of which only seven, including Pte Rupert Barlex, were subsequently returned by the Red Cross as being prisoners of war. Barlex, by now trudging eastward through the November rain to a huge POW compound in Vendhuile, remembered how *"after a time, we were moved into one big camp. This was a huge corrugated iron shed. The Shed was not well roofed and large icicles, quite six foot long, were hanging from the roof. When we awoke in the morning, we found the one blanket supplied to us frozen hard... Through the terrible treatment which we received the strength of the camp was reduced by quite sixty per cent within a few weeks through deaths and illness.*

Whilst there I developed blood poisoning in my hands [...] it went into my arm and, although my arm was slung up in a wire frame to keep it rigid, I was compelled to work with my other hand at the point of a bayonet..."

Chapter 24

Missing. Presumed...

In the confusion of battle the presence of an individual soldier at the CCS was not always immediately reported. When roll calls were taken, the whereabouts of the unanswered names were not always known. In this war those men were multiplied by the thousands and the army simply termed them as 'missing'. It was common practice for the War Office to issue telegrams to the next of kin naturally hungry for news following major engagements. When William and Harriet Carson, at home in Congleton, Cheshire, received that dreadful knock at the door and signed for their son's 'missing' telegram they were unaware that Captain Charles Graham Carson MC, the former medical student at University of Manchester, had been carried out of the Quadrilateral to a casualty station badly wounded and very close to death. As commander of C Company, he had reached his objective but had been hit in the chest.

The missing telegram was second only in its dread to the news confirming a loved one's death. Occasionally, a follow up to the missing telegram reported the soldier to have been found alive, usually wounded. Or, there were telegrams reporting the soldier as a prisoner of war. But, for many and just as today, the term 'missing', 'believed killed in action', means only one thing: no known grave. The painful anxiety of Carson's parents was given faint hope almost immediately by another telegram stating that Captain Carson had been taken to a military hospital in Rouen. But their relief was short lived. They soon received yet another knock at the door and with it a third and final telegram, sent with sympathy. Charles Carson's wounds were far too severe for the army surgeons to do anything with. A fine man, who specifically requested the Hammers as his unit, died aged twenty-two, on Sunday 19th November 1916. His headstone in the CWGC on the southern outskirts of St Sever bears the simple inscription "Thy will be done".

Whether or not a soldier received a proper burial in a marked grave was pretty much determined by where and in what circumstances he met his fate. If killed on ground occupied or captured by his comrades then his body (or what was left of it) would be recovered, identified if possible and given a military funeral and its location recorded. If identification was impossible then that fact was recorded and a marker 'Known unto God' was placed on the grave. Sometimes, particularly in the case of front line burials, the grave site might be in disputed territory held or recaptured by the enemy which would subsequently receive the attentions of artillery, finally destroying most traces of any graves there. Great efforts were made to record the original locations of these small informal plots and this enabled the Imperial (later, Commonwealth) War Graves Commission to re-establish the sites after the war. A marker was then placed stating a certain soldier as 'known to be buried in this cemetery'. There are several examples of this for the West Ham men on the crown of Redan Ridge because for those missing in combat, it was largely a case of remaining just that. It was too dangerous to attempt any sort of immediate battlefield recovery and very often there were simply too many to try and recover in any significant numbers.

For the West Ham Battalion, those with no known graves are commemorated alongside their chums from Delville Wood, on the Thiepval Memorial to the Missing of the Somme. The names include L/Cpl John Levi Coventry. He was twenty years old and had grown up on Park Avenue in East Ham. Pte John William Fitch was thirty-four years old and grew up in Tucker Street, West Ham. Charlie Gibbs was a promising soldier, appointed corporal, and came from Chargeable Street in Canning Town. He was nineteen.

Pte Cecil John Wells lived on Mountfield Road in East Ham. The thirty-eight year old worked in the Royal Docks as a labourer. Pte Harry Musgrove was another nineteen year old and came from Chevet Street in Homerton, not far from thirty-one year old Pte Henry John Dipple who lived in Bethnal Green on Morpeth Street. From Harrow Green in Leytonstone John Clifford Furlong was twenty and had enlisted at Stratford. He wouldn't be returning to his parents at Trinity Road. David Richard Balcombe was born in Limehouse. When he enlisted the thirty-six year old was living with his wife in Tidey Street off Bow Common Lane. Pte Martin Thomas Austin from Queen's Road in Walthamstow was twenty. He was killed firing one of the Brigade's heavy machine guns.

Of the West Ham Battalion officers, four remain missing to this day. Captain Edwin Milward Charrington was twenty-five years old and extremely determined to fight on despite losing his nose to a German shell in 1915. Overcoming severe discomfort and shocking disfigurement, he still confidently put himself forward at every opportunity. Colonel Carter "*had the greatest regard for him and a high opinion of his capabilities as an Officer*". A very popular man, "*beloved by all who knew him*", he was seen to be killed while leading the first wave. Though this fact was reported, his body was never found. Neither was 2/Lt Cyril Lionel Bishop Lyne who had been born in Stratford. He was twenty-four and, after returning from Canada to be commissioned straight into the Hammers, was there onboard the Princess Victoria a year previously. He was one of those wounded alongside Papillon and Len Holthusen when the HQ dugout was crumped in Delville Wood back in the summer during his stint as Adjutant. Here at the Quadrilateral, Cyril was reported wounded and sent to make his way back to the Regimental Aid Post. He never arrived.

2/Lt Bernard William Finn had only turned up at the West Ham Battalion a few weeks previously and took part in the disastrous recce of the Quadrilateral with JD Robinson. 2/Lt John Greville Fulkes had also only been with the Hammers for four weeks although he'd seen action as a Military Medal winning Company Sergeant Major in the Royal Fusiliers. Thirty years old and originally from Ilford, he was last seen going over the top with Busby and D Company in the second wave.

Three West Ham Battalion officers were somehow bought back to British lines. 2/Lt Frederick Garnet English was thirty-four. Another recent arrival, English had been immediately attached to the West Ham Battalion. Twenty-seven year old 2/Lt George Manners Gemmell lived with his 'well to do' parents in Forest Gate at Hampton Road and after a chance meeting with some members of the Hammers had applied to be an officer with the battalion early in 1916. Perhaps William Busby had a hand in persuading George to come, as he noted his arrival with some satisfaction in his diary. A true original of the West Ham Battalion, Busby was awarded the Military Cross on their first trench raid. A product of his age and all around splendid character, we shall not see his like again. "*His wholeheartedness was seen in whatever labour he undertook,*" wrote his father and *"no half measures suited him. Whatever he felt was worth doing, he believed was worth doing well, he put his best into it and therefore made it a success..."*

Busby died as he would have wished, keenly leading his 'boys' of No14 platoon and the rest of D Company into action. He was hit in the head by bits of a German shell, a small 'whizz-bang'. Beside him, and hit in the right side by fragments from the same explosion, was Pte J Clark from Emma Street in Silvertown. Under fire, as the men of No14 Platoon tended to their officer and the others littering the battlefield, Busby was heard by Clark to whisper *"Goodbye, my lads, I hope you will get through alright..."* It was they, his lads of D Company, who struggled to carry his body back, through that awful gripping mud and the incessant rain, to give him a 'proper' Christian burial. Back home, on hearing the news, his 'boys' of the West Ham Scouts immediately renamed themselves Busby Troop and changed their neckerchiefs to khaki in his memory, a Remembrance proudly upheld to this day. CSM Charlie Blowes, one of the first three hundred volunteers, later wrote a sincere letter to Mr Busby, describing William as the *"ideal officer"*. George Gemmell, Fred English and William Busby lie close to each other, and in good company, at Serre Road No2, the largest cemetery on the Somme.

Despite the unceasing enemy artillery fire raking No Man's Land and the widespread scavenging by hordes of rats, identification was not always impossible. Lt Henry Blamaires Wilcock was twenty years old when he followed Captain Charrington over the top on November 13th. When Charrington was killed Wilcock *"immediately took command of his Company, leapt over the wall and [...] into action"*.
That act was the last time anyone saw him alive, witnessed by several men who subsequently survived. He was consequently reported as missing and a telegram was sent by the War Office, to his father on the 21st November. The Reverend WH Wilcock of the Rectory, Tolleshunt Knights in Essex read a fairly standard explanation: *"Regret to inform you Lt HB Wilcock Essex Regt is reported missing Nov 14th. This does not necessarily mean that he is either killed or wounded. Any further reports if received will be wired immediately"*. The telegram was followed up by a personal letter from Harry Carter in which he described Wilcock's last known actions and confirmed what his parents had feared the most.

As winter eventually put an end to the fighting around Redan Ridge and Serre, the battlefield was trawled by the Divisional Salvage Companies trying, as their name suggests, to reclaim items of stores, equipment or weapons which might possibly be re-used. The 32nd Divisional Salvage Company were searching the area fought over by the West Ham Battalion when, on the 30th November, they found the decaying body of Lieut Henry Wilcock. The discovery, confirmed only by his personal effects, was reported as well as the location of his subsequent battlefield burial on *"the Old British Front Line Area, Map Ref: 1/40000, Sheet 57D K.35a.6.7"*. Just before Christmas another telegram was sent to Reverend Wilcock: *"Deeply regret to inform you Lieut HB Wilcock Essex Regt previously reported as missing is now reported to have been killed in action on or about Nov 13th. The Army Council express their sympathy"* The effect of receiving such news can only be imagined, especially on people with little concept of army ways. This was, after all, almost a Citizen Army and those left behind were thrust into an unknown spiral of uncertainty. In a painful letter, written on New Year's Eve to the BEF Casualty Base *"in the hope that you will be able to give us some particulars of our son"*, Henry's mother Mary Ellen Wilcock expresses this uncertainty. *"...it is now over 3 weeks since the War Office reported him to have been killed and we have not heard a word from either the Colonel or the Adjutant. Both have been written to, also the War Office and the Sec for War replied telling us that they had no particulars at the War Office about Lieutenant Wilcock's death. We shall be most grateful if you can tell us how the conclusion has been arrived at that our son was killed in action on or about Nov 13th...*

Since we had this news he has been reported killed so some further information regarding him must have come to hand or this latest report could not have been sent. Has his body been found, or his disc, or was he actually seen to be killed? It has been an awful time of distress and sorrow to us, and I am sure you will understand how much we are longing to hear why our dear son is reported killed. Anxiously awaiting your kind reply." Lt HB Wilcock is another buried at Serre Road No2.

There were also instances, where a soldier was reported missing and no body found, yet his death was accepted due to the irrefutable evidence of those who were there. Captain James Murray Round MC had led B Company in the first wave to attack the Quadrilateral on that morning. He and his men were initially successful but heavier and heavier German counter attacks pushed them back. They were finally pinned down under the redoubt's machine guns. A great many casualties were sustained and only a handful of B Company men were taken prisoner. James was posted as missing and his father Francis Round, a JP in the Essex town of Witham, received his telegram. It began the heartbreaking chain of letters and enquiries, to official and non-official sources, to anyone who could possibly shed some light on exactly what had happened that fateful morning. As Christmas came and went Francis Round went back to the Red Cross who were still receiving notifications of those men who had become prisoners. Then, on 27th February, 1917 the Agence Internationale des Prisonniers de Guerre forwarded a postcard. It was from Company Sergeant Major TR Walker, presently a POW at Dulmen in Germany, dated 21st February. In it he stated that Captain Round's batman, Cpl JJ Clarke witnessed the death. James Round was *"seen to have been killed"*. Clarke was later moved to a POW camp in Minden. A few weeks later, a letter was received by the War Office, from the Red Cross, with information from Pte William Ryan, a POW at Munster Camp. There was *"no mistake,"* he had seen Capt Round killed, in fact *"I moved him to see if he was really dead..."*

Faced with such evidence James Round's family were forced to accept that he was gone. A memorial service was held at the family church in Witham. The War Office changed 'missing' to 'Killed in Action' and gave the date of death as 13th November, 1916. But to his parents he was still simply missing. Finally, on 22nd July 1917, his body was found by yet another battlefield 'tidy up' operation, identified and laid to rest, amongst his men, in the ever growing cemetery on the Serre Road.

His family were handed the personal effects found on his body: fifty-five French francs, a souvenir two Franc note, his ID discs, a leather cigarette case and personal diary. Later in the year his elder brother was also killed, aged twenty-one.

The Round family lost three of their sons in the Great War.

Chapter 25

Be Prepared

Frank Keeble finally returned to the Hammers, after his recuperation, on the 16th November. He was stunned by the missing faces. One of his first acts was to settle up the outstanding mess bill for Charles Carson who had been his first Company officer when the Hammers were raised back in Stratford and a very close friend.

Following a brief rest at Vauchelles les Authies the weary remnants of the West Ham Battalion were moved to a training area north east of Abbeville in the gently rolling hills of Normandy. As the entire Division followed and centred itself on Brailly, the Hammers settled down in the wooden hutments at Gapennes on the 27th November. Some began small celebrations of having made it this far. One group, sitting together with a smiling officer who might just be William Brown-Paterson were frozen in time by a photograph entitled "the Somme Ancre Pushers". Sitting beside Cpl Tom Tozer, Sgt JJ Ash has his cap at a dapper angle. The part played by the Hammers in the Somme battles had cost them dear and they were not alone in suffering heavy losses. Badly mauled, they began a period of rest and, for those lucky enough to be next in line, leave. "*I got my first leave on 28th December 1916,*" remembers the West Ham Battalion tailor Ernie Kurtz. "*Home in England on 30th December to see little Doris for the first time on her 1st year's birthday... At that time, leave was extended to ten days so you can bet I had ten happy days! We invited all the family and friends and had a merry time!*" This may also be the period when Ernie Kurtz changed his name. There had been continued and violent anti-German resentment in East London and it had increased considerably after the many thousands of Somme casualties began coming home. By August, a number of Kurtz families, living in North East London had changed their name by deed poll to Curtis and some published announcements of the fact in the London Gazette. Ernie's wife Caroline may well have decided that a name change was the best option for her young family too. Whenever it occurred, and for whatever reason, by the end of his war Ernie Kurtz had become known as Ernie Curtis. And it quite possibly saved his life.

While Ernie had a party, the troubled leave of another Hammer was reported in the Stratford Express. Pte Arthur Thompson arrived back in West Ham to find his home in darkness. His wife and his children were gone. Frantically, Arthur searched for them, amongst friends and neighbours, fast becoming a desperate man. Then, he learned the awful truth. His wife had died of pneumonia, his children placed in a home. Another original, and one of the oldest at forty-five, Arthur Thompson was understandably distraught. A brave man's spirit was broken and on his leave he very quickly "*took to drink*". He was eventually arrested for being drunk and disorderly and appeared at West Ham police court on Friday 2nd January 1917. The court was presided over by the no-nonsense Henry Palmer, the very man who had magnanimously provided the finance for the West Ham Battalion King's Colours (which still hadn't been delivered) almost two years before.

Sympathy for Thompson's story dissolved quickly as the court heard that a telegram *had* been sent to the front, but it obviously never reached him. One has to wonder if such news would have been any less tragic if it had arrived, but at least he would have had the support of his pals. Chairman of the magistrates Palmer called him *"a disgrace to your uniform, getting beastly drunk"* but did let him off with only a warning. Arthur Thompson returned to the front and exactly what was going on in his mind can only be imagined. He survived the war, returning to West Ham in 1919 to try and piece his family together again.

At the end of his leave, Ernie Curtis *"told Carrie not to see me any further than the garden gate. The scene is quite bad enough at the stations with the sweethearts and wives, I can tell you. As soon as you get to France, in and out of the old trucks taking you up to the Line again where your Division is, you don't feel very happy. You know the war will never end and that is how we all feel. Your troubles and fears get worse the longer one is out there, although you might appear to look a veteran..."*

Back at the front, Sgt Jenns now had a new acting Adjutant to sign off his work after the death of Cyril Lyne. Eric Campbell Musson was the son of a French widow and, although born in Jamaica, had grown up in the pleasant surroundings of Park Cottages in Westhampnett, a small village outside Chichester. He had been serving in France since July 1915 before he'd undertaken officer training and had arrived together with Captain Round and Charrington prior to the Hammers' action in Delville Wood. Jenns also notes in the war diary the numbers of reinforcements arriving, drafted in from England. A few of these men were recovered wounded returning to the front. Mostly though, the drafts were conscripts and the majority, by definition, didn't want to be there. Despite basic training at home they were for the most part ignorant of 'army ways', of being 'handy' and the other small things that made military life easier – even here, out on the churned up battlefields of France. They were not the idealistic volunteers of 1915, hungrily absorbing all available knowledge and experience that might make them better soldiers. They equally weren't given much choice about where they served or with which unit. It was not unknown for conscripts to be trained wearing the badge of one regiment only to be reallocated on arrival in France to another. An example arrived at the Hammers' HQ, in the short, sturdy form of Pte Enoch Edward Bentley. A Lancastrian born and bred, Bentley was a married man from New Pleasant Street, Acre in Haslingden where his father had a grocers shop. Enoch was himself a weaver at the Alliance Mill in nearby Baxenden. He was thirty-seven and had grown up in the area, it was all he knew. Called up in June 1916, Enoch now found himself among a draft of two-hundred and fifty-one "other ranks", arriving in dribs and drabs, to replace the dead and wounded of the West Ham Battalion.

The surviving Hammers veterans were every bit as alien to him as France itself.

Chapter 26

Another Bloody Year

On January 1st, 1917, the King awarded Captain Dick Collier the Military Cross. Being part of the New Year's Honours there was no citation which would normally outline the reasons it was given. It is believed to have been awarded not only for his continued good work (including spending time as commanding officer at one point) but primarily for the way in which he looked after the King's good friend Papillon when he suffered his breakdown from shellshock. The King had personally presented Papillon with his DSO at the Palace at the start of November and no doubt a good recommendation was made for Collier. A few days after the list was published, Papillon was himself 'Mentioned in Dispatches' along with Harry Carter, and a couple of the originals, Sgt L Windsor and Sgt J Alexander. For the rest of the Hammers, still billeted in Gapenne, time was spent bringing the replacements and conscripts up to speed through field training, practising trench attacks and increasing their accuracy on the firing range. There were also boxing tournaments. The whole battalion was paraded and platoons were re-arranged to spread the veterans of the Hammers among the conscripted replacements. They then practised attacking trenches again and again. On the 7th, names began trickling in of those few men captured at the Quadrilateral including two more NCO's from among the originals, Sgt Major Todd and Sgt Foreman while Sgt Caulfield gratefully said goodbye to the snowy dangerous trenches for a while and headed to England for the extra responsibility that would come after officer training. 2/Lt Brown-Patterson MC also resumed the role of acting Adjutant in charge of Jenns.

There was then more bitter cold snow on the 9th as the Hammers marched fifteen miles to Boisbergues arriving in the early evening. The next day Carter gave a long lecture on the merits of march discipline to every man. Carter was a bit of a stickler about march discipline. Over Christmas eight new officers had arrived to make up the deficit, including Captain Ritson and 2/Lt Sacre. Claude Wilson Ritson was born in Newcastle but had emigrated seeking a better life and was working as a civil engineer in Canada, on the miles of new railway tracks being laid. At the outbreak of war he, like so many, returned to England and enlisted. Antoine Reboul Sacre was just eighteen years old and a vicar's son from East Hanningfield in south Essex. He had no previous military experience. Later they were joined by, among others, thirty-two year old Calcutta born 2/Lt Baboneau, a short-sighted colonial officer and magistrate who had been working out in British North Borneo for a number of years. His company desperately wanted him back and wrote many letters to the War Office requesting his return. He was a bit of a hero to them, being the sole speaker and published author of the local languages and dialects. More importantly he was responsible for quashing the violent 'Rundum uprising' by local tribesmen in 1915. After his remote company station was surrounded and attacked by murderous head hunters,

Baboneau made a gruelling two week escape and evasion through the thick mountainous jungle, leading a small group of survivors as they were chased the whole way night and day. He then led a massacre of the ringleaders after his company soldiers arrived in reinforcement and the tribesmen were cornered in a cave. Now in France, thoroughly out of his element, Noel Blake Baboneau soon began feeling the ill effects of malaria, compounded by the general trench conditions.

Two more fifteen mile marches took the Hammers to Bouzincourt where they went into the Brigade reserve lines and for the next week or so they were busy clearing roads and occupied as working parties. One of the originals felt a need to leave the trenches and consequently Pte Middleton was reported as *"deserted"* on the 14th. Luckily there were a number of replacements milling around to any fill gaps like these. Among the recent arrivals was Cpl Manningtree from Dedham in Essex, who had already seen action and been wounded at Loos in 1915. Assigned to B Company it became one of those odd coincidences when he told his commanding officer Frank Keeble where he came from. Keeble exclaimed *"Why, you must know my old man!"* back on the farm in nearby Brantham. He did. It seemed to cheer Keeble's spirits and due to his combat experience Cpl Manningtree was put in charge of a Section.

The Hammers then began moving again and finally slumped down in huts at Ovillers. On January 21st Arthur Daly left the command of Brigade, going home on an extended leave. He had become thoroughly exhausted by the war and the responsibility his rank brought but would end up being mentioned in dispatches seven times. Meanwhile many of the Hammers were being utilised as working parties. Keeping busy with the usual mundane yet dangerous elements of trench life was the only way of staying relatively warm. Despite the freezing weather, at 6.45am on the 22nd the whole battalion was 'stood to' outside their huts for half an hour, most likely as a group punishment from Carter for some undisclosed reason. It was followed by two days of hard physical exercise and gas drills. On the 24th January, they were back in the frontline, entering the mud filled right subsection of trenches in the Courcellette sector. A & B Company were first in. The conditions were absolutely terrible requiring the next few days to be spent generally trying to improve the trenches, baling out the water and fixing up the wire in front. They were also out in No Man's Land, night patrolling in the quagmire. By the 28th they left the trenches and went back to billets at Bouzincourt spending the following two days practising bayonet fighting, Lewis gunnery and bombing while relaxing with further boxing tournaments. On the evening of the 30th Carter marched all officers off and made them practise *"compass reading at night"*, obviously in an effort to improve the skills of the recent arrivals.

A full ceremonial parade opened February 1917 and on the 2nd there was the chance to have a bath at Senlis. This was followed by a shooting competition, yet more drill and extra instruction under Carter. Working parties were still being sent out but Major Winthrop, who had been in hospital suffering with sciatica for the last few weeks, was now sent home to England. He had arrived at the Hammers in March 1915 but would not be returning. One officer still around from the early days in Stratford was Major Arthur Gracie Hayward, who had won his Military Cross leading the first trench raid in 1916. Hayward now took command of the battalion as Harry Carter went on a senior officer's course for a week. There were handovers elsewhere as 2/Lt Ernest Sherman took over the role of assistant adjutant. Sherman was the young officer sent out by Carter to report on the carnage at the Quadrilateral back in November and was now writing up the war diary as cover for the absence of Frank Jenns.

In either Hayward's first or Carter's last act in command of the West Ham Battalion one of them recommended Jenns for officer training.

Chapter 27

Home Fires

Jenns left for officer training back in England on Valentine's Day, 1917. Subsequently, the war diary no longer lists the names or service numbers of the men wounded, including the two who were injured the day before while forming part of a huge working party. It's unknown what the injuries were, but the combination of barely trained conscripted recruits with the appalling weather was having dire consequences, even in some cases with frostbite. Major Hayward ordered foot inspections to be carried out and a few of the remaining veterans no doubt tried to pass on tips to any who were listening. More worryingly, it was also found necessary to have extra rifle inspections too. Another of the originals chose to leave on the same day as Jenns, with Pte Thurston being reported *"deserted"*.

The West Ham Battalion then moved back to Ovillers as support for the Brigade. They hit their bunks at 1am but by 5.45am on 17th February they were hurriedly assembled *"in consequence of actions in the Courcelette sector."* This was an allied attack, behind a creeping barrage, to take the last remaining frost bitten high ground on the Ancre battlefield, securing the height advantage still currently held by the Germans. Despite fierce fighting the objectives were taken and as the new frontline moved forward, the Hammers found themselves taking over flooded trenches in the muddy left subsector outside Miraumont which the enemy was in the midst of abandoning. The men began strengthening the advanced posts in the freezing night, building splinter proof shelters and reconstructing positions to face the other way. They now had a clear view down over the valley plain and could clearly see the Germans in Miraumont and Pys pulling back out of range.

For those like Jenns at home in England, the evening of Friday 19th February was very memorable, but for all the wrong reasons. The old Brunner Mond factory, at Crescent Wharf in the heavily populated Silvertown area, had been re-opened by the government a year or so earlier to manufacture high explosives. Now, after an initial fire in one of the outbuildings, fifty tons of TNT flashed into a huge explosion at precisely 6.52pm, rocking the Borough. The detonation was reportedly heard up to one hundred miles away while the sheet of flame from the explosion was said to be visible for thirty miles, with the shock wave taking a full minute to arrive. The blast killed seventy-three people, sixty-nine of them instantly and the youngest wasn't yet five months old. Over four hundred people were wounded and it remains the largest explosion ever witnessed in London. Nearly eighty-thousand houses were damaged by the concussion wave and flying debris. Of those, nine-hundred homes were completely flattened. The factory site remained levelled for many years and none were willing to build there. Today, it is still flat, with the Crescent Wharf footprint now the Thames Barrier visitor's centre car park. It is impossible to know how many of the West Ham Battalion, either out in France or at home on leave, were directly affected by this shocking yet avoidable event. It is likely there were quite a few.

Back at the mud and blood of France there was still some activity as the German artillery calculated the updated angle to distance ratio from their new positions. The shell hole craters, filled to the brim with a poisonous muddy soup, were capable of taking a man and drowning him within minutes or if really unfortunate, hours. There were also snipers holed up in their well prepared hides and over these few days two new officers and thirteen men were killed, including Pte John Delaney from Stepney and Pte James Launder from Bethnal Green. Two more struck from the roll of West Ham Battalion originals.

Today Delaney lies buried in Regina Trench cemetery while Launder is one more remembered only by name on the Thiepval Memorial to the Missing. Killed the week before was thirty-four year old L/Cpl Spicer who had won his Military Medal at the Quadrilateral back in November. He left a wife at home in Blackthorn Street, Bow and only his name remains on the Thiepval memorial. Another of the dead was Pte Enoch Bentley, from Lancashire, who had only arrived a few short weeks before. Six others were listed as missing and thirty-one were wounded out here as the push forward to follow the Germans by Brigade continued. One of the wounded men was as a result of a self-inflicted shooting. The overwhelming majority of casualties however were sent to hospital with trenchfoot. It was a preventable condition to a degree, and was simply caused by lengthy immersion in muddy water. If left untreated it could turn gangrenous and require amputation. In a few cases men deliberately exposed their feet to the conditions as a way to escape the madness and terror of the line. A staggering eighty men left the Hammers ranks with the ailment at the end of this short tour.

The remainder of the battalion moved to the rubbled yet bustling town of Albert on February 23rd. It was the busiest and largest military hub on the British part of the Somme battlefield and the Hammers began cleaning themselves up after arriving caked in mud. There was also the opportunity to have a bit of relatively peaceful sleep. Foot drills and inspections were very regular now though, and the CSM's and senior NCO's were smartening them all up in their usual manner and style. Carter returned and dragged all the junior officers out for more squelching about in mud on battlefield map reading exercises. A few additional fresh officers were arriving, such as 2/Lt's Austin and Tonkin, while those who had only been here a few weeks, like 2/Lt Antoine Sacre, were already being hospitalised from the conditions which were very often responsible for severe dysentery and other debilitating sickness. There was only one death over this rest period and it wasn't due to enemy action. Pte Henry Moss, a recent replacement from Friston in Suffolk, died from an attack of epilepsy on 2nd March. The Hammers then crunched back in bitter icy wind to Ovillers about three miles away. At 6.30am on Sunday 4th they formed one huge working party in an effort to clear the roads through Courcelette and by the end of the day the divisional commander was "*much impressed by the splendid work done. The progress made was little less than astonishing in so short a time...*"

While they had been away from the front, the gains made taking the Ancre Heights had meant the line could actually cautiously advance. On the 11th March the West Ham Battalion entered positions on the left of the Loupart sector and began preparations to support the taking of the last remaining German trenches. Their efforts weren't to be required however. Night patrols had disbelievingly noticed a lack of German troops. It was swiftly realised that they were actually making a clandestine retreat. Cautiously following the Germans everyone remained on their guard. The enemy were ultimately heading for the "Hindenburg Line", positions they had been preparing secretly for quite some time which were very well constructed and implemented everything that had been learnt in the last few years of trench warfare.

Following them, the Hammers were staggered when they encountered some abandoned enemy dugouts in the old front line, where a few were lined with brightly coloured wallpaper in places. Beer, wine, cake and other home comforts were seemingly freely available. The Hammers were quickly snapped out of daydreams by the discovery of innumerable and various improvised explosive devices or *"booby-traps"* as they were known at that time. They had been carefully placed and left behind with the intention to maim or slaughter a souvenir hunter. Five men were killed in this period, including two nineteen year old originals who had sailed over together on the Princess Victoria. Pte George Green was from Stanford Rivers in Essex while Pte Arthur Allerton was from Duck Farm in Stebbing. Arthur had enlisted in the Hammers because his father was a native of Limehouse. They are two more of the many Hammers listed on the Thiepval Memorial to the Missing. Twelve other soldiers were wounded during this slow and nerve wracking advance, never knowing where a sniper might lurk or a wire might be waiting to be tripped.

The area of the new No Man's Land they were walking into should have been relatively unscathed by the war. But the Germans, carrying out the orders of their withdrawal plan to the letter, had not only left traps. They had also relentlessly destroyed anything of use, whether by snapping pickaxe and shovel handles or by thoroughly poisoning the local water supply. Houses were pulled down and as the last men retreated to their new positions, crops and stocks which hadn't been confiscated were burnt in their wake. Some of the French locals, who had upheld a relatively healthy business this far back during the static years of war, were disgruntled. A few openly blamed the allies for their misfortune.

Finishing their tour in the Loupart sector the Hammers moved to reserve in Dyke Valley camp. Despite arriving at 4am they immediately set about drying and cleaning themselves and their kit again. On the 15th March there was a job no doubt relished by a civil engineer like Capt Claude Ritson. They set about the important task of laying brushwood tracks and fixing up the roads so that the artillery could be brought up into range. They were also laying fresh duckboards for the infantry to walk over. After two days of extremely hard work their length of the labours was proudly christened the "Essex Track". Carter expressed his appreciation, especially for the work done by Ritson and said that every man in the battalion was not only clearly keeping up *"the traditions of the Essex Regiment"* but they were all obviously *"trying to go one better"*. Carter placed on record the excellent behaviour of the West Ham men and officers during the advance which he described as being *"a great strain on all ranks, who had already undergone a severe strain holding the posts..."*

They slopped back to Loupart Wood and took over four wet lines of previously German trenches just south west of Sapignies for a short uncomfortable yet uneventful tour. As the British advanced, the Germans pulled back and Sapignies was thoroughly and deliberately burning by the time the Hammers returned to Courcelette nine miles away on the 20th March. They spent yet another night *"drying clothes"* and *"cleaning arms and equipment"* while scratching away at the body lice. Shuffled about, they ultimately ended up at relatively comfortable billets in Warloy and by the 23rd March engaged in a thorough clean. It meant the first full refit for every soldier after an audit was held by Major Arthur Hayward. Ernie Curtis in the Hammer's tailoring hut was nearly overwhelmed by the *"too numerous"* tasks that were soon piled all around him. *"One sergeant and a private to do the repairs for just over a thousand men was not so easy!"* The battalion cobblers were equally as busy. Harry Carter intended to leave them all fighting fit in health and kit before he transferred to the officer training school in Aldershot.

On the 29th, a letter, following up a telegram, arrived for Carter. It was from the daughter of Pte Charlie Fox. He was one of the early volunteers from Tidal Basin, a forty year old coal porter wounded at Delville Wood back in July. In the twelve year old's plaintive language and simple handwriting she begged for her father to be allowed home. Her mother had just died and the five children desperately needed him back to sort out the family affairs. Most urgent was payment of the bill from the undertaker who had buried her. Carter sympathetically allowed Fox to have a short period of leave.

A series of moves into billets occurred over the next few days before the Hammers finally arrived in Huclier. They had more training for the replacements before Carter finally left on the 6th April. He was replaced, as they moved to Ourtin, by a highlander Lieut-Col CT Martin. His second in command was Captain AD Derviche-Jones MC and for the next ten days the additional replacement soldiers arriving in small and large groups were quickly brought up to scratch with drill. Leaving Ourtin, the Hammers returned to the rear reserve area of the trenches at Roclincourt. They continued their fine work laying duckboard tracks towards the Oppy sector with the divisional commander again impressed enough by their efforts to make official notice. Ritson must have been really proving his worth as finally the Corps commander commented how he was *"much struck with the organisation and work being carried out..."* In the evenings the dugouts were continually inspected for their cleanliness and feet were washed, rubbed and treated to prevent more cases of trench foot.

On the 8th April they heard the incredible noise of the opening artillery barrages being laid down prior to the latest offensive, designed to punch a hole in the German line and thrust towards Cambrai. Some objectives would appear difficult for the infantry to accomplish, like the taking of Vimy Ridge, while others looked to be simpler affairs. In the event, the attack was successful and the longest advance of the war was made, despite most of the combat taking place in bitter snowstorms. In the subsequent repositioning of troops, the Germans were forced to relocate their forces and by the 13th April were once again pulling out of the lines back to freshly dug positions. By the next evening, the division, hot on their tail, were in some spots less than five-hundred yards from the freshly laid German defensive wire.

It was the usual all-grabbing spiteful thistle bush of immense proportions.

(Trustee's of Catsfield Church)

Lt-Col Pelham Rawstorn Papillon, DSO, JP by RG Eves, painted in late November 1917

The steamship Princess Victoria

Joe Cooper of Limehouse (Authors Own)

Dick Collier, Transport Officer (Collier Family)

Oscar Ollett of Bocking and his grave painted by Sgt EE Warr (Essex Regiment Museum)

The tireless West Ham Battalion Pioneers

Thomas Crispin.

L/Cpl James who won the Military Medal
twice with the Hammers

(Keeble family)

Frank Keeble's menu prior to the Hammers first trench raid in July 1916

(Essex Regt Museum)

Men of the 6th Brigade trench mortars, including a number of soldiers from the West Ham Battalion

(Keeble Family)

Frank Keeble, MC + Bar

(Essex Regt Museum)

EM Wilding, MM

William Busby, MC

George Harry Ross

Capt James Murray Round, MC

Capt Claude Wilson Ritson

2/Lt Arnold Hone, MC, post-war

(Michael Holden)

(Imperial War Museum)

Waterlot Farm and High Holborn, prior to and after bombardment on 8th August 1916.

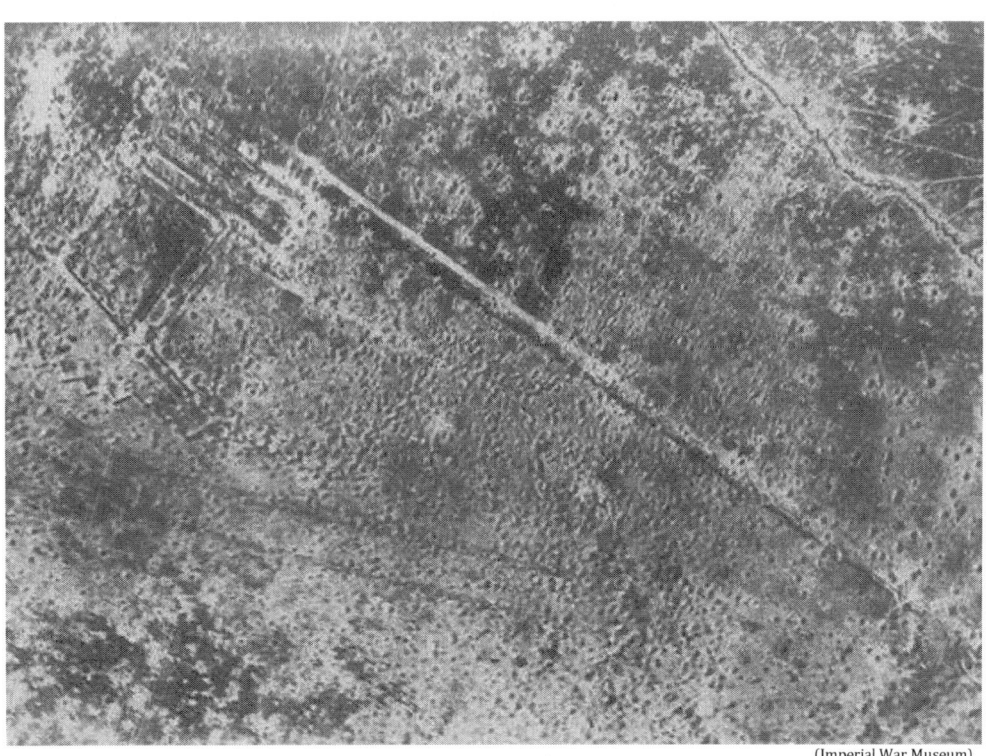

(Imperial War Museum)

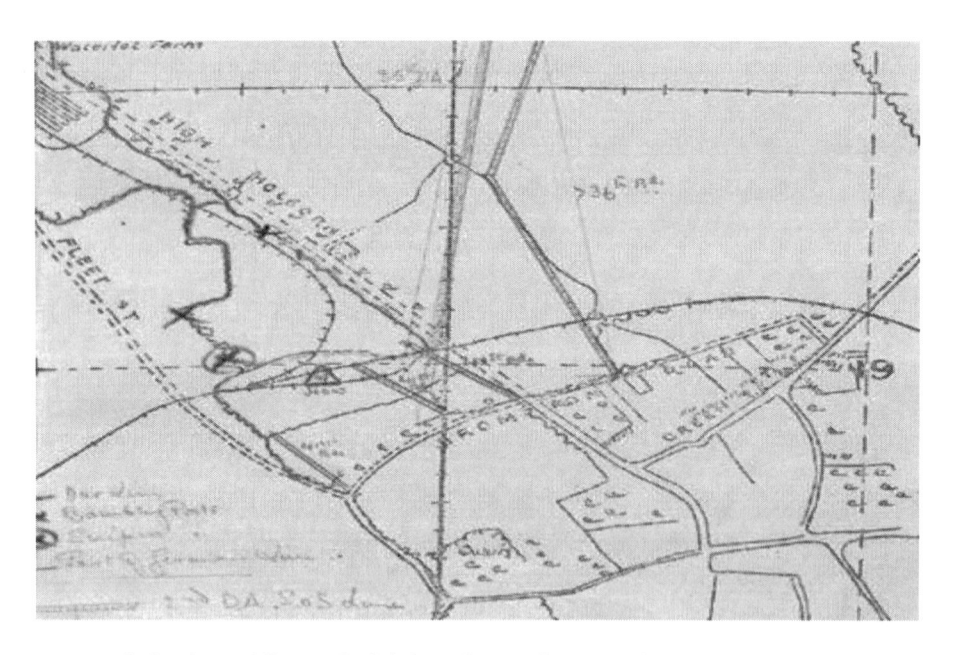

Captain Rounds sketch map following the failed attack on Guillemont with 'Green Street' trench on the right.

(Essex Regiment Museum)

Photograph taken in Gapenne at the end of the Somme fighting. The officer is unidentified,
JJ Ash, DCM, has his hat at a dapper angle and is seated beside Tom Tozer, MM.

Charlie Songhurst, MM

(Folkard Family)

Frank Tyhurst Folkard, wounded at Delville Wood

(Bunting Family)

Captain Eric Bunting

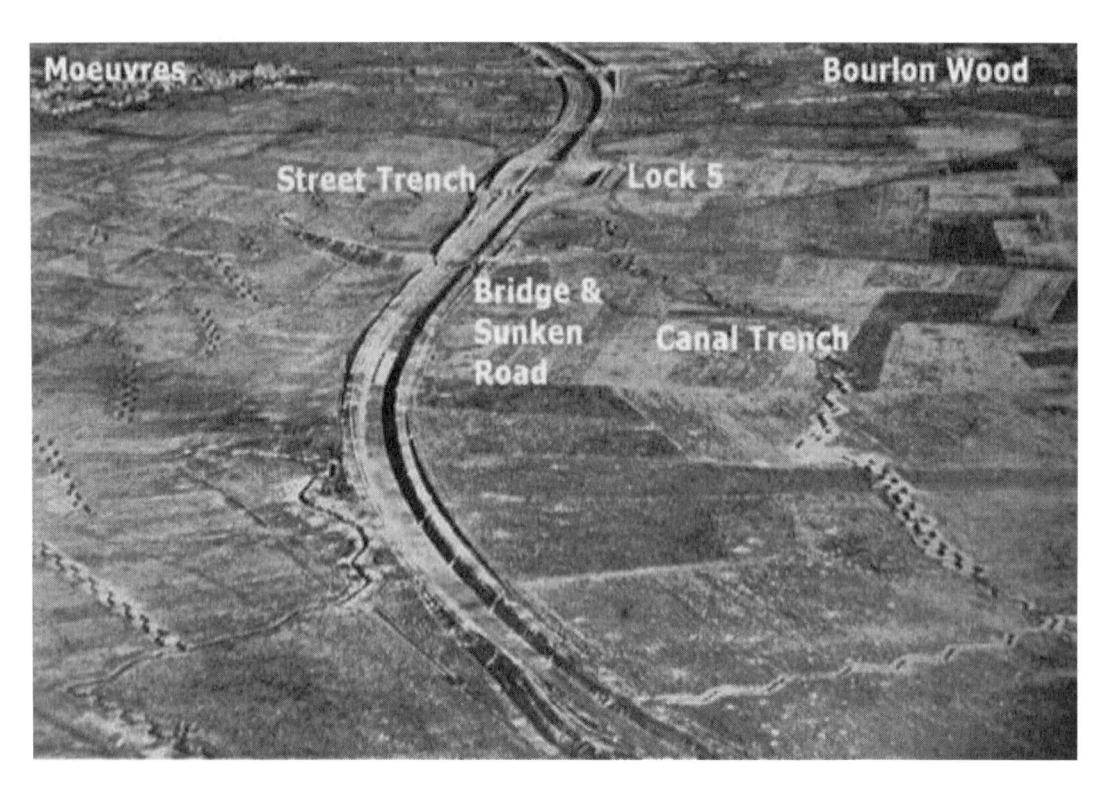

Aerial recce photo of the Canal Du Nord positions at Moeuvres.

Dedicated
In Memory To
The Sacrifices Made By
THE WEST HAM PALS
of
13th (Service) Battalion
THE ESSEX REGIMENT
('The Hammers')
France & Flanders Nov 1915 - Feb 1918
"UP THE IRONS!"

THE MAYOR & CORPORATION OF WEST HAM
request the honour of the Company of

1295 Sergt A D Moore D.C.M

to DINNER & RE-UNION

of the

13TH (S) BATTALION, ESSEX REGIMENT,
(WEST HAM)

on the 21st June 1919, at 6-30 p.m

at the

CONNAUGHT ROOMS,
GREAT QUEEN STREET, W.C

(Essex Regiment Museum)

"The Magnificent Last Stand of the Essex" at the Lock and Sunken Road, by Richard Caton-Woodville, published as a double page spread in a February 1918 edition of the Illustrated London News.

Part 3

Moving Shadows

Oppy & Cambrai 1917 - West Ham, 1919

Chapter 28

"No Friends Out Here!"

Back at Roclincourt, the Hammers continued laying the tracks for those following in the advance. Some were tasked with clearing the way ahead. Cpl Manningtree remembered when he was *"detailed off to take three men with me and take all the equipment off the soldiers and the pay book and all the civil sort of things. Off the dead, yes… They'd been there a day or two. They were stiff, y'know... One got a hole in his head and shoulder, another got a hole in his feet. We slung 'em in the far shellhole..."* Due to his actions these men would be unlikely today to have a known grave. This is perhaps the reason why Manningtree, post-War, lamented that it was *"a rotten thing I done…"* He ended the duty with *"a pack of books under me arm, as thick as that. Letters and... Still, I always had faith. That go a long way. I ain't religious, far from it, but …"*

Some of the veterans then welcomed a familiar face. On the 16th April in his new uniform no doubt already muddied and snagged, the freshly commissioned 2/Lt Frank Jenns arrived back at the West Ham Battalion. He took up his old role, officially, as assistant Adjutant from 2/Lt Sherman and resumed writing up the war diary. Running battalion HQ and signing off the diary as his acting Adjutant was Lt William Brown-Paterson MC, formerly the Hammers signals officer who had won his Military Cross with Arnold Hone at the Quadrilateral back in November. He had been replaced as the signals officer by Lt Archie Wells. One person who didn't come back off leave however was Pte Charlie Fox. After sorting out his family affairs, he was now listed as AWOL and being watched for by keen-eyed policemen on the streets of West Ham.

On the 18th April 1917 the Hammers prepared themselves to move back into the Brigade's left subsector frontline trench which was by now facing Oppy village and its wood. To their south, preparations were underway for the next step in the advance which would include vicious combat for the town of Gavrelle immediately followed by the inevitable stiff counter-attacks. Here facing Oppy, the lines were being pounded by German artillery as the Hammers struggled, during the morning of the 19th, to dig communications trenches and consolidate the forward positions. Five men were killed and another seven were wounded. Four of the dead were originals, manning these advanced posts. L/Cpl Tom Tinning was thirty and from Canning Town. He was buried in Orchard Dump Cemetery right beside Pte William Johnson from Mile End. L/Cpl Wright was from Clapton and today he is another with only a name remaining on the Arras Memorial. Also from Canning Town was twenty year old Pte William Poile who had been working with the Royal Engineer tunnellers when he was killed. Today he lies in Achiet-le-Grande Communal cemetery. For the next two days they held the line and developed what was known as "New Trench", only three-hundred yards from the German front and over one-thousand yards long. Major Derviche-Jones was supervising the construction. Giving cover was a platoon, with two officers, fifty yards in front of the new trench.

The German shelling on the Hammers lines began like clockwork, heavily at 9am. It lasted for an hour before it became *"intense"* and remained intense for the rest of the morning and afternoon. It then tailed off noticeably and practically ceased altogether at about 7.45pm. Night patrols were still being sent out to discover anything of value and Cpl Manningtree remembered an incident around this time when *"every Company had sent out a patrol, bar B Company. So the old sergeant major come to me, he said "I got something right up your barrow, boy... Something good! They want to know who's in front of us, what regiment of Germans..."*

Unusually, rather than stealth, Manningtree *"took a section with me and two Lewis guns."* As the group crept their way dangerously closer to the German advanced posts, something happened which quite clearly required a very swift resolution. It became *"another rottenest thing"* Manningtree took part in, if not led. *"Do you know what we done? Killed the lot..."* Despite taking no prisoners they had also fulfilled their mission. As they cut identifying shoulder straps and searched the dead enemy for anything of military value within the cordite smoke, the German reply from the front line trench was naturally swift and aggressive. Suddenly, *"we were pinned down, with rifle grenades, 'cos they knew we was out and they knew our distance..."* Back in the Hammers' lines it was no doubt thought that, judging by the Lewis fire and the German response, the patrol was surely dead or captured. They went on high alert but the night subsequently became quieter. Out in No Man's Land, Manningtree's party had continually *"dodged about"* and evaded capture, hiding for the whole of the following day. They *"lay out there, in shell holes, till it got dusk."* The group then made their way back to the Hammer's lines. Getting close to the home trench, *"we were challenged, "Halt! Who goes there?" I said "friends". He said, "We aint got no friends out here!" and they started firing at us! You don't know what I said to them!"* It took a while to make their way safely back but when Manningtree saw Keeble *"I didn't half walk it into him! He said "We didn't know if you were dead or alive!" I said "no, and you didn't care! You might have told them we was out there!"*

As the darkness of a chilly evening crept up on the 21st April, the clockwork routine of German shelling finally drew to a close. Out in No Man's Land several shell holes were occupied by those men in advance of the long 'New' trench being constructed, regarded as an *"outpost line"*. In front of the right-hand length was a half platoon with a couple of Lewis guns and twelve riflemen, led by eighteen year old 2/Lt Antoine Sacre, the vicar's son from East Hanningfield. Far away to his left was the other half of the platoon, led by the malarial thirty-two year old 2/Lt Noel Baboneau. Major Derviche-Jones had warned Baboneau to use *"the utmost vigilance"* on this end of the new trench, as he could see how vulnerable it was due to its distance and angle from the covering fire of the British frontline. Baboneau placed his troops in various positions which Derviche-Jones was happy with and he returned to the British lines.

Suddenly at 9pm, from seemingly out of nowhere, a heavy and unexpected barrage fiercely opened up on the rest of the West Ham Battalion. It cut off the advanced posts, where one of the lookouts now spotted the dreadful outline of some keen German trench raiders heading their way at speed. About fifty fierce looking Bavarians with clubs and revolvers were aggressively charging at them in three groups, perhaps eagerly seeking revenge for Cpl Manningtree's little massacre. On the right, swiftly getting his Lewis gun into action, a section led by one of the originals, Cpl G King, fired at a group of about twenty Germans. He shot and killed one man at a range of forty yards and the Lewis gun sent the rest diving for cover. King then led his men back into the uncompleted new trench where he met his officer, 2/Lt Sacre, and the other section.

They all realised that another group of twenty or so raiders had entered the trench at the midway point and a firefight quickly drove the Germans to the left and down towards Baboneau's half of the platoon. As 2/Lt Baboneau arrived from out front, Sacre sent up the SOS signal flares. Immediately, there were four red lights sent up from the German frontline and within a matter of seconds their artillery laid down a full five minute barrage, behind the newly dug trench preventing reinforcements from approaching. It became the orange and blue flashing backdrop as all along the shallow trench men tried to take what cover they could. In the chaos, Sacre saw another party of Germans advancing on the far left of the trench where Baboneau's troops were. They entered it, unopposed. Then, on top of the German artillery, the British artillery eventually responded to Sacre's SOS and threw down a viciously brutal barrage. Terrifyingly, most of it was landing all along the length of new trench, a fact later described as *"unfortunate"* by Lt-Col Martin.

The British bombardment ceased after fifteen minutes and Baboneau promptly went to the left, alone, along the trench to regroup his half of the platoon. He moved carefully for a good distance but didn't encounter anyone. Towards the far end, in the swirling smoke and cordite of the recent barrages, he couldn't see very much at all. Then, from out of the darkness came a whispered question: *"Hast du sie?"* ["Have you got them?"]

Baboneau answered with two shots from his Webley revolver, heard a man crumple and swiftly returned to Sacre and the others.

They then made what would be later regarded as *"an error of judgement"* when they decided it was best to pull their men back to the British frontline, in effect giving up the trench to the Germans. Arriving breathlessly at C Company's position at 10pm, they reported the situation. Fifteen minutes later, as word got back, Captain Ritson was very urgently sent from HQ with strict orders to *"strongly occupy"* the lost ground. Colonel Martin's order's to Ritson regarding Baboneau and Sacre were to *"send them straight back to the trench they had evacuated"* as it could almost be viewed officially as pure cowardice in the face of the enemy. At 2am Ritson, the two officers and the remaining members of the platoon crept forward into the advanced outpost area on the right. On their arrival at the trench, it was all quiet, eerily so. Sacre and Baboneau were leading at the front and, cautiously entering the combat area they discovered German grenade dumps, with tools and also rifles close by and ready for action. Progressing further along, they became aware of six bodies lying about, five British and one German, all dead. Within the smoke and half light they realised that another man was semi-conscious. It was an ashen faced German officer, silently bleeding out.

As they searched the length of the trench and the ground in front it was apparent that the rest of the Bavarian trench raiders had gone. The remaining twenty-two men of Baboneau's platoon were also gone, taken prisoner. Ritson distributed the men along the trench in tactical positions and warned them to stay alert and listen for his commands. At 4am, a five man patrol led by a German officer cautiously made its stumbling way on the left, through No Man's Land towards them. They were spotted by Ritson's group who held fire and let them advance until the Germans had slipped quietly down into the trench and made their way along to the left. Ritson and his men then opened a close-range rapid-fire but in the chaos the Germans incredibly managed to kill one of his soldiers before they withdrew and began running back to their line. Captain Ritson quickly brought up a Lewis gun and over the next few minutes at varying ranges effectively shot them down, in the back. As dawn broke the Germans shelled the trench continually, badly wounding four. As the afternoon wore on, Ritson noticed that Baboneau was showing all the signs of suffering from an acute attack of malaria. Within an hour, he had collapsed and was taken out of the line. He eventually returned to England for recovery but never returned to France.

The next day the Hammers were finally taken out of the line and placed back at Roclincourt. Despite being in the rear, the shelling killed one of the replacements and wounded another. On the 24th, word was urgently sent that a counterattack was expected from the Germans. It would be coming from Oppy village and consequently the Hammers were rushed up into the support trenches. The men geared themselves up for action but they were finally sent back at 7pm, unused. Counter-attacks were actually being directed on the towns either side of the Oppy sector, as the Germans attempted to recapture the ground they had earlier given up in the opening stages of the battle. The following evening, Captain Frank Keeble had the chance to return to the pleasant surroundings and comforts of Brantham and left on leave while Lt-Col Martin headed over to Brigade HQ. It was for a conference to lay out the plans to capture Oppy and the ground around it before the Germans could build up enough strength of forces to resist. The attack would go in at 4.25am on the 28th April, with the West Ham Battalion leading the way on the right, beside their old friends the Footballers on the left.

Made up of professional players but having suffered virtually similar battlefield experiences as the West Ham Battalion, the Footballers ranks were noticeably short of the many famous faces from a year ago. Either dead or maimed they were destined never to play the beautiful game again.

Chapter 29

Midfield Mayhem

The West Ham Battalion left the billets at Maroevil and marched for three hours back to Roclincourt. There they had a hot meal and a rest, before moving up to assembly trenches at dusk. The men *"appeared cheerful and confident of success"* which was perhaps only natural after gulping down their rum rations. They were also issued chocolate and cheese sandwiches intended to last them for the next two days. A few had noticed how far undermanned they were, due not only to the missing men of Baboneau's platoon but also from the shelling, dysentery, TB, frostbite and trench foot injuries of the last month. This was compounded when the Brigade ordered that one hundred and eight men should be left behind as "ten per centers".

Those making the attack were all too aware of the wider gaps in their ranks but assurances from above that the wire was cut tempered the general disquiet. Some of the Hammers veterans no doubt gave that a wry smile. They had heard it all before. The attack would be the usual affair and in three waves. After a bombardment, the first wave had to charge at the German front line trench, take it and hold it before the second wave would join them. Together they would closely follow behind a creeping barrage, and advance beyond a length of road leading from the right of Oppy village. The third wave would be following up to take a parallel road a little further on. In total they were expected to advance a distance of more than a thousand yards. The three waves were split into two lines each, with bombers and riflemen going first followed by Lewis gunners and men armed with rifle grenades. Word was sent along the lines that this was expected to be a tough fight as the Germans intended to defend the spot with vigour. Strong counter attacks would follow any gains made by the Brigade. As they got into their jump off positions at 2am, the Germans were already shelling the lines.

At 4.25am the British artillery opened up, specifically targeting among others the German front line. This was quite effective, but the Germans had already implemented their tactic of leaving the front trench lightly manned by machine guns sheltered in deep dugouts while the rest of the troops waited some distance behind before they would rush back to the trench at the end of what they knew to be a preparatory bombardment. Consequently, when the Hammers went over the top and arrived at the German lines at 4.38am they quickly dealt with the machine gunners and took the first trench. Eighty or so prisoners were sent back to the battalion lines. It wasn't all successful however. On the right, part of B Company led by Captain Ritson, encountered the German wire and found it to be mostly uncut. As a result, they were swiftly trapped and mown down by the machine guns, in an echo of the attack on Guillemont. There was great loss of life and this hitch would prove to be one of the decisive factors.

The second wave moved on to take their objectives but began being chopped down by machine guns, this time not only on the right but from within the wood on their left where the Footballers were attacking. Some Germans were seen on the roofs of houses in Oppy village with machine guns as well as a multitude of snipers hidden in the trees. Meanwhile the protective artillery barrage moved forward and consequently removed its protection from the Hammers, especially those on the right. With Ritson's part of B Company firmly decimated and unable to secure the extreme right flank, a large group of Germans began doggedly grenading and driving the survivors back. Cpl Manningtree was in one element of B Company which had actually managed to get forward through the wire and remembered how *"we took the first objective and always had a mob behind to clear up the dugouts, because when we used to shell them the German got in his dugout, out of the way..."* A few Germans re-entered their old frontline and began shooting at the backs of the advanced British. *"They* [the 'moppers up'] *were so pleased to think we took the first objective easy, they forgot the dugouts! We took the second* [objective] *and look round and there was Germans aback of us!"*

The attack by the Footballers was going equally disastrously with the intensity of machine gun fire from the wood slowing their attack. It was impossible to get support troops up to help deal with the problems, especially of Ritson's B Company who were now overrun. The German barrage on the British frontline was extremely heavy and the troops of the third wave waiting to go 'over the top' were not considering leaving the relative safety of the trench. Within these chaotic lines the signals officer, Lt Archie Wells, was back in from No Man's Land for a moment. Somehow he used his authority or experience and *"organised the support troops under heavy fire"* before he yelled a personal battle cry and *"repelled a counter attack"* on the right. By about 5.50am, as the dawn broke, the Germans had rolled through the wood on the left in very large numbers. Now they began aggressively working their way around the flanks of the Hammers and Footballers to meet up with any survivors in their old trench on the right.

The positions manned by those few Hammers who had managed to move furthest forward were naturally coming under intense counter-attacks and on three, nearly four, fronts. In an advanced observation post more commonly called a smoking shell crater Lt Sherman was surrounded by dead and dying, both British and German, as he sent back situation reports on the invaluable field telephone. He was the Hammer's Lewis gun officer and now had a grandstand view of the effect his well trained men like Sgt JJ Ash were having, setting *"a fine example of courage and determination"* out here on the battlefield. Formerly a cashier at the Beckton gas works and one of the originals, Ash was using his favoured Lewis gun with a supreme skill. He was accurately cutting down Germans left and right and despite the men around him being killed, picked out *"a better 'ole"* and advanced single handed, holding this new forward position for the next few hours. Nearby was Pte AJ Harvey, a recent replacement doing equally as much damage. Harvey was surrounded by his dead comrades too but *"kept his Lewis gun in action with the greatest coolness"*. Both men were however fighting a losing battle for ammunition and had to resort to stripping the dead and hurriedly reloading between attacks and shellfire.

Lt Archie Wells, the signals officer, was by now back out and about *"under heavy fire"*, continually repairing the telephone lines as they were cut. He ensured that *"due to his fearless energy"* contact was maintained with the advanced positions like Lt Sherman's. It was impossible to call in artillery support as the battlefield was so utterly chaotic and between 6 and 7am, the Germans retook their positions in the lost ground.

Around 9am, word was sent to what was left of the West Ham Battalion up front, disorganised and exhausted, to fall back and consolidate the old German frontline. They attacked the position and reoccupied it. By 10.45am they were taking increasingly heavy attacks from along both ends of the trench, on the right from where B Company should have been and at the other end on the extreme left where the Footballers were beaten back after an incredible rally. At 11.15am those that could, decided to pull back to the British lines. Many of them were shot in the back making the attempt. Manningtree witnessed how *"some got killed, some got captured and some got away. I managed to get away that day…"*

Hours later, as the roll calls were made the silence of unanswered names was shocking. Once again, many of the officers had been seen killed. Among them was Captain Claude Ritson, leading B Company. Three 'other ranks' were already listed as killed. They had been brought back early in the action by the fearless stretcher bearers. Lt Sherman and Archie Wells were both badly wounded but immediate evacuation was required for 2/Lt Antoine Sacre. His injuries would see him eventually leave the army. Seventy-eight 'other ranks', including Sgt JJ Ash, were wounded in varying degrees, from mere bullet grazes through to double amputations. But by far the largest number were simply 'missing': eight officers and two-hundred and forty other ranks. Lt William Brown-Paterson MC, the acting Adjutant, was one, moving forward during the battle to find suitable locations for the new battalion HQ. He was never seen again and his body never found. Somewhere close to Brown-Paterson went 2/Lt Frank Jenns, doing a similar job. For whatever reason, other than that he hardly ever mentioned officers anyway, when writing up the war diary Jenns doesn't record that he himself was also wounded. It is shown in his service file, however. Whether slight or more serious he remained patched up at duty and naturally became the next acting Adjutant. Jenns also appears to have possibly been recommended for a medal in the Oppy fighting, but it is yet another anomaly. As an officer, he would most likely have received a Military Cross for any bravery or decisive action. Yet, the query card is regarding a Military Medal, awarded only to the other ranks. Any confusion might have been caused because Jenns was a ranker who became an officer in the same battalion, another element of his service which was contrary to the usual army conventions.

As the Hammers were relieved and made their way back to the dugouts in Roclincourt, Lt's Sherman and Wells were awarded the Military Cross while Sgt JJ Ash and Pte Harvey received the Distinguished Conduct Medal for their coolness under fire. Three men were awarded the Military Medal for their conspicuous bravery, including one of the Hammers originals, Pte WJ Peacock. In the late evening, news came through that earlier in the day West Ham Utd had won their last match in the Southern Combination League and were crowned Champions for the 1916/17 season, ahead of Millwall in second place and Chelsea third. The celebration was muted among the veterans out here, especially when they heard that Bob "Pom-Pom" Whiting, the former Thames Ironworks goalkeeper lately playing for Brighton, had been killed with the Footballers that morning.

The total number of West Ham Battalion dead from the April 28th attack on Oppy was one hundred and twenty-five. Of those, the vast majority were replacements but a number of originals had been killed. Thirty-nine year old William Jolly was one. He was still mourning his younger brother Joseph who was killed with the Hammers last August in the attack on Guillemont. Both men had grown up in Plaistow and enlisted together. Equally, James Cotten from Tidal Basin was killed aged thirty-one. His elder brother Percy, a Military Medal winner, had been killed as a sergeant with the Hammers when they attacked the Quadrilateral last November. Other originals killed at Oppy include Charlie Bullen from Barking, just nineteen years old. Fred Lancaster from Bird in the Hand Court off Devons Road, George Keer from Mile End, Bill Lane from Stratford and George Smith from Custom House. Not many of them have graves.

Lt-Col Martin was sent to take over command of the Brigade and Major Derviche-Jones took over the Hammers for a short while. Four new officers arrived, bringing one hundred and sixty soldiers with them to begin instantly filling the gaps in the depleted ranks of the West Ham Battalion. One of them was the popular Lt Reg Box, a shipping clerk with pre-war military experience who had grown up locally at Sandringham Terrace in Leyton. By now they had moved on to Ecurie but Oppy Wood and the village still had to be captured. With so many troops already killed or seriously wounded the only option was to form a 'composite' unit drawn from three of the four battalions in the Brigade. The Footballers wouldn't contribute as they had been very literally annihilated on April 28th. Three officers and one-hundred and twenty 'other ranks' were supplied for this next attack. It went in on May 3rd, but was another devastating disaster. Six of the West Ham Battalion were killed including Robert Cameron, an original from Islington. He died of his wounds and today lies buried in Duisans British cemetery. Sixteen men were wounded and the cheerful Sgt George White, one of the earliest volunteers, lost his right leg above the knee. Fortunately, he was found (possibly by another original and friend CSM Charlie Blowes) and evacuated off the battlefield, eventually arriving back in England with his 'Blighty'. His recovery would be long, painful and at times experimental as the limits of prosthetics were advanced and developed.

Martin didn't return from Brigade, meaning the Hammers now had a new commanding officer, Lt Col Harris, their fourth since arriving in France. Major Derviche-Jones meanwhile moved over to take command of the King's. One of Harris' earliest duties was to sentence the recently recaptured Pte Charlie Fox to twenty-eight days of field punishment for overstaying his leave attending to his family affairs. The recent loss of so many of his friends while he had been on the run would have been punishment enough. As what was left of the battalion moved back again to Roclincourt, training was carried out for all the new replacements and this continued for the rest of the month as they were brought up to something resembling full strength.

Frank Jenns got a short respite when he went home on leave for a week on the 19th May and asked Alice to marry him. Writing up the war diary fell to another original, Lt Norman Lang, the Hammers' 'honorary' Quartermaster. On the 21st May, Captain Keeble returned to the Hammers and once again was stunned by the missing faces. Most of the officers he had played snooker with at the Alexandra Mess in Stratford High Street were long gone, dead or shell-shocked into submission.

This time he would really have noticed the lack of familiar faces from within the ranks.

Chapter 30

Mundane Routine

By June 1st the Hammers had moved a short distance to Ecurie. One of the replacements was killed and another wounded by being in the wrong place at the wrong time when a German aeroplane unexpectedly dropped a single bomb by hand on their billets. The Hammers were joined by a new second in command, Major McFarlane-Grieve just as they returned to the new frontline. It was little more than a short, stout wall of sandbags in front of a shallow ditch. They were in the 'red line' of the Arleux sector and patrols were sent out in case of any further retreat but for once, the Germans were *"very quiet..."* The tour ended without incident and the Hammers returned to Roclincourt.

The Germans weren't being so quiet back on the home front however. Some truly shocking news arrived for the veterans when they heard how June 13th had become a hot and stuffy day for the pupils at Upper North Street school in Poplar. A few of the children had already lost their fathers, brothers or uncles in the war and the teachers were working hard to keep them relatively happy. High above them, the German airforce made ready to unleash its first daylight air-raid on London. In the bright, hazy sunshine, a number of large Gotha bombers were spotted, *"scintillating like so many dragonflies..."* Releasing their payloads the crews had no idea, nor little care, where the bombs might land. One bomb screamed down and crashed into the school roof. It went straight through the upper floor of a classroom full of older children and shot out through the ceiling of the class below, landing in the midst of youngsters busy making paperchains. Eighteen of them, average age of five years old were killed a fraction of a second later when the bomb exploded. The Gotha's began a slow alteration in their course and headed back to home base, happy with their success and looking forward to chilled champagne.

The funerals were attended by the bereaved families and the stunned school children who'd survived the raid. Fathers openly wept and mothers continually fainted, in an era when emotional displays were frowned upon. Also in attendance were many thousands of residents, thronging outside the church. Hardly any of them could sing the hymn *"There's a friend for little children"*, let alone finish it. The King sent his deepest sympathy to the area and a memorial was later unveiled in Poplar Recreational Ground, depicting an angel on a pedestal. Living around the corner of the school and possibly a pupil there was young Maggie Cooper. In the close-knit community many of the dead would have been known to her. It was yet more shocking trauma for the slightly built but plucky six year old. She was still deeply mourning the loss of her father, Pte Joe Cooper, an original member of the advance party who was killed by a trench mortar back in April 1916. Maggie subsequently carried an understandable yet pathological fear of anything resembling an aeroplane up to her death in 1988.

As events like these became etched on the local memory, back in France the Hammers began a journey by bus to Bethune, a town well remembered by those few original Hammers who had made it this far. Although it was now just rubble, some were billeted in the ruins of what was the old tobacco factory, with its ghosts of Christmas Day 1915 when they were still new to it all. As they moved again, into the Givenchy sector around the town of Gorre, they spent the month in and out of the line and Frank Jenns returned, resuming his role writing up the war diary. Many of the originals would have noticed that since the advance, some of these familiar trenches had collapsed and become grown over with weeds. There were even wild flowers in blossom out in No Man's Land, as if blood really did make the grass grow as the drill sergeants used to scream at them.

They set about consolidating and repairing the old positions by day and night and they were slowly coming back up to strength and fitness in the process, although one of the originals died of illness at base hospital. Pte John Edward Bayliss was forty-one and from Tudor Road off Mare Street in Hackney. He is buried in Etaples cemetery. The Hammers then found themselves in more positions from the early days, back in the area around Windy Corner. Here there was specific training for the snipers, observers and bombers. Men were also supplied to the Royal Engineers to assist the tunnellers.

On the 6th July, Major MacFarlane-Grieve returned to his Highlander battalion for a couple of weeks and his place as second in command of the Hammers was taken over by an old face and friend, Harry Carter, recently returned from a spell teaching at Aldershot. Being a man of high military standards he wouldn't have been impressed when, in the support area, Pte George Greeno was somehow *"accidently wounded by a revolver shot..."* Jenns gives no indication as to who shot George in the thigh, but the fact he doesn't say "by comrade" might imply the fault lay with an officer, receiving an unlucky reminder that the Webley pistol issued at this time had no safety catch. Greeno, like Jenns an original member of C Company, was currently serving as an officer's batman. He had spent most of the early time in France as a signals runner under Len Holthusen, commended along the way for the part he played in the Hammer's first trench raid. After the wound from the accidental shooting was treated Pte Greeno returned to the Hammers and eventually survived the war.

That evening a German raid was expected to be launched, indicated by the heavy artillery barrage targeting specific points on the front. B & D Company, personally led by Lt-Col Harris, moved up at 9.30pm to give support to the Footballers who were holding the trenches of the old British line. Nothing came of it however and they ended up returning to billets. At that time the Footballers were playing chaperone to some recently arrived and cheerfully plump Portuguese troops who were only now regarded as just capable of manning short lengths of the front.

The next day Captain Dick Collier, the transport officer, began learning the duties of Adjutant under the guidance of Frank Jenns. By now it is easy to believe that after being in the role for so long Jenns was a thorough expert in all the myriad elements required for the administration of a combat battalion. Although he wasn't naming the dead and wounded anymore, he did find a space to mention an award to one of the originals. L/Cpl FA James had already won the Military Medal back at Deville Wood and now received a second one, a 'bar', for his actions at Oppy. Later that evening, Lt-Col Harris again took B Company, this time with C Company, to be ready in position to support the Footballers and the Portuguese. The Hammers moved into the left subsection, at 9.30pm. By the early hours their lines were being shelled before they realised it had become a heavy box barrage placed around them. They were unable to give any assistance when, moments later, the Germans commenced a vicious trench raid on the Portuguese and elements of the Footballers.

As dawn broke on the 9th things quietened down and after an uneventful afternoon the rest of the Hammers moved up and took over from the Footballers at the usual 9.30pm. They had a night of *"intermittent shelling on both sides"*, which killed one of the recent replacements, and it became the constant background music as they fixed up the trenches, wired and patrolled uneventfully until the 14th when they moved out to Gorre and let the Footballers move back in.

In Gorre they spent more time acclimatising the conscripted replacements and generally drilling and practising while at night they formed a working party and attended to all the usual dangerous chores. A sports day was held with football and boxing and general resting before there was a keen-eyed rifle inspection personally led by the dreaded Armourer Sergeant on the 19th July.

At 9.30pm like clockwork that evening, the Hammers made their way back to the trenches, exchanging with the Footballers in the familiar left subsection. They immediately began fixing up the wire in front despite *"enemy machine guns and snipers active throughout night..."* Twenty-eight of the recent replacements were pulled out and sent to *"the divisional draft training school for twenty-one days intensive training"*. It might be an indicator of the varied standards of soldiering at this time. The consolidation work to the positions carried on and it generally got quieter until the 24th when the Footballers returned. The Hammers went into the support lines at Givenchy and billets at Windy Corner once again.

On the evening of the 25th, Lt Eric Bunting got himself and twelve men ready for a planned operation. They would be providing a diversion for the King's who were mounting a large trench raid in the area. Although he had been onboard the Princess Victoria back in 1915, Bunting's name was, typically for an officer, never mentioned in the first year's war diary. He most likely had been away carrying out a liaison role up at Brigade HQ but tonight he would definitely be seeing action on the Western Front. Sometime before 10.00pm his party crept over the parapet and moved stealthily through the British wire. Bunting and his men got seventy yards away from the German line. Checking his watch he nodded for the men to prepare to attack. Each man was a *"rifle bomber"*, a specific role and requiring a good eye for accuracy. On their rifles, where the bayonet was usually fixed, they had in place a steel device which held a small grenade and fired it much further than it could ever be thrown. At precisely 10.30pm each man sent over six bombs in rapid succession. As the first of seventy-two grenades hit and exploded, a red flare went up from the Germans and their artillery launched a vicious barrage on the front line. Simultaneously, the Brigade's trench mortars opened up on the German line and the King's began their successful raid. Bunting withdrew his men to relative safety although one was wounded along the way.

Back at the support lines in Windy Corner training was still being carried out and working parties supplied. There was light shelling generally but on the morning of the 27th the Germans began intermittently sending over *"shells of large calibre"* right on the battalion HQ positions where Jenns was based. Thankfully, no-one was injured. Officers were still coming and going, including the return of an original from the advance party, Lt Gilbert Simpson from Forest Gate. Meanwhile, long serving solider of the Essex, Captain JGH Kennefick, went on leave back to Tipperary in Ireland. Lt Farmer the new medical officer arrived while 2/Lt JD Steele left for some hands-on instruction with a nearby artillery battery and Captain Jessop returned from leave. The names are unfamiliar as by now the overwhelming majority of the officers are replacements, each bringing many differing levels of experience. They are often away, on courses of instruction to bring them up to speed or enjoying the privilege of regular periods of leave. They must have presented many opportunities for questions of ability from those remaining few grim faced original West Ham Battalion veterans.

On the 29th July, at 9.30pm yet again, they moved up to relieve the Footballers in the left subsection. They took up their favourite spots and positions, noting what changes had been made out in No Man's Land. It was more wiring and patrolling at night, made difficult by the recent downpours of heavy rain, but writing up the war diary Captain Collier notes *"general situation very quiet..."* and they handed over their trenches back to the Footballers in the rain of August 3rd. They returned to Gorre and carried out a period of intensive training, especially the Lewis gunners and riflemen but they were back at the left subsection by the 9th as the August weather worsened. It was another quiet time until the 15th when they left for Windy Corner again. It was here that one of the replacements was wounded while fixing up a trench firestep when he had dug out a small unexploded bomb which then went off. Meanwhile the training intensified for the snipers, bombers and other specialist soldiers in the battalion and whispered rumours spread that they were being sent to Passchendaele and the Batle of Ypres. But on the 21st they entered the same trenches yet again, nodding hellos to the old faces in the ranks of the Footballers. There was *"normal machine gun fire and sniping at night"* for the whole of this tour but by the time they handed back to the Footballers on the 27th it had been noticed that the Germans were now reinforcing their wire. One bold group had to be dispersed with machine gun fire before German trench mortars flew over in retaliation.

As the Hammers moved back to billets at Gorre there had been some incredible thunderstorms to rival the artillery duels. Now it was getting windy too, with gusts strong enough to blow a helmet off, and when the rain fell, it was heavy. In this wind and rain Lt JD Robinson was evacuated to hospital for two weeks with a mild case of tuberculosis. By the end of August the Hammers were still hard at training. Captain Collier ended his period learning the role of Adjutant and his handwriting is replaced by that of his good friend and neighbour, the recently promoted Captain Eric Bunting. By day their range time continued and the shooting was improved. At night there were cross-country marches, by compass and wearing gas masks. They were for everyone, including Jenns and Bunting in the Hammers HQ. With the start of September they returned to the familiar trenches of the left subsector at Givenchy and began re-wiring the muddy ground to their front. Aircraft were flitting about in the sky. Ominously, the shelling of both sides was getting heavier, artillery duels taking place with the British specifically targeting what the acting Adjutant Capt Bunting describes as *"tender spots in the enemy line..."*

The German reply could in itself be incredibly nerve shattering, especially when an accurate cluster of twenty *"light shells"* and eight *"77mm"* landed on the Hammers' positions. With huge sighs of relief from those closest, they turned out to be 'duds' and failed to explode.

Chapter 31

Enter the Lock

On 7th September, the West Ham Battalion left the line, walked along the south bank of La Bassee canal and went in as reserve at Bethune. They spent their time cleaning up and generally repairing themselves. The inevitable boxing and football matches were arranged, but the war continued and towards the middle of the month they were back at Windy Corner. After moving into the left subsector again on the 24th a party, led by Lieut FJ Southern with a few men from each Company, were sent to assist the Brigade's trench mortar battery for a minor operation that took place on September 27th. It was *"completely successful"*. The next day, there was some unusual excitement when the Hammers witnessed a British observation balloon shot down. They had seen a similar fate befall a German balloon a few days earlier but on this occasion the *"occupants descended by means of parachutes..."*

Frank Jenns packed his kit for a welcome period of home leave and to finally have the pleasure of getting married to Alice. As he said goodbye at midnight on Sunday 30th the trench gas alarms were anxiously clanged and the uncomfortable claustrophobic masks went on. The Germans bombarded the positions for the next three hours. At daybreak, while the morning mist cleared to reveal the last remnants of noxious chemical clouds sinking low into shell holes, a well disguised patient and cold German sniper slowly scanned the trench lines. A slight movement caught his eye as he sighted the briefest parts of a man, carefully adjusting himself for duty and unaware of being watched. Through powerful optics the sniper noted something, probably with some satisfaction. Judging by the specialist badge on his jacket cuff, the target was a valuable prize, a dreaded Lewis gunner. With barely a blink, the sniper shot him through the head. L/Cpl Peter Warwick slumped to the bottom of the trench and left a trail of blood as he was quickly removed to the CCS at Gorre. He was clearly very dead before he got there. He had been a twenty-four year old butcher living at Woodfield in Stansted village, last at home on leave to his mother only two months before. His Company commander wrote to her that *"it has been a great loss to the company, as your son was held in great esteem by all and was a steady and capable section leader. It is very difficult to offer you any consolation in such a great loss but I hope it will relieve your grief to know that his death was almost instantaneous and he was buried in the presence of the whole platoon. I hope you will accept my sincere sympathy."* Warwick now lies in the Anglo Indian Military Cemetery.

The Hammers then moved north, to Lozinghem. They spent the whole of a bitterly cold October training again and it was more of the same: 'close order' drill; physical training; bayonet fighting; rifle exercises; tactical instruction; lectures. They concentrated on their 'musketry', and it was noted with some satisfaction that practically all were achieving the firing rate of thirteen rounds per minute and many were achieving the pre-war regulation rate of fifteen rounds per 'mad' minute.

A platoon from D Company then took part in a Brigade marksmanship and Lewis gun competition. Finally, together with the rest of the Brigade, they were inspected at Raimbert by the First Army Commander on October 15th. This visit fuelled further speculation that they were bound for the Ypres sector and the final push to the top of Passchendaele Ridge. The rumours finally ceased altogether when the whole Division moved once again, to yet another training area, this time near the town of Auchel, east of Bethune. It was here that Frank Keeble learned of the death of his younger brother Harold in a flying accident on 27th October over Kent. 2/Lt Keeble was killed alongside 2/Lt Sidney Hunt. Their DH4 aircraft *"side slipped after a vertical bank too near the ground"*. Frank Keeble left for his brother's funeral in England a few days later. Somewhere along the way he would have passed Captain Dick Collier and Lt Eric Bunting returning from their leave.

Early on November 5th the Hammers were ordered to move and quite a distance too. Ernie Curtis would *"never forget that forced march"* for *"three days until we got into Belgium… I collapsed at our journey's end…"* They were now in Houtekerque and *"hung about for three weeks under canvas"*, where there was yet more practice and training before they *"got sudden orders to entrain at once"* and the whole Division undertook an extremely tiring train journey. *"We started at 2am with rations [and] heard rumours of going on the Italian Front. When we finished our journey, we found ourselves on the Cambrian plains…"*

While the Hammers had been travelling, the initially successful planned attack on Cambrai was beginning to flounder against determined German resistance. They had slowed the British advance as it reached the outer defences of the Hindenberg Line. Bourlon Village, fiercely fought over, was flattened. What rubble remained was engulfed in flame from end to end and currently in the hands of the enemy. Bourlon Wood and the high ground to the northwest remained in British hands who were now rushing fresh Divisions up for the fight. Both sides had suffered heavy casualties in the determined defence by the Germans which had immediately exploded into a fierce and determined counter attack.

Captain Frank Keeble returned from the funeral as 2/Lt Frank Jenns arrived back from his wedding just in time for them to rejoin the West Ham Battalion as they undertook another long, painful march through driving rain. It soon turned to sleet before becoming an almost blinding snowstorm. The Division was completely assembled by mid-afternoon on November 26th, 1917. Colonel Harris had now left for England and Major (acting Lieut-Colonel) James Walsh had taken over command of the Hammers. Another pre-war 'ranker' Walsh had made his way through 1914 and by October 1916 was second in command to the Footballers when Harry Carter had replaced Papillon. Walsh now received a telephone message from Army HQ ordering him to move the West Ham men towards the Bapaume area. With evening approaching, the guides led them along the bitterly shelled Bapaume–Cambrai road.

As one of the lead elements of the Division, the West Ham men finally took over from the Irish Division, south-west of Bourlon Village in the early hours of the 27th. The icy, slimy trenches were nothing more than ditches, nearly a foot deep in liquid mud. It wasn't to be the only uncomfortable element. In B Company, Cpl Manningtree remembered overhearing *"our officer [Keeble] asked their officer of the Ulster's, "Which is your..? Well, where's your front!?"*

The reply was disconcerting: *"All around you!"*

On the night of the 29th November 1917, in subsequent adjustments, the Hammers took over a position to the south east of the village of Moeuvres, astride the dry Canal du Nord which at that time was still under construction. It was a difficult position to defend, being what the Division history described as *"a kind of gigantic dry moat about 80 feet broad at the top and 40 at the bottom. The steep sides of this moat and the bottom of it were of brick. In consequence, communication between the British troops east and west of the canal was most difficult and hazardous... The bed of the canal was dry and if a man wanted to cross it he had to slither down a 28ft slippery wall and climb up the other side by means of a rope while the enemy opened a galling fire on him with machineguns and rifles..."*

Taking over the front line trenches, Walsh immediately established his HQ in a solidly built concrete bunker, positioned in a short stretch of 'sunken road' on the east bank of the canal, beside a destroyed road bridge and approximately two hundred meters south of Lock No5. Badly knocked about, and little more than earthworks besides the partially constructed canal, Lock No5 was a key feature in the defence of this position on the right of the front line. It jutted out like a stubby finger pointing towards the Germans. B Company, under Capt Keeble MC, was assigned to defend this right bank of the canal, including Lock5, as well as a stretch of Canal Trench which ran south parallel with the Canal Du Nord. To the south, his area of responsibility also included the remnants of the bridge across the canal and the eastern section of 'Sunken Road'. He placed his reserve platoon here. Keeble immediately gave orders to improve the defences, ordering the digging of short sections of trenches to the north and east of Lock No5, for use by the Lewis gun crews and the rifle sections.

He also explored the *'underground passages'* below the Lock and placed some of his men in them. That evening, Keeble found time to take out a patrol to reconnoitre the open ground to the east *"with a view to taking it over"* the next night. During the patrol, on a piece of slightly elevated ground, he left one of his infamous practical jokes: a stuffed hare, upright and alert, wired to a stake and placed directly facing the Germans in the distance. Keeble had bagged it with his shotgun back in Lozinghem, and the pose was the speciality of a Belgian taxidermist.

Captain Harry Duff's A Company was in Canal trench to the south in support of Keeble's B Company. Duff equally assessed his situation and set A Company improving the defences, before he too went out on a recce into the open ground to the Hammers right. He reported *"no hostile patrols encountered"* and *"the night"*, he said, was *"quiet"*. It would seem he also had plans for extending his position the following evening. D Company, under Captain Herbert Turner Jessop, held the area on the left bank of the Canal, immediately opposite Lock No5. On Jessop's left he was facing the enemy in the shattered rubble suburbs of what was once the town of Moeuvres. To Jessop's lower left were the right hand elements of the King's, holding their section of the line. D Company also occupied Street Trench, again parallel to the canal and running south down to just short of the 'Sunken Road' which made its way due west and south of Moeuvres. Captain Jessop dispatched 2/LT Edward Leslie Corps on a mission to check the state of the barbed wire defences in front, as this was an obvious path of assault by the enemy. The rest of D Company set to rebuilding the position and fire steps. Their support was C Company, placed on the left bank and lining the Sunken Road up to the shattered bridge position. C Company was under the temporary command of Lt Alan Nethercott.

The West Ham Battalion settled into their new surroundings and tried to keep themselves warm.

Chapter 32

"Most Noteworthy Courage..."

By 6.00am on 30th November, the lookouts reported to Keeble that his stuffed hare was beginning to receive the occasional pot shot from the enemy. Half an hour later the German artillery began to put down a *"desultory"* bombardment on Lock No5. It also hit a section of the dry waterway to the south of the lock, with a few shells landing harmlessly in the area of Canal trench. After an hour, the intensity of the shelling increased noticeably when joined by the heavy artillery, Minenwerfer and some mustard gas rounds. They prepared for the inevitable assault. The cries of 'stand to' sounded up and down the lines.

D Company had endured an increasingly heavy barrage with the only relief being that some of German gunners targeting them were overestimating the range. Despite this, the second in command Captain John Durns Steele, was wounded. Captain Jessop ordered the men to move Steele and other casualties to a dugout and then take the best cover available. He saw no sense in exposing the entire Company unnecessarily but left one sentry in each fire-bay. At 8.45am Jessop dispatched Lt Corps to a 'forward observation area', nothing more than a shell hole with a height or cover advantage, from where to watch the enemy. In the early morning mist what Corps saw through binoculars was stunning. Two entire German regiments had gathered close to Quarry Wood. Long lines of heavily armed infantry began moving forward at 9.25am, crossing the Moeuvres-Bourlon Road and threading their way through their barbed wire, gathering in the open ground just over a thousand yards away. When Jessop heard Lt Corps's incredible report, SOS flares were immediately sent up by the signallers of D Company. In less than thirty seconds the snappy British artillery showered a heavy rain of shells down on the German ranks. D Company watched with gut wrenching apprehension as the German formation convulsed before re-forming itself into 'artillery formation' (sections-in-file) and began to move stoically towards them. On the right hand side of the canal with Lock No5, Frank Keeble realised his B Company was about to take the full force of what was shaping up to be a heavy and determined attack on his sector of Lock No5 and Canal Trench. Whistles pierced the air, calling the West Ham men to their battle positions. The German infantry came, in almost Napoleonic fashion, as the British artillery, called in by Jessop, wrought havoc in their ranks. With each shell fired, a few degrees was notched down the trajectory scale, grabbing yet more lives. B Company lined the fire-steps, watching the enemy advancing astride the canal. Keeble steadied his men, ordering them to hold fire. Approximately seven hundred or so German survivors levelled their rifles and charged across the frosty and shell scarred ground. Mixed among them were flamethrower units, by now coming into the range of the Lewis gunners.

It was 9.30am. Keeble let them come on while his men looked through the iron sights of their rifles and chose who to kill first. The speed and aggression of the Germans increased with adrenalin, but still Keeble let them come. Then at a point less than two hundred yards from the British line, he yelled the command to engage. B Company exploded into a murderous and sustained fire on the exposed German infantry. The slaughter poured on them was horrendous and, with flat, open country to their rear and no cover except the occasional shell hole or fold in the ground, the German casualties were considerable. Keeble later put *"a moderate estimation"* at five-hundred of the enemy killed.

Meanwhile, on the left bank Jessop ordered D Company to open fire on those Germans attacking his position as well as in support of Keeble's B Company over the gap on his right. The response was more combined *"vigorous"* rifle and Lewis gun fire. Its ferocity, intensely practised the month before, brought the advancing Germans to a shuddering, bloody halt after a quarter of an hour of carnage. B & D Company had held the line but, while the immediate crisis had eased, it certainly had not passed. Keeble sent a signal to HQ informing Walsh that he had *"beaten off the attack"* and a desperate search for ammunition was immediately underway as they had *"eaten up"* nearly all their rounds. The Lewis guns were running out before empty magazines could be reloaded and now, at 9.50am, every round had become vital. A mere three-hundred rounds were desperately discovered by B Company at the back of a battered dug-out and immediately loaded in the drum magazines of the hot Lewis guns. The pockets and pouches of the dead and badly wounded were being searched for ammunition and field dressings.

Surviving German troops began to regroup themselves and annoyingly to return fire. An isolated few took scant cover in shell holes or behind small banks of earth lining the track ways crisscrossing the field. Others desperately huddled in holes shared with the many dead. They kept the Hammers on constant alert, sniping and bombing while some attempted pointless and suicidal attacks by stealth. Behind them in the distance, the next mass attack commenced from the German lines. Murderous volleys were again unleashed, especially on those German infantry attempting to make their way along the brick lined canal bed towards the bridge position. Pte Anselm Duckett from Colchester and a small group most likely located in the 'underground tunnels' beneath B Company, kept up an astonishing rate of accurate Lewis gun fire on these Germans and specifically targeted the enemy troops who were supplying their throwers with grenades. Ultimately, by sheer weight of numbers, Pte Duckett's party was forced to relocate back to Lock No5 above where casualties were mounting.

Up here in the lock with Keeble the Lewis guns were busy making roman candles of the enemy flamethrower units but at the same time the grenades were being used up quickly. Cpl Manningtree particularly remembers this morning and how they were continually *"bombing one another to pieces, as close as I am to you..."* Just south of Keeble's position was No8 platoon of B Company in the forward stretch of Canal trench. They were now facing an enemy attacking from the direction of Bourlon Wood to the north east. It had become an attack on two flanks as some Germans had swung wide around the Lock to avoid B Company's intense fire. No8 platoon was led by the ever cheerful Sgt Leonard Fisher. Nineteen year old Len Fisher was another of those in the West Ham Battalion who had grown up in and around Papillon's old family seat at Lexden. No8 Platoon had also been Frank Keeble's very first command, back when he was growing his moustache as a fresh faced 2/Lt at the Alexandra Mess in Stratford High Street. He held a close affection for them. No8 Platoon was now totally out of ammunition and under intense fire from a machine gun the Germans had somehow brought up. Len Fisher gave the dreaded command to fix bayonets.

At 10.20am everyone's situation got a great deal worse when the German artillery placed Lock No5 and the surrounding area inside a 'box barrage'. Captain Duff, commanding A Company to the south in support, had been watching Keeble's situation deteriorate and sent a platoon with several boxes of rifle cartridges to resupply B Company, in particular No8 Platoon. They were under the command of 2/Lt EC Hall, only twenty-two years old but an 'Old Contemptible' since 1914. He was a West Ham man through and through, born in Meanly Street, Manor Park and living along Beachcroft Road in Leytonstone. Hall was assisted by Sgt Tom Peartree, a twenty-five year old Military Medal winner from Chobham Road in Stratford. The timely arrival of this reinforcing platoon was especially critical as B Company were currently in the midst of beating off the remnants of the latest attack but expending the very last of their ammunition. The fresh supplies were hurriedly distributed but Keeble had lost nearly half his Company in the attacks. Hall's men were now desperately needed at Sgt Fisher's position on B Company's right and they were immediately put in action against the determined attacks pushing from the north east. Sgt Fisher and the platoon, by now joined by Pte Duckett and his Lewis gun, actually lay out in the open in front of their trench and "*completely repulsed*" the Germans "*by the intensity of the fire...*" They slaughtered hundreds, stalling another attack on that flank, despite coming under withering German machine gun fire and rifle grenade bombardment which had made casualties of many of them.

At 11am James Walsh was out in the thick of it checking his men and positions. He called Hall, Peartree and Fisher away from Keeble's position and ordered them to get down to the B Company reserve platoon as quick as possible. It was currently serving as the machine gun garrison in the canal bed, taking the Germans head-on and killing many at the Sunken Road and smashed Bridge position. There were no officers there and Walsh seriously suspected they might retreat at any minute. He informed Lt Hall and the two Sgt's that they were now expected "*to fight to the last, with bayonet only, if necessary...*" Walsh makes a point to personally remark in his after-action report that the three men took this news "*extremely well*", showing a "*magnificent demeanour*" and being "*absolutely determined to fight to the last...*" Len Fisher had a "*remarkable*" smile on his face. On their safe arrival at the Bridge a few minutes later, they were swiftly involved in stemming a flood of Germans storming up the dry canal bed. It was an intense and brutal action, led by a belt-fed Vickers machine gun belching fire at close range and grenades pitched with the accuracy of cricket outfielders. Together, they created heaps of dead and dying.

Back at the Lock, the scales were beginning to tip and B Company's fight no longer hung in the balance. Keeble was being forced to reconsider every option of his position. These attacks had consumed much of his remaining ammunition and he very reluctantly made a final decision: he must abandon the Lock. After a quick explanation to the Sergeants at sometime around 11.15am the survivors of B Company, now just numbering roughly forty men, began a fighting withdrawal from Lock No5 down towards Duff's A Company positions to the south in Canal trench. The remaining men of No8 Platoon gave them a diminishing covering fire but not all of B Company at the Lock got away in time. The Germans were very swiftly on top, overrunning the position by grenade, bayonet, pistol and boot. As what was left of Keeble's Company came scrambling away they swiftly ran out of ammunition completely and made the rest of their escape under a fierce hailstorm of unanswered bullets. No8 Platoon then rallied before they too were forced to join Keeble's tail and fall back towards the 'sunken road'. Meanwhile, Hall and those at the bridge position had seen the narrow escape. Even though the ammunition for their Vickers machine gun and grenades were almost spent countering this persistent attack coming up along the canal, they still had to protect the right flank in order to secure the safety of what remained of their pals in No8 Platoon.

The men steadied themselves and for the second time that day Len Fisher gave the order to fix bayonets.

Midway through his terrifying withdrawal Captain Keeble met Lt Harry Cook of C Company incredibly coming the other way. Cook had miraculously managed to move forward under the shellfire in an attempt to make contact with B Company at the Lock but Keeble quickly told him, in no uncertain language, of the dire plight of Jessop and D Company, especially regarding ammunition. On his return to HQ, Harry Cook saw what he took to be D Company, on the other side of the canal, fighting a desperate action over in a section of Street Trench and receiving heavy assaults to their front. It was clear that they were in danger of being surrounded and ultimately cut off by groups of German infantry who were working their way along the west bank of the canal. Lt Cook, who had commanded D Company back in May and knew them all well, arrived back at Company HQ and immediately telephoned Walsh at Battalion HQ to report the situation. Cook then dispatched a corporal, believed to be the experienced former soldier Joe Beardwell, and eleven men with five boxes of rifle ammunition to D Company at the Lock. They were never seen again.

Keeble, withdrawing at top speed and under sustained fire at his back, led his remaining men through the smashed Bridge position towards Sunken Road, to the east of the canal. The Bridge platoon led by Hall, Peartree and Fisher (who was actually described later as having maintained '*the utmost cheerfulness*' throughout the proceedings), had tenaciously held the position, during a fight of truly epic proportions. Only Fisher, Peartree and four other men survived. 2/Lt Hall lay dead, buried beneath a smoking, bloodied heap of Germans inches from the hot Vickers. Fisher and Peartree, with no time to medically attend to the more seriously wounded or note the names of the dead, joined Keeble and the survivors moving back towards A Company's position in Canal Trench. Sensing, perhaps for the first time, that the British were short of ammunition a coloured star shell flare was fired to lift the German artillery box barrage. Their infantry now swarmed closely after the retiring British and were busily engaged in setting up heavy machine guns in the Lock.

On the other side of the canal, D Company was holding their tenuous position but both flanks were now dreadfully exposed. Captain Jessop watched horrified as the German infantry overran B Company's position at the Lock, exposing his right flank on the far side of the empty waterway. The Germans then set up three machine guns and began arching their fire over onto Jessop's position, just as a major assault was launched at him on the left from within the rubble of Moeuvres. The best shots of D Company took out one machine gun team with accurate sniping and scared off the other two. Breathlessly the last runner to get through brought orders confirming that the Brigade was being pushed back on his lower left flank. The report added that, if or when D Company were driven out of the position, they were to *"counter attack immediately..."* One can only guess what went through Captain Jessop's mind on receipt of that message.

With Keeble's B Company retiring and D Company effectively cut off, the Germans now began a flanking attack on C Company whose few remaining NCO's desperately organised a defensive line. Sgt Bill Ranner had been behaving *"with great coolness under very heavy shellfire"*, at one point single-handedly digging out three men buried alive. He was also working tirelessly, plugging the gaps as each man fell. Bill Ranner was an original of the Hammers, enlisting in February 1915 and rising through the ranks with his coolness and practicality. This he was now exhibiting in abundance, personally directing the defender's fire. Sgt A Moore from Westerham Road in Leyton was another member of Henry Dyer's first three hundred in C Company. Moore doggedly defended his section of trench, now no more than a series of shell holes, even as his machine gun crew were being killed around him. He stalled the Germans as long as he could, but two whole platoons had been practically annihilated as the storm-troops steamrolled through the leading British defences.

C Company's action temporarily halted the German advance, but again at a heavy cost. The other two platoons had been lying in the open in a desperate attempt to evade the deluge of shells from the box barrage and had then, somehow, held the overwhelming German advance to their front. Incredibly, they even attempted two counter attacks, including a bayonet charge, led by Lt Alan Nethercott. L/Cpl Charles equally displayed immense bravery when he bombed his way up Street trench towards D Company, followed by more of the West Ham Battalion. He held the gains, despite Germans in the open ground above him on both sides of the trench. He '*displayed a most noteworthy courage*' and continued bombing until finally dragged back to the Hammers lines, badly wounded. C Company suffered such heavy casualties that they were forced to pull back to avoid being cut off themselves. They were met by C Company of the Footballers coming up in support to assist them. Together they stubbornly gritted their teeth one more time.

Back at D Company, the telephone wires linking to HQ had been cut by the incessant shellfire very early in the action, despite the single-minded efforts made by the signallers to re-establish links. Captain Jessop dispatched two runners, in an attempt to get through to Walsh to report his situation and clarify his orders. In the next moment, a cluster of German high explosive shells screamed in and 'crumped' the sides of the trench and his dugout. Command now devolved on Lt JD Robinson, one of the few remaining 'Temporary' officers among the Hammers who had only recently recovered from tuberculosis. Robinson was immediately summoned from the right flank, where he was reorganising the defence. On looking around he realised they were about to be cut off by the enemy incursions from the direction of the canal.

The surviving men of D Company were equally aware that they were surrounded. Robinson duly shortened the line and commenced a harassing action in the form of sniping to conserve ammunition. He held a hurried consultation with the other surviving officer, Lt Corps, before informing Company Sergeant Major Edwards and Platoon Sergeant's Phillips, Fairbrass, Parsons, Lodge and Legg that he had decided to consolidate the position. They would continue resistance for as long as possible and hold their ground at all costs until relieved as per the original orders. Regardless of it being hopeless, the men of D Company, on being given this news by their sergeants, were in excellent spirits and in absolutely no mood to give up an inch of ground. They repaired the fire steps and reorganised themselves for all round defence. Some were using the bodies of dead Germans as extra cover. The resultant redoubt was immensely strong and easily defended. Yet the German hold on both sides of the canal was rapidly strengthening all around them.

On the right bank, Capt Keeble and his B Company survivors finally tumbled breathlessly over the relatively safe parapet of Canal Trench, held by A Company. The lack of ammunition meant Keeble's group had been unable to return fire and the Germans had been following very closely behind, gaining on them. This now allowed Captain Duff and his men of A Company to step up and pour down a withering 'point blank' fire on the enemy advance. The Germans boiled up to the parapet of Canal Trench, straight into the maelstrom unleashed by every man of A Company capable of using a rifle, revolver or grenade. The courage of the Hanoverians faltered, stuttered and failed in the face of this withering concentrated and accurate tempest unleashed by the West Ham men. Decimated, they fell back and took cover, leaving heaps two or three feet deep of dead and wounded inches from the parapet.

Duff allowed Keeble and his survivors to catch their breath and reload before rallying the party to help form a block in Canal Trench, just as the Germans caught their own 'second wind' and resumed the assault, with more troops coming up bringing a renewed vigour. But the Hammers weren't finished. Keeble had been busy, organising a bayonet platoon consisting of the survivors of his B Company and a few chosen men from A Company, like Pte Hugh Bannon an original from Upton Park. As a former Grenadier with Boer war service in South Africa, he knew exactly what to expect from the enemy and precisely what was expected of him as he fixed his bayonet to his Lee Enfield rifle. They were quickly joined by a burly party from the South Staffords under the command of 2/Lt Charles Hinde, who had also brought much needed ammunition and grenades.

The attackers slowly crumpled under the terrible onslaught delivered by Duff's A Company and at around 12.10pm Captain Frank Keeble MC stood up. No doubt with adrenalin running at a high through them all, Keeble bellowed a yell and led his small bayonet party 'over the top' in an awe inspiring charge. Sgt Farmer, another of the remaining originals, went on to display *"a magnificent example of outstanding courage..."* Also in the bayonet charge was the popular and capable twenty-two year old Captain Reg Box. He had attended the council High School in Leyton and had previously been in command of B Company during the absence of Frank Keeble in April. Reg sprinted forward the fastest, now lobbing grenades before clambering triumphantly onto the German's leading edge. After shooting a few he raised his Webley revolver in the air and, yelling his encouragement, watched as the improvised bayonet platoon followed up. With an energy created from well drilled co-ordinated thrusts of primeval butchery they effectively threw the enemy back terrified down the Sunken Road. It relieved the immediate pressure on Duff's men, buying them time as they hurriedly prepared their positions in Canal Trench for defence on two sides. They rearranged sandbags and grabbed ammunition where they could find it. Magazines were feverishly reloaded with loose bullets by shaky hands, dry, cracked and cut. Some men were shivering from cold, shivering from dysentery, shivering from hunger, the shock of imminent death or from the effect of pure adrenalin.

Just when it seemed that the small victory was theirs, the impact of Keeble's death defying and spectacular counter attack by bayonet was reversed. Still on the leading edge, yelling down at the enemy, Reg Box suddenly became the focus of a storm of fire from every German there. His body was lifted before it crumpled in a bullet riddled heap. With a roar, the Germans counter-attacked and Keeble's men were forced to fall back to Duff's position in Canal trench.

Thousands of the enemy were streaming towards them from the direction of Lock No5.

Chapter 33

One Last Shout

Back at the surrounded position of D Company the Germans were seen at the rear in some numbers. The probing attacks began. It was obvious that neither of Jessop's runners had made it through. The Germans were using part of the captured Street trench to attack elements of C & D Company but were met with such fierce determination by the Hammers that they were soon forced back. D Company even managed to capture more than a dozen Germans and took them prisoner, placing them in the care of the reserve platoon led by Sgt Lawrence Legg, a twenty-four year old original from Forest Road in Walthamstow. Assaults on the left of D Company were met with equal 'West Ham' resolution but the rifle ammunition and grenades were starting to run worryingly low. Privates Smith and Nightingale particularly distinguished themselves on the right flank, being seen to catch and hurl back scores of German grenades at their attackers coming up from the canal bed. SOS flares shot skyward again. Lt Robinson, perhaps feeling the lonely isolation of an encircled commander, wrote in his message book that *"we have had orders from the Battalion to the effect that we are to hold on at all costs and we hope communication will be obtained with headquarters, even though the runners who have returned report that the enemy has worked round our rear from the flank. Our position, forming a natural strong point on all sides, has cost the enemy great loss in his endeavour to capture us..."* D Company sent up their eleventh SOS flare of the day. All lines of communication were cut and the lead element of the Brigade, the West Ham Battalion, were to all intents and purposes split in half with one Company completely overrun.

Back at Duff's A Company, ample reserves of rifle ammunition and grenades now began to arrive for Keeble's men, brought up from HQ through an unceasing German bombardment. They were organised by the very capable Company Sergeant Majors EC Brock and W Cockrain who *"displayed great courage and perseverance in constantly organising carrying parties and sending them off to the companies heavily engaged"*. This *"coolness and ability helped the forward companies to maintain themselves..."* Brock and Cockrain placed the supply chain squads under the command of men such as Cpl Charlie Lucas, like Brock another original and also a member of the Battalion Police. Without this extraordinary effort, Duff's A Company position would very likely have fallen. This, in its turn, would have threatened the entire allied front line. The situation was critical.

Keeble was personally commanding the bombing block in Canal Trench, a mere ten yards from the Sunken Road held by the Germans. Sgt Farmer was still in the thick of it, displaying *"proof of marked skill"* with his grenade throwing and *"encouraging his men..."* Keeble, together with Farmer, Sgt Fisher and the bayonet platoon, once again went 'over the top' at 1pm. Their attack was met by a hail of rifle grenades. They continued bombing the German troops occupying Sunken Road but were again forced back, not only by sheer numbers but because the Germans had by now brought forward another vicious machine gun. Duff re-organised the defences.

One platoon from A Company together with three from the South Staffords dispersed for a length of the Canal Trench running south. They formed a strong garrison as did two platoons of A Company and one of the South Staffords manning the east–west section of trench. The Germans made repeated attacks, from 1.30pm on Canal Trench from the Sunken Road but they were met with an insurmountable resistance from Keeble and the West Ham men, by now very well supplied with ammunition.

Above them all, in the November sky, an intense dogfight was taking place.

Lt HL Hughes, the intelligence officer, was dispatched from HQ with orders for the commander of C Company, Captain Aylmer, almost a duplicate of those sent to the unfortunate Captain Jessop: *"counter attack immediately and retake the ground lost"*. This was highly unlikely in their depleted state, and depleted they certainly were. A roll call was ordered by Captain Aylmer, to which Sgt's Ranner and Moore, the two surviving NCO's, reported a total of only three officers and twenty-five other ranks. Nevertheless, despite the failure of two previous efforts, Captain Aylmer was preparing them to attack again when the timely arrival at his location of men from both the South Staffords and King's changed his odds somewhat.

Another truly heroic bayonet charge followed and the composite Company incredibly recaptured a small section of the line. The cost to C Company was another ten men killed. Further orders were then received from Walsh, ordering C Company to place themselves under the officer commanding the Kings who were equally heavily engaged fighting Germans to the south of Moeuvres village itself. Captain Aylmer was also asked to inform the Kings that it was Walsh's intention *"to retake the Sunken Road if at all possible, thereby restoring the line..."*

The German attacks finally tailed off as night arrived. Both sides were completely exhausted but there was to be no 'stand down'. As darkness fell, Walsh in HQ was feverishly trying to create a semblance of order out of the chaos. Brigade was also desperately trying to make contact with forces west of the canal and they were both asking the same question: where was D Company? Nothing had been heard of them since 10.20am that morning. At 8pm, they got their answer. From in front of the West Ham lines crawled a mud drenched and weary Sgt Lawrence Legg accompanied by another soldier, his identity now lost. Legg, who had been guarding the prisoners captured by D Company, immediately headed to Walsh at HQ. In the smoky and flickering light of the cramped damp dugout his report was heard in a wide eyed hush. He described the 'council of war', held four hours earlier by the remaining officers and NCO's who were determined to fight to the last but were now surrounded and extremely low on ammunition. Legg had volunteered to attempt to get through the German line and bring desperately needed reinforcements. The attempt had been regarded as a 'forlorn hope' but, as military history has often witnessed, it succeeded.

The news spread like an inspirational wildfire throughout the Hammers and to the whole Brigade. Numerous signal flares were sent up to indicate to the survivors of D Company that Legg and his companion had made it through. They were heard giving a hearty cheer. All through the night, *"violent attacks"* were made to reach the beleaguered Company. Frank Keeble personally led three attempts to reach them but first he had to retake the Sunken Road. He didn't have any success. With the first grey streaks of dawn appearing over Bourlon Wood everyone realised that the surrounded men were doomed.

At 7am, in their small redoubt the few survivors of D Company tidied themselves up. The wounded were moved to the battered dugout and placed alongside the patched up German prisoners. In the chill quiet of daybreak, they all knew what was about to happen. Out of ammunition, physically exhausted and with some suffering dysentery and other trench life illnesses, the nineteen survivors fixed bayonets. They sat collecting their thoughts and waited. Twenty minutes later, a roaring mass of German soldiers surged up from the cover of the dry canal lobbing grenades while more appeared from the dead ground in front of the position. It was all over very quickly.

Ernst Junger was a young officer there at the very end of the fight. In his memoir 'Storm of Steel', Junger remembers an officer, most likely JD Robinson, following his handful of men into captivity. Junger stopped him but, when asked questions concerning the position and its defence, Robinson stood to attention and saluted, rather embarrassing Junger. He was politely directed to Captain Jessop, *"a young man of about twenty six, with fine features, leaning against the shelter door with a bullet through his calf. When I introduced myself to him he lifted his hand to his cap, I caught a flash of gold at the wrist. He said his name and handed over his pistol. His opening words showed me he was a real man. 'We were surrounded'. He felt obliged to explain to his opponent why his Company had surrendered so quickly. We talked about various matters in French. He told me that there were quite a few German wounded, whom his men had bandaged and fed in a nearby shelter. When I asked him how strong the rearward defences of the line were he would give me no information. After I had promised to have him and the other wounded men sent back, we parted with a shake of the hand..."*

D Company had held out, in an epic defence, isolated and fighting almost continuously, for twenty-two hours.

As the day wore on, HQ realised that the Division, though bloodied, was unbowed and remained defiantly astride the Canal du Nord. Considering the weight of the attack, it had lost surprisingly little ground. German attacks continued throughout the day until, towards evening, fresh units began to move up and take over the front line from the battered and now much depleted Brigade. The Divisional reserve was divided either side of the canal in expectation of further assaults and the Hammers were relieved on the night of 1st/2nd December as the fighting continued, but without the ferocity of the previous two days. While the West Ham men were placed in support trenches by the village of Graincourt, the Germans made two or three further attempts to turn the line on the 2nd/3rd December, but were frustrated by more stubborn resistance. Pte Charlie Nicholson, an original volunteer was one of those killed during the assaults and was buried in Hermies Hill cemetery. The stuffed hare Frank Keeble had placed out in the dead ground to tease the enemy was also finally removed, battered and *"chipped about"*, by a German working party. Keeble was by now being treated for his wounds in hospital. He was forever tickled that it had taken them three frustrating days to work out his joke.

Dawn broke on the 5th of December with the Brigade, including the Hammers, now in reserve at Lebucquere. Four men had been killed overnight. It was noted in the Brigade war diary, that the conduct of Keeble and Duff was beyond praise and that *"the determination shown by these gallant Officers not to yield one inch to the enemy had a greatly stimulating effect on their men..."* Keeble, Harry Duff, Alan Nethercott and CSM Brock were awarded the Military Cross. For twenty-two year old Frank Keeble, an original volunteer to the West Ham Battalion, it was his second.

CSM Cockrain, Sgt's Fisher, Peartree, Ranner, Moore, Farmer, Rogers, L/Cpl Charles and Pte Duckett were each awarded the Distinguished Conduct Medal. Colonel Walsh received the Distinguished Service Order while other men, like Sgt Legg and Cpl Lucas, received the Military Medal. Edward Hall's name is strangely absent from the list of honours. Born in Meanley Street, Manor Park, the twenty-two year old was a West Ham man through and through and one possibility may be that he was recommended for a Victoria Cross, which was ultimately refused.

The casualties sustained by the Hammers during the six days of fighting were heavy indeed. Nine officers were reported wounded or missing. Sixteen other ranks were confirmed killed, probably those who actually reached an aid post but had not survived the attempts to revive them. Seventy-eight men were reported as wounded. Fred Lathangue was one of them, hit yet again on his right wrist. Since landing in France, Fred had been wounded in every major engagement of his home borough's battalion. Fred had first been hit in the face and hand at Delville Wood, then on the right wrist at the Quadrilateral followed by a wound to the forehead during the second attempt to take Oppy village. Here at the canal, he'd been caught yet again on the right wrist. Two hundred and sixty-nine men were reported as missing. Of these many were killed but also included those who could not be returned other than as 'missing' because HQ was not, at that time, aware of their fate. Some, like Cpl Manningtree of B Company, had actually been taken prisoner when the Lock was overrun. *"When I was captured… they gave us a stretcher. Four of us was taking a big old German wounded bloke, somewhere. We got to take him 'somewhere', we never knew where because we didn't understand German. Our people was retaliating with shells and bullets. I could hear the bullets swishing around* [so] *we chucked him in the trench, stretcher and all!* [laughs] *...last day of November 1917..."* Somewhat dangerously, Manningtree was literally covered in battlefield 'trophies'. *"I'd got a German officer's girdle and a nine inch goat's foot dagger and a prismatic compass, a jack knife, and a pair of scissors and a hundred Mark note. It was a good job they din't examine me then!"* He had also taken a dead man's sidearm, a *"Mauser"*, which had already been sold on *"to an officer for fifty Francs... As we were going along the road, we kept stopping to let the traffic come, y'see. I got rid of everything I could and, by the time we got where we was going, I'd got rid of the lot of it! I thought 'safety first', boy!"*

Letters now had to be written to the grieving families back home. Colonel Walsh wrote to Reg Box's parents living at Baxter Avenue in Southend, telling them *"your son behaved splendidly on that day, and we [...] have lost a gallant comrade and a fine type of an English gentleman..."* Another Officer told them Reg *"was liked by the men, which is the supreme test... You have every reason to be proud of your son..."*

The West Ham Battalion had been in France a little over two years and had earned a solid reputation as a fighting unit. But the faces had changed dramatically since those heady days of the volunteers who had first landed at Boulogne. There were precious few West Ham originals left. The fight at Moeuvres had reduced them drastically.

Gone were men like Fred Bailey from Bow and George Gibson of Canning Town, two of the very first to enlist with their names on Henry Dyer's front page appeal for volunteers in the Stratford Express. L/Cpl Jimmy Blanks had been under age when he had originally enlisted. Twenty-six years old, Pte William Beattie was from Walthamstow. Pte Ernie Cooper wouldn't be going home to Royston Street in Bethnal Green. Pte Bowyer of Stepney, Pte Seaman of Clapton... more with no known grave.

Their names are among the thousands inscribed on the Cambrai Memorial at Louveral.

Chapter 34

Goodbyee

On December 8th 1917, the Hammers were back in the trenches west of the shattered village of Demicourt but Ernie Curtis, the battalion tailor, had pulled what he thought was bound to be a 'cushy' task when *"I was sent down to look after the stores, which were dumped in the village of Dysognies ('Dogs Knees' we used to call it)..."* He prepared himself for a welcome respite, a whole ten days in the comparative 'quiet' behind the lines. However, the location of the billet was not so relaxing. *"There were batteries of heavy artillery all around our dump. Jerry soon got the range of our guns..."* The Germans caused continual havoc in the dump and inflicted many casualties on the gunners. By the end of his ten days, Ernie had gone deaf in one ear from a particularly close call which blew out his eardrum, along with *"shattered nerves... I couldn't tell you how our billet didn't go to smithereens!"* The Hammers were finally moved into a support role on the 20th December and required their stores. Ernie was waiting for two lorries to arrive so he could begin loading up, but *"it took the motors over ten hours to get up to us, the shelling was so heavy. Our old motor driver wanted to get away before we got all our stuff on, but we wouldn't let him do that. I asked him how he would have liked to have been there for ten days, like I had, waiting to get blown up and dare not leave the place! Just as we were ready to get away, a shell dropped on the roadway. No-one was hurt. Our luck was in again... After a few days I began to feel like my old self, but I've never regained my hearing!"* Four men were killed this day, most likely by shelling. Included among them is another of the originals. Pte William Fisher was thirty and had grown up in Huxley Road, Leyton. He was buried close to Charlie Nicholson in Hermies Hill cemetery.

By the evening of 23rd December they moved back into the front line. There they spent their second Christmas away from home. Two men were killed by shelling on Christmas morning including another original. Pte PJ Llewellyn was a twenty year old from Gordon Road in South Woodford and proud to be *"a native of London"*. He had first been wounded at the fight for the craters back in June 1916 but now he was buried at Rocquigny CWGC. Frank Keeble returned from hospital and received a very welcome gift from his parents back at the farm in Brantham. It was a whole, cooked, Christmas turkey, seasoned to perfection and swiftly delivered through the ever efficient army postal service. A batman organised the table in his dugout, creating a very presentable festive spread. Dining was still one of the most important events to young officers, a chance to regain some memory of 'normality' and of home. Satisfied, Keeble went out on his rounds and to deliver some invitations to help carve the turkey. He had been gone less than a half a minute, just turning the corner of the trench, when a lone high explosive shell screamed in and, almost spitefully, thoroughly 'crumped' the shelter. Thankfully there were no casualties buried beneath the smoking and shattered wreckage of earth, wood and corrugated iron sheets, but the turkey was obliterated.

When the Hammers marched out to billets in Hermies they enjoyed a belated Christmas dinner. Roast pork and fruit for dessert, washed down with five hogsheads of beer that the ever resourceful Lt's Norman Lang and Tom Brind had brought up from the town of Albert. On the 29th there was a field court martial for one of the regular officers after Captain Kennefick had regrettably been found drunk on duty. John George Hammerton Kennefick had a lifetime of service to the Essex under his belt. He had been with the West Ham Battalion since mid-1916 and, with periods of acting as second in command, had watched as so many of the familiar faces disappeared. This was compounded by his personal life after he lost his elder brother, killed in action with the Essex in July 1916. Back home in Tipperary, his father had then died a few days before the failed attack on Oppy. As the last son and heir to his mother, he now had a lot to live up to. His maternal grandfather was General Hammerton, who at the battle of Waterloo had led the famous "44th", a battalion which would go on to form the original Essex Regiment.

New Year's Day 1918 dawned bitterly cold. Squalls of driving rain and sleet added to the misery. On both sides of No Man's Land, men shivered in the vice like grip of a cruel winter. In Paris, the Seine froze over for the first time in over a century. The West Ham Battalion, settling back into trench routine, provided countless wiring parties and endless night patrols. It was commonly thought, perhaps naively, that 'Fritz' was totally exhausted. However, quite the opposite was true. The weary German troops who had fought so hard throughout 1917 were gradually being withdrawn for rest and reorganisation. Replacing them were fresh units, newly arrived from the Russian Front. The collapse of the Russian war effort, through a communist revolution, had released thousands of tough, well trained and experienced German troops. They were now being reassigned to the Western Front.

Captain Duff, home leave finally over, made the tedious journey to the Hammers trenches, resuming command of A Company. He arrived just as they were leaving. The West Ham Battalion then marched, through intermittent shelling and sleet, back again to their billets in the village of Hermies. The following day on the 4th January 1918, they moved once again, marching along icy roads to the rear. In the village of Rocquigny, they occupied a hutted camp and again began the training and assimilation of the many replacement soldiers. Officers came and went: Captain Harry Mulkern and 2/Lt Edwin Paterson left for England on leave, while Lt Charles Ware left for Le Touquet on a Lewis gun course. Lt ML Farmer, RAMC, the medical officer, returned from a short spell in hospital and Captain (now acting Major) Arthur Hayward MC returned from a gas course at Albert.

The war dairy records the internal movements of a battalion settling down, with new faces and a varied range of skills and abilities. Training at this time was a return to basics – very basic, in some instances. Feet washing and rubbing, in particular. As the originals in the Hammers knew from hard experience, an infantryman's feet were an extremely important piece of kit, requiring special care. Training continued, as more replacement drafts trickled in, sometimes accompanied by brand new officers and typically the experience they brought with them equally varied. 2/Lt Harry Fairbank was a former corporal, in France since 1915 where he subsequently saw a great deal of action. On arrival at the Hammers, he was assigned to help rebuild B Company, almost wiped out at the Lock. 2/Lt Thomas Ginder was another former corporal and although he had seen no overseas service he had shown promise as an aspiring officer. Ginder was posted to C Company. 2/Lieut Fritz Denham was a young man, commissioned straight into the West Ham Battalion, despite having no previous military experience. He too went to C Company.

On the 8th January Colonel Walsh left for England, on a well earned leave. Command devolved again to one of the very few remaining original officers of the Hammers, Major Arthur G Hayward MC. It was at Rocquigny, while busy sandbagging the huts against the attentions of enemy aircraft, that news began to filter through of the fate of some of the men during the epic fight at Moeuvres. 2/Lt CW Phillips, previously reported as 'missing', was confirmed by the Red Cross to be a prisoner of war in Germany. On the 11th January, more news arrived, again via the Red Cross. The four officers of D Company, thought to be dead, were also reported to now be prisoners. Captain HT Jessop, Lt JD Robinson, 2/Lt EL Corps and 2/Lt RJ Trebilco were all in Germany. Then there was further cheering news. The mother of Cpl Robert Jack, another original member of D Company thought to have been killed, was thrilled to receive a letter at the family home in Rendle Road, Custom House. It had been written on the 12th December, asking for a parcel to be sent to Robert's prisoner of war camp at Minden, Westphalia and was published in the Stratford Express under the headline *"West Ham Battalion hero in Germany!"* Robert Jack had enlisted on the 20th January 1915, and after attending the council school in Tidal Basin had been an employee at the Loisier and Nicolines factory in Silvertown.

By comparison, the news from home was not good, with an open questioning of the conduct of the war. This, along with incessant and damaging manoeuvring by the politicians, was threatening an imminent major reorganisation of the army. By the middle of January, it was the common belief in the military that a large scale German assault would come in the spring of 1918. To make matters worse, the War Cabinet, in Downing Street, had agreed to a proposal from the Supreme War Council to the extension of the British line south to St. Quentin. In addition, it had been proposed that both the British and French armies withdraw seven divisions each, to form a 'strategic reserve' ready to meet any major attack head on. Haig was horrified. He held a private 'pact' with Marshal Petain that each should come to the others aid wherever and whenever the situation demanded. He believed, not unreasonably, that such a decision should remain with the professional commanders in the field.

Furthermore, the British advance at Cambrai and the subsequent German counter offensive had all but totally destroyed two of the divisions earmarked for any such extension of the front line and it was increasingly obvious that there would be no further reinforcement of his armies, at least not in the foreseeable future. It was already, however, a political 'done deal' and Haig reluctantly accepted that the only way to achieve the necessary build up of fighting strength at battalion level was to amalgamate some units and disband others, using the spare officers and men as reinforcements. This would mean a major reorganisation of the army at a time when they should have been resting, training and constructing defences against the inevitable German onslaught expected in a few months time. None of this was known or understood by "the poor bloody infantry" on the ground, of course, and the adjustment to army life at the front continued for those new to the West Ham Battalion.

The Royal Artillery band were appearing in the cinema hut, but as fifteen men from each Company including Jenns and the HQ Company were ordered to attend you have to wonder whether they were any good. Perhaps there was little appetite for martial music anymore. Wiring lectures, innumerable demonstrations of various kit and tactics for all ranks with range practice were a daily routine. On the 14th January, twenty six more soldiers arrived as replacements, while a further one-hundred and forty-five joined the depot battalion. They were also shown on strength by the current Adjutant of the West Ham Battalion, the newly promoted Captain Eric Bunting. He left the following day for leave in England, sharing the journey, as he had done throughout the war, with his near neighbour Captain Dick Collier, MC.

Frank Jenns took over the familiar role of Adjutant once again. No4 training area rang out to the battlefield commands soon to be uttered in earnest as they drilled, marched, practised rapid reloading and fire control. 2/Lt's HA Mulkern, EA Paterson and MS Claydon all returned from leave. Claydon left again almost immediately, taking twenty-five OR's with him for an attachment to Australian tunnellers, continuing the subterranean war. As this training progressed, news filtered through that an original had died of the wounds he'd received at the canal fighting. Pte William Smith was born in Silvertown and had enlisted in Canning Town in February 1915. He died on 10th January at no9 General Hospital outside Rouen and was buried in St Sever Military Cemetery. By the 24th, the training period was over and the Hammers were moved, by light railway, to Metz and a sector known as the Highland Ridge Line, just northeast of Arras. They went into the support lines and most were engaged on building and improving the defences, under the watchful eye of Captain Greenwood of the Royal Engineers. A further thirty-five other ranks arrived at Battalion HQ, more replacements to rebuild D & B Company.

Preparations were in full swing for the grand scale reorganisation of the British army in France, a truly massive undertaking. It was decided that each Brigade would be reduced, from the 1914 establishment of four battalions, down to three. The theory was that they would be stronger in numbers and therefore better able to both withstand and mount counter attacks, as per the supreme war council directive. While the reorganisation was an undoubted logistical nightmare for Haig and the general staff, it meant very real heartache to those battalions eventually selected for disbandment. The decision had already been taken that the Regular Army and Territorial battalions would not be affected. This meant that almost all of the units chosen were to be 'Service' battalions, like the Hammers and the Footballers. It was a distinction which had progressed through the long bitter conflict, from a stigma and mark of disdain to being a matter of hard gained respect. They were 'Kitchener's Men' and extremely proud of it. The West Ham Battalion, like all the other Service battalions, had been volunteers answering a nation's desperate plea. They had proven themselves in battle, time and again, suffering horrendous casualties. True, they had absorbed a great many replacements, but still, at their heart, was a last remaining core of plucky civilians, the pals who had answered Mayor Dyer's appeal so long ago.

On the 28th January, the Hammers returned to the front line, back once again in the Artois at La Vaquierie. This was a relatively 'quiet' sector with only the occasional enemy shell to threaten the end of another life. But, it was still a combat zone and that week's casualty return up to Brigade showed six had been killed and twenty seven wounded. One solider was 'missing'. Jenns also noted *"considerable air activity"*, as the RFC flew sortie after sortie, watching for any build up of the German forces. The Hammers were ordered to provide working parties of one hundred and twenty-five men with four officers from A & D Company. They were then tasked to repair Farm Avenue and Nelson Support trenches. Night patrols and wiring parties went out into the still highly dangerous, nocturnal realm of No Man's Land.

Ernie Curtis had some good news, though. It cheered him up considerably. Home leave was back on, and he was to go next. *"I had been out in France for 28 months, so you can bet I was looking forward to my second leave! It's only us chaps know that pleasure... You are mad with joy! When you see old Blighty's shores, the old white cliffs of Dover, oh it's great! Then, when you are in the train bound for London, it's like another world after leaving the front, where the war was still raging in all its grim determination to slaughter man and beast. Well, I got home on Saturday, about 6pm. The babies started crying when they saw me in all my clobber!"*

They returned from leave at the end of January but Colonel Walsh brought news with him that was sure to sadden the few originals left. The West Ham Battalion was to be disbanded. The following day they were relieved by their old Brigade friends and regular army unit, the South Staffords. They had heard the news, causing much back slapping, hand shakes and sympathetic murmurings. The shelling, usually accompanying each change over, began. It hastened the Hammers out of the line, for the very last time. They marched back to the support area around Villers Pluich and it was there, on the last day of January 1918 that Walsh formed the entire West Ham Battalion on parade, into three sides of a square, and officially delivered the news. They were to be broken up, and then posted to other units piecemeal. A telegram was read, from Haig himself. He acknowledged the *"fine work consistently done"* and it is possible to feel, within its simplicity, the heartfelt sorrow of a professional soldier at the demise of a fighting unit. There was hardly a dry eye among the surviving originals. The hardships, horrors, good times and bad, they had endured it all, side by side. Each man had his own memories. From those patriotic and brave sunny days with Papillon, route marching along leafy Stratford Broadway and proudly around the Borough through to the stormy grey days of training on a bitterly cold Salisbury Plain. The tangible nervous excitement as they sailed to France onboard the troopship Princess Victoria, where they witnessed the horror of the HS Anglia being sunk. So long ago. Their baptism in the Artois. That 'show' up the slope of Vimy Ridge, those 'stunts' on the Somme. That truly awful summer and autumn of 1916, which saw the violent end of so many chums at Delville Wood and Guillemont before ending tragically, facing the 'typewriters' of the Quadrilateral in the thick November fog. 1917 had seen them in continuous duty, dominated by the carnage at Oppy Wood and indomitable spirit shown by every Company at Moeuvres. Oscar Ollett, Charles Carson, Harry Ross, Bernard Page, William Busby and all those other fine 'young gentlemen' who should have had a whole carefree life of possibilities ahead of them. There were the family men too, equally worthy of an opportunity to watch their 'chicks' blossom and present them with grandchildren. Instead, they were each nothing more than a fading photograph on a dusted mantelpiece, bordered by the black ribbon of mourning. One last smile for the family, proudly wearing the uniform they died in.

The breaking up of any strong, well established unit was not a simple process and the West Ham Battalion was no exception. There were literally hundreds of loose ends to be tied. Company stores were gathered up, repaired or repainted before being distributed, with the relevant paperwork, among the remaining battalions of Brigade. Records and other files were collected, collated and carted off. Finally, or perhaps such matters are never final, the Company Quartermasters had to account for enough missing kit at the final inspections to sink the ship that had first brought the Hammers overseas. The phrase 'lost by enemy action' has haunted many a clerk for years.

One last Battalion dinner. The smart officers and polished ranks, together, toasted the King, all the Colonels and the Borough but only the West Ham Battalion itself was cheered to the very echo by those last few surviving original volunteers. Over the next few days, like a slowly thinning mist, the Hammers simply faded away. It was, perhaps, some small comfort that most of the men went to other battalions of the Essex Regiment. On the 11th February, one unit received three officers and nearly one-hundred and twenty soldiers. Among them were a few originals, including 2/Lt Frank Jenns. He was fortunate to promptly get just less than a fortnight of home leave with new wife Alice. Some of the West Ham men went by choice where possible, to other units or regiments. Capt Frank Keeble eventually applied to join the tanks where Reggie Howell, his good friend from the old days and early member of the Hammers, was now a Major. Most of the volunteers continued seeing action, at times intense, but by now some had been given new service numbers and in that way have become lost to history, especially after so many records were destroyed by fire during the Blitz of 1940.

A total of one-hundred and fifteen battalions were lost in this way, some thirty per cent of the New Army, with a further thirty-eight subject to amalgamation. Nineteen 'composite battalions' were created, with no particular identity. Perhaps the saddest aspect to all this upheaval and juggling was that not one extra rifleman became available for duty in the front line. In each disbanded battalion however, was a small nucleus of men who were not posted elsewhere. The army, in its foresight, had decided to form them into 'entrenching battalions' to work on the Brigade frontline defences. Not to be confused with the labour companies, or even the pioneer companies, these men were all fighting fit and ready to replace losses in any frontline unit at any time. There were twenty-five such battalions, kept under strict army control, preventing them being used and swallowed up by hard pressed divisional commanders.

When the long expected German offensive 'Operation Michael' arrived in mid March, several were heavily engaged in the defence of the trenches they had fortified. Some even took part in counter attacks and more of the surviving veterans from the old West Ham Battalion were killed or wounded. Sgt Legg for example, who had got the message through about D Company at the Lock was killed before he was even presented with his Military Medal. It was eventually sent by post to his grieving parents. Pte Hugh Bannon is another. An original member of A Company, named on Henry Dyer's front page recruitment appeal back in January 1915, he was involved in yet another epic stand by early April 1918. This time he was defending Arras and during the fierce German attacks he was shot in the face through the cheeks, lost some teeth and had part of his lower jaw blown away. He was fortunate enough to be evacuated out to a field hospital. Not being allowed to write any personal message on the standard Army postcard sent back to relatives by wounded soldiers (under the threat of the card being destroyed) Bannon incorporated something into his signature: *Hughdontworry*. He eventually returned home and slowly recovered.

It was on the 10th (*Service*) Battalion ("West Ham") of the Essex Regiment was erased from the Army List.

Finally, the war ended in November.

But not for everyone.

Chapter 35

Captivity

Ernie Curtis was one of those who had stayed within the Essex regiment on the Hammers disbandment. After so long as the battalion tailor, here he was back as an infantryman. *"It was a game! I was sent straight up the line and there I was... Six days in at a stretch and come out for three days, then up again. We were doing this for five weeks when all at once the German's started their great offensive on 21st March 1918. I went through the hoop for a couple of days. Why I am still alive is a masterpiece to me!"*

Ernie was gassed during the initial assault before his fourth line trench became the front line. While *"wondering when my packet was coming"* he had another very near miss as a German shell landed on the spot where he had been standing moments before. The explosion buried him alive. Finally managing to claw his way out in terror, he realised that *"my poor mate Joe was dead as a doornail. That was another one, just covered over with a waterproof sheet where he lay..."* As the never ending assault raged on all around him he was strafed by enemy aircraft, one of which was brought down, before a mass of German infantry advanced on the tenuous positions. *"That was a grand sight, but awful..."* Men who tried to make a run for it were shot down by machine gun fire.

Ernie and another former Hammer *"started blazing away at Jerry. The chap next to me was getting very excited and kept on saying "Look at them, you cant miss them!" They were coming over in hundreds... All at once something hit me in the face. I thought I'd copped it. I quickly turned round. It was my mate at the side of me. A bullet went right through his head, shrapnel helmet as well. He never uttered a sound. A few seconds and then that pallor of death spread over his face. I watched him for half a minute, when the blood started trickling from his temple. It makes you feel very grim. This was one of the most trying times of my life..."* Exhausted, Ernie was finally forced to surrender but he *"was so dead beat I couldn't hold my hands up long... I had a peculiar feeling. How often I had read of Jerry being taken prisoner, 'mercy kamerad'. Well, we didn't ask for mercy. We had fought until there were only a few of us left..."* With the enemy none too hospitable towards those captured soldiers with a German surname, Ernie was no doubt grateful for his earlier change from Kurtz to Curtis. *"By jove, I can tell you I kept my eyes rolling in case they stuck us. From that time until the Armistice I was on a starvation diet..."*

Corporal Manningtree, describing his subsequent journey to captivity, remembered how *"they put us in the wagons. Cattle wagons, shoulder to shoulder, thirty of us. They put us in those trucks Thursday morning and we din't come out of them trucks until Saturday morning. Standing room only..."* These men, caught during November's fighting at the Lock, had no toilets, no water, no heat. Just that dreadful feeling of anticipation in the pits of their empty stomachs as they progressed deeper into enemy territory. That night, *"the train stopped at a station. There was two tubs of sauerkraut, that's the German's national food, and [it was] all we got to eat..."*

On arrival in Berlin, they were paraded through the snowy December streets in their rags of uniforms. But Manningtree had noticed something particular about the state of the enemy here in their homeland. *"You can believe me: there weren't a crust, there weren't a crumb, there weren't a currant, in any of the hostels or hotels. They were down and out!"*

Marching through the December sleet to Minden camp in Westphalia, one of the first things the Germans needed to do was remove the trench 'wildlife' from the prisoners. Most men were a walking lice infestation, or, as Manningtree explained, *"we was varminous! They sent a mobile incinerator* [and] *baked the clothes. We stood there in our birthday suit till they done 'em. When the stuff came out that 'old fridge', they fell to pieces. So I didn't have a shirt on for three months. All I'd got was army cardigan, as rough as... They took our boots away and gave us clogs. They took our boots for their soldiers..."*

By contrast, Ernest Linney's first night as a POW was spent locked in a church just behind the front line. A late replacement member of D Company and survivor of the epic last stand, Linney had been marched, carrying the wounded, to the church where they then received medical treatment and even some hot soup. All the while he was keeping a brief diary on scraps of paper, with a stub of pencil. On December 2nd they were bundled into cattle trucks and shared similar experiences to those of Cpl Manningtree before being packed, cold and hungry, into the cotton factory at Le Cateau on the night of 5th December. They then endured another terrible train journey before arriving at Minden camp on the afternoon of December 9th. The Red Cross were notified and POW writing paper, known in German as 'Kriegsgefangenensendung', was made available to the ragged men. Christmas was celebrated with the issue of Red Cross parcels, one between four, and a not so large bowl of thin soup for dinner. An example of the typical parcel contents comes from Pte CW Ellis, one of the originals listed on the Stratford Express front page, who was hoping to survive and return to Lawrence Avenue in Manor Park. Ellis sent a 'parcel received' return postcard, to Mrs Payne at the Ilford Women's Prisoners of War Society. On it he ticked off a packet of tea and biscuits, some sausages, sardines as well as bone beef, syrup and sugar. There was also a luxury, soap.

Prisoners of War were expected to work. Not to any military end but rather on the land or repairing schools and hospitals. Ernest Linney recorded the issue in the New Year of warm hats and coats before being marched out of the camp back to the railway station. He was bundled, along with many others, into more cattle trucks at midday. They arrived exhausted at Munster camp in the late evening. They were now to become a work party, bound for occupied Belgium. Although delayed for a week, they still received issue of loaves of bread, milk, cocoa and biscuits together with more Red Cross parcels. There was a little more of the hot, thin soup. At 9am on January 17th 1918 they were again shunted by train and travelled all day. They passed through Namur, arriving at Mons in the early hours of the following day. Next to Lille, and another railhead, before they arrived at Hallam, near Tournai in Belgium. They were immediately set to work on the frost bitten land.

Cpl Manningtree meanwhile had been sent to Sneidermule camp in north Germany, where *"agreement was drawn up between the British and Germans that no rank over a lance Corporal was forced to work. But he could volunteer. Well, there was seventy of us in Sneidermule: Officers, NCO's, Sgt Majors and Regimentals."* None of them stepped forward, so *"they got rid of us and sent us down to Poland."* The conditions were far from pleasant, with no replacement for the clothing lost during the initial delousing. *"We had a winter there and our camp didn't have no fire in. No coal! All we was left with was wood and peat. We used to go into peat bogs and make our own peat bricks. We had to cook outside* [and] *we had to dig our own latrines. That was your training!"*

Curtis, Manningtree and Linney would have encountered the malnourished men who had by now spent more than a year as a POW, some even longer. Pte Rupert Barlex, captured during the Hammers 1916 assault on the Quadrilateral where he saw his brother killed, had been moved from Vendhuile to Maretz. *"There we had a new Commandant whose orders were very drastic... The French civilians tried all ways and means to get food to us and were brutally treated in consequence. We were reduced to picking up crusts lying on the roadside [...] dropped intentionally by the kind hearted French people. Orders were given that any man found taking anything from the French civilians would be shot. Several men were shot for this supposed crime..."*

While in the camp at Maretz, Rupert Barlex witnessed two men escape but they *"were brought back after several days. They were punished by being confined to a dark room and at meal times they were brought out, strapped to a railing and had to remain in that position while the whole of the men in the camp drew their rations. They were then released and put back in their cells."*

Everyone in the camp knew what the punishment would be for any further attempts, yet *"they escaped again but were only away for a few hours. When caught they were beaten with sticks, whipped, kicked, buffeted about and knocked unconscious."* The severity of the beating caused the camp doctor to be called and the two men were sent to hospital, but *"if they survived after this treatment they must have been wonderfully strong..."* Barlex, continually suffering from *"a considerable number of boils"*, with *"at one time five in very vital places"*, himself became the subject of the camp brutality. He was *"compelled to work"* but *"had to stop several times through pain"*, and remembered one instance when *"a German Officer was near. I was kicked and hit in the ribs until I lost consciousness. When I recovered consciousness I was compelled to continue my work..."*

The eventual end of the war didn't mean an end to the constant discomfort. As Cpl Manningtree points out, *"after the Armistice, the Red Cross parcels stopped, y'see..."* However, there was still a final opportunity to disrupt the former enemy, at the moment of freedom. *"When we was all lined up, ready to come away, an old German interpreter wanted sixteen of us to stop back and clear the camp up..."* Despite offering to *"pay you and feed you well"*, he was left in a Teutonic frustration when *"he never got a volunteer."* In fact Manningtree and the other NCO's *"pulled all our huts inside out, to make a fire!"* and razed the place to the ground. Then began the long journey home and eventually, *"we come to Danzig [and] has a stop there for our ship moored in"*. After the deprivations of the camps, it was natural to seek diversions. *"One of our mates could play the piano, "how about going in the café?" he says, "we can have a tune." We was in there, drinking and playing piano [when] a boy come in. He said "comrade's en vuit!" Our mates had gone with the ship!"* Not only that, the kitbags containing their few precious possessions had also been stolen.

They managed to join a Danish Red Cross ship and *"left Danzig, the 21st December, 1918. Come across the Baltic, called at Copenhagen and picked up some Officers, then come on to Leith and landed at Leith Harbour on Christmas Eve. We had to lay out there until Christmas morning."* Dressed in rags and somewhat emaciated, *"we came down from Leith to Ripley in Yorkshire to get clothed in khaki. There was hundreds of us..."* But there was to be no warm welcoming committee, despite the Season of Goodwill. Neither did the authorities *"put on a Special Train for us. We had to muck in, with the civvies..."* Ever resourceful, *"three of us shared a toilet. That was our seat, on the toilet. When somebody came in and wanted to use it, we had to get out and come back!"*

As they returned to West Ham, the East End and their homes in Essex, with the few survivors bearing the scars and wounds of France inside and out, they never got a victory parade from the borough. The battalion didn't exist anymore. Harry Sharman, who was gassed back in early 1916, was *"maintaining a distress fund"* for those of the Hammers who were now encountering *"hard times..."* Around four-hundred of the surviving originals attended a reunion and dinner at the Connaught Rooms in June 1919. The Stratford Express described it as *"the butterflies homecoming"* in an obvious and affectionate reference to Papillon. George Cattermole, still in France and unable to attend, sent *"his love to the battalion"* as did JD Paterson, by now in Gibraltar and steaming his way back to the Malay States.

The very first toast of the evening was *"to absent friends"* which was drunk in absolute poignant silence. Then the festivities began, with speeches made by Ernest Wild, the Temple barrister who had originally paid for half the cost of the Colours and was now not only an MP but had also been Knighted. The Hammers were described as *"a very happy little family"* with *"great and mutual confidence between officers and men, largely due to the influence and personality of the commanding officer"* which was supported by many shouts of *"Good old Colonel!"* and heartfelt cheers. Papillon took his ovation then stood up and his speech praised the Hammers, especially the way in which there had been hardly *"any crime"* and he never had a need for harsh discipline - which truly was the envy of other battalions. *"My old pals,"* he said, raising his glass, *"I wish you all long life and the best of luck!"*

The following year, the King's Colour for the Hammers was finally delivered to Colchester barracks. It was immediately 'laid up for Eternity' in the regimental church at Warley. It still occupies a high corner, up the back. The 'home-made' colour, hand stitched and embroidered by the wives and girlfriends, has been missing since the summer of 1915. Eventually, the cap badge of the Essex Regiment itself vanished from the parade grounds of the British Army, through amalgamation to become part of the Royal Anglian Regiment in 1958.

Although no connection in documentary evidence can be found, it seems a very fitting *coincidence* that 1958 is also the first year West Ham United appear to have adopted a three turret castle, very similar in design to the old cap badge, as an integral part of their new club logo. Up until the 1930's, United had only ever used an artistic sketch of the locally famous one turret Boleyn Tower to represent 'the castle'. A three part fishtail scroll at the bottom was also added, mirroring the original Essex cap badge.

At 11am on Remembrance Sunday 2009, a black granite memorial plaque to the 'West Ham Pals' was unveiled by Sir Trevor Brooking OBE at United's Boleyn Ground. The stone was donated by local undertakers HL Hawes. There was an honour guard of soldiers from the Royal Anglian Regiment in the presence of the Essex Regiment Association, the East Ham branch of the Royal British Legion, 'Busby' Troop of Newham Scouts, more than seventy relatives and descendants of the original volunteers and many club supporters. The Last Post was played perfectly by a Royal Anglian bugler recently returned from combat in Afghanistan.

In a radically altered, almost unrecognisable, area and with news that the football club may relocate away from the heart of Green Street and the beloved Boleyn Ground it is hoped that the West Ham Battalion are no longer forgotten.

We Will Remember Them

Back Home Again

Pelham Papillon returned to his wife and children at Catsfield Place in Sussex, slipped back into the life of land owner and JP quite comfortably and re-established Crowhurst Cricket Club. His physical recovery was long, with the endless round of medical board assessments where he joked that his deafness (he could hear a watch tick at two feet yet was stone deaf in busy traffic) could still be used *"to an advantage"*. His portrait was painted in the last two months of 1917 by his brother-in-law, the prolific artist Reginald Eves. Papillon's eyes are staring off into the distance, contrary to Eves' usual work where the subject stares directly at the viewer. His head is also turned slightly, hiding the external scars of Delville Wood above his right eye. In 1921, Papillon changed the name of one farm on his Crowhurst estate to Green Street Farm. It's not yet known whether he did this as a mark of personal Remembrance to the men of his West Ham Battalion, or perhaps for those who fell close to Green Street trench while attacking the wire of Guillemont in 1916. He was visited at home by HM The Queen in 1935, by which time he had become President of the Crowhurst British Legion and vice-president of the Hastings branch. He died peacefully five years later, when the country was once again at war with Germany. He now lies buried in the beautiful churchyard at Crowhurst. It is fitting that beside his grave there is a CWGC headstone, almost as if on guard duty. It is for Papillon's son-in-law, Pilot Officer Stephen Olers Hankey, son of a lifelong friend from the South African war of early life. Hankey crashed his Lysander in fog a few miles to the south of Crowhurst while engaged on the dangerous task of extracting French secret agents from German occupied territory in 1941.

George Cattermole the former Royal Navy Petty Officer in the Boer War and colourful Sergeant Major of the West Ham Battalion had moved to the Royal Fusiliers after disbandment, becoming their RSM. At the end of the war he stayed in France, joining Graves Registration, one element of the effort to give all of the fallen an Imperial War Grave. He located many a man on the old battlefields who wouldn't have a known resting place today. By 1924 he had seen enough of the battlefields and emigrated to Australia where he became a gardener with the Sydney Parks Department. He was known for always wearing his bowler hat at an angle and he still had his personal souvenir from France, the pistol he had taken from Leutnant Hammerich in the Hammers first trench raid. In 1939 George shaved ten years off his age and enlisted to defend the motherland in a third war. He served for a year in the Australian Forces before he was finally rumbled and honourably discharged due to *'evident'* old age.

George White, who lost his leg in the second attack on Oppy, suffered a lifetime of uncomfortable pain with his injury. George was visited quite often after the war by some of his West Ham Battalion chums from the old days, especially **CSM Charlie Blowes** of Amity Road. Both men were originals named on the front page listing the first volunteers. In 1924 Charlie presented George with a walking cane, silver topped and inscribed *"From Your Pals"*. During WW2 George again put himself in the line of fire from the Germans, this time as a foreman in charge of bomb fuse manufacturing at the Woolwich Arsenal. It was possibly one of the most dangerous places in London during the Blitz. He died peacefully aged fifty-nine *"after much suffering, patiently and cheerfully borne"* at Whipps Cross hospital in 1949.

JJ Ash, the former chief cashier at Beckton Gas Works who won his DCM with the Hammers at Oppy, was another who emigrated to a peaceful future in Australia.

Frank Keeble went back to the farm in Brantham and enjoyed his life, eventually passing the land over to his son. Frank considered that he'd had a 'good war', as did his close friend and regular visitor, **Reggie Howell**, who had moved over to Tanks back at the end of 1916. At home, Keeble kept items from the Hammers' trench raid where he had won his first MC as well as the telegram invitation to the Palace to receive it. His Webley pistol and the Zouave Buffet menu were eventually framed (after repeated requests, it had taken him nearly the whole of 1917 to get the menu back from within the confidential staff papers of General Kiggell), while a bullet holed Pickelhaube hung above the fireplace and entertained the grandchildren. His shrapnel helmet went in the attic along with his linen trench map of the Canal Du Nord sector and an aerial 'recce' photo of the Lock. He also saved one particular notebook, containing the names and home addresses of his very first command in the West Ham Battalion, the men of No8 Platoon.

A few years after the Great War, Frank bumped into **Corporal Manningtree**, who had been a member of B Company and captured at Lock No5. Manningtree remembers, on the platform at Brantham railway platform, asking him *"How ever did you get away?"* Keeble held out his hands, shrugged his shoulders and smiled broadly, as if to say *"I have no bloody idea!"* Manningtree was held captive for *"one year and thirty three days"*, before he *"had a month's Demob and two months to recuperate. I'd been at home a fortnight and I got a job. I stuck it 37 years…"* He was tracked down years later by Keeble's son who recorded an audio interview from which this material was drawn. Sadly, Manningtree is an alias in the book as his true identity remains unknown to this day.

Samuel 'Dick' Collier returned to his fathers business in Marks Tey near Colchester, mining and delivering aggregates to the construction industry. He inherited the company and managed it well, in his turn passing it to his son and daughter. His brother married the sister of his friend and fellow West Ham Battalion officer **Frank Folkard**, who had been severely wounded at Delville Wood. Both men then served in India, with Collier in the Transport Corps and Folkard with the 3rd Rajputane Rifles. He stayed with them until 1924, stationed on the still volatile North West Frontier where he became an expert in the native languages. In later years both men returned to England, with Folkard becoming chairman of the Copford branch of the Royal British Legion. During WW2 Dick Collier commanded the local Home Guard unit with Frank Folkard as second in command. **Eric Bunting**, who always shared his leave with Capt Collier and was Adjutant in the last few months, also returned to the nearby family business at his father's garden nursery. It had made a name for itself importing Japanese lily pads at the turn of the century. He later inherited and then handed on the business to his son Peter who diversified and in turn passed it on to his two sons who today run it equally as successfully.

After becoming Brigade Transport Officer, **Robert Shrapnel Biddulph-Pinchard** was sent back to Britain suffering trench fever in April 1917. By October he had requested a move to No2 horse transport depot on Blackheath. Post-war, he became a chicken farmer but the business went bankrupt in 1923, so he returned to the army and worked throughout WW2 and beyond as a civilian garrison engineer on Salisbury Plain. He died in 1970.

Robert Swan was sent back to the UK in January 1916 to face a medical board which immediately placed him on a month's leave. Having been *"found unsuited for active duties"* he was transferred into the hands of Captain Leo Dyer, the Mayor's son back at base depot, with the specific order that *"this Officer should not be sent out with reinforcements proceeding overseas..."* Surprisingly, Swan was immediately transferred as temporary second in command of the 98th Training Reserve battalion in Aldershot and proceeded to be an instructor, obviously contrary to Arthur Daly's orders of *"no close contact with troops"*. Swan eventually took overall command of the drill school in July. By September 1916 he had successfully pleaded his case for an overseas combat posting to erase the 'blemish' of his dismissal and was later wounded in action. He went on to receive the Russian Order of St Anne with swords and bow for his role tackling a fire when stationed at a base in Archangel. By wars end he had been promoted to Lt-Col and awarded the military OBE.

Herbert Turner Jessop was released from captivity and returned to teaching. He had made every effort to get individual recognition for the men of D Company, but sadly every effort was in vain. He was, by 1932, still in uniform, promoted to Major with the Officer Training Corps at the University of London. In 1952 he published his findings on "Photo-elasticity and Aircraft Research" in the new jet age and died in 1967 at his home in Thurrock.

Ernie Curtis, the Hammers tailor, returned to east London following his time as POW. Sadly, in an echo of the experiences of many, he discovered that his wife Carrie had died of a ruptured appendix and, as the family believed he was already dead, scattered his children to relations and sold the family home along with all his possessions. As a result, Ernie suffered a severe mental breakdown on his return to Blighty.

Len Holthusen, who had been badly smashed up when the HQ dugout was hit during the action of Delville Wood still suffered with his wounds after the war. He had sought recuperation in Westcliffe On Sea, but sadly he died, aged 34, at the Millbank Military Hospital in November 1920. His brother **Alan Holthusen** had also moved to Westcliffe to be near his brother, living there until his death aged 65 in 1950.

After his short spell with the Hammers, **Reverend Westerdale**'s stint on the Western Front ended when he was admitted to hospital and sent back to England for recuperation from severe exhaustion. By September 1917 at Chisledon Camp in Wiltshire he was badgering the secretary of the chaplain's department at the War Office, reminding them constantly that he wanted to return to *"the front at the earliest opportunity. A young, unmarried energetic man like myself ought not to be kept at a small home camp longer than is necessary. At least that's the way I look at it for there must be many older men than myself needing a rest."* Westerdale wrote two books of memoirs about his time in the trenches, firstly as a medic and then as a chaplain.

Sid Lathangue served in the Hammers until the traumas of late 1916 when he was invalided out by wounds. He eventually left the army with the Silver War Badge which was awarded for 'services rendered'. All three Lathangue brothers survived the war.

Noel Baboneau returned to an unchanged Borneo, stepping back into his colonial role. There was still a simmering resentment to his part in the events of the Rundum uprising pre-war. In 1920, as a phone call interrupted his game of golf, he was fatally shot in the head from very close range on the steps to his home. His murderer was a trusted tribesman, Lima, who was working as a local police constable with access to the house. Lima then put the gun to his ear and killed himself on the steps. A short biography was written a year or so later by his good friend, the war poet Owen Rutter.

Anselm Duckett, who had proved so effective with his Lewis gun, was transferred on the disbandment to the 11th Essex. He was wounded while on patrol on 5th July and by September 1918 he was recovering at a camp in Shoreham, regarded as *"a man of quiet disposition and a good soldier"* by his commanding officer. A few days before the end of October 1918 he received his DCM for the fighting at Lock No5. For whatever reason, Anselm promptly hung himself from a rafter in the barracks washroom. He was 38 years old.

The **Alexandra Temperance Hotel**, in Stratford High Street, which served as the officer's mess for the Hammers in 1915, closed not long after the end of the war. It passed through many uses, mostly on behalf of Newham Council and today it serves the community as the Discovery Children's Centre.

And what of our diarist, **Frank Arthur Jenns**, who religiously mentioned what happened to the men and yet hardly ever noticed the officers? Only through his meticulous work in that first year could so much have been done to remember the volunteers he served alongside. Promoted through the ranks of the West Ham Battalion, from Private to Second Lieutenant, it is his handwriting which opens the Hammers war diary in 1915 and it is his handwriting on the very last page of 1918.

When the Hammers were disbanded Jenns's new Essex unit was *"holding the line at Albert..."* On April 5th during a sudden, unexpected and intense German offensive, huge co-ordinated attacks were unleashed all along the frontline. The whole area around Jenns position received bitter German assaults using every weapon type available. Multiple gas shells were followed by waves of masked storm troops brandishing flamethrowers while above in the sky brightly painted aircraft were strafing and bombing the trenches already flattened by incessant heavy artillery.

Overnight on the 5th/6th April, Frank was seriously wounded and stretcher-bearers carried him back to No37 Field Ambulance. Three days later came the dreaded knock at Essex Road in Manor Park where his young wife received the telegram baldly stating *"deeply regret to inform you..."*

They had only been married back in October.

Alice never remarried, had no children and lived alone in Waltham Forest until she died peacefully in 1985. It is not known whether she was ever able to pay a visit to her husband's grave in the peaceful CWGC cemetery at Varennes.

Original Volunteers to
The West Ham Battalion

Dates of Death up to Disbandment

(This list is incomplete and while every effort has been made to ensure accuracy, the authors cannot be held responsible for any omissions)

Officers

Surname	Forename	Service Number	Award	KIA/DOW	Cemetery	Memorial
Keeble	Frank	Captain	MC+Bar			
Busby	William Walter	Captain	MC	13-Nov-16	Serre Road No2	
Howell	Reg	Lt				
Harford	H Cardinal	Major				
Winthrop	Henry	Major				
Paterson	John Donald	Captain	MC			
Swan	Robert	Lt				
Sharman	Harry Handley	Captain				
Carson	Charles	Captain	MC	19-Nov-16	St Sever	
Folkard	Frank	Lt				
Bunting	Eric	Lt				
Collier	Dick	Captain	MC			
Simpson	Gilbert	Lt				
Lang	Norman	Lt				
Page	Bernard	2/Lt		09-Aug-16		Thiepval
Ross	Harry	2/Lt		09-Aug-16	Delville Wood	
Trumble	Frank	Captain				
Pinchard	Robert Shrapnel Biddulph	Captain				
Brind	Tom	Lt				
Papillon	Pelham	Lt-Col	DSO			

Other Ranks

Surname	Forename	Service Number	Award	KIA/DOW	Cemetery	Memorial
Abbey	C	18674				
Adams	Edward	18227		17-Nov-16	Etaples Military	
Adams	F	18364		23-Jul-16		Thiepval
Adams	AG	18973				
Adams	WR	19333				
Agass	C	17273				

Alcock	Albert	17580					
Alexander	J	17576					
Allen	Daniel	17534					
Allerton	Arthur	18231		13-Mar-17		Thiepval	
Allway	Harold	17498					
Ames	R	18042					
Amies	WJ	17991					
Amner	WJ	19381					
Anderson	Ernest	17740		02-Aug-16	La Neuville British		
Andrews	AFJ	18679					
Arber	W	17159					
Arber	F	17854	MM				
Archer	Henry	17575					
Argent	F	17349		01-Jul-16	Ecoivres Military		
Ash	John Joseph	17348	DCM				
Asser	George	18589		18-Mar-16		Arras	
Atkins	JCT	18311					
Ault	Samuel	18538					
Austin	Martin Thomas	18859		13-Nov-16		Thiepval	
Austin	FW	18261					
Avice		17689					
Ayers	Hubert	17574		30-Jul-16		Thiepval	
Aylott	WH	17254					
Baggott	J	18381					
Bailey	Henry George	17532		13-Nov-16	Serre Road No2		
Bailey	Fred	17135		30-Nov-17		Cambrai	
Bailey	Thomas	17138					
Baker	Henry Thomas	18044		29-Jul-16		Thiepval	
Baker	George Henry	17573		09-Aug-16		Thiepval	
Baker	William	17418					
Balaam	Albert	17842					
Balcombe	David Richard	18835		13-Nov-16		Cambrai	
Baldwin	C	18379					
Ball	WA	17741					
Bancroft	G	17308					
Banks	Henry William	17613					
Bannon	Hugh	17272					
Barber	Edwin John	17995		06-Mar-16	Loos British		
Bardens	Fred Samuel	17451		30-Jul-16		Thiepval	
Barker	Albert Edward	17215		29-Jul-16		Thiepval	
Barlex	George Alfred Charles	17165		13-Nov-16		Thiepval	
Barlex	Rupert	21231					

Barlex	James	18663				
Barnes	Ernest E	17581				
Barnett	J	18036				
Barsby	H	17701				
Barth	Paul	3 3032				
Bartley	FD	18358	DCM			
Bass	A	17347				
Bates	GH	18828				
Bayliss	John Edward	17572		25-Jun-17	Etaples Military	
Beattie	William Robert	17531		30-Nov-17		Cambrai
Beazley	Henry Ralph	18463		19-Feb-16	Le Touret	
Beck	Charlie	18260				
Beckwith	W	17392				
Bedford	James Norman	17530		07-May-16	Loos British	
Bell	SA	17996				
Bellinger	Norman W	17391	DCM MM			
Bennett	TJ	17151				
Benson	George	17346				
Benson	W	17390				
Benton	Alfred Frederick	18143		13-Nov-16	Bertrancourt	
Berney	John F	17700		01-Jul-16		Arras
Berson	William	18156		01-Jul-16	Cabaret Rouge	
Bifield	GW	17214				
Birch	W	18161				
Blackaby	WJ	17389				
Blackman	GD	18056				
Blackwell	WS	17963				
Blake	WJ	18686				
Blanks	James	17529		30-Nov-17		Cambrai
Blattmann	CAH	17496				
Blowes	TW	17536				
Blowes	Charlie W	17116				
Blythe	A	17114				
Blythe	R	18594				
Bolton	Albert Edward	18816		01-Jul-16		Arras
Bone	William	18180				
Bonfield	J	18109				
Bonser	WT	18055				
Boswell	J	18099				
Boulton	William	18354		28-Apr-17		Arras
Boulton	Stephen John Nathaniel	18076		28-Apr-17		Arras
Boundy	Arthur	17583				

Bowyer	Alfred Henry	17699		30-Nov-17		Cambrai
Bradfield	L	18142				
Bradshaw	A	17481				
Braham	J	17156				
Brailly	Charles	17271				
Branton	A	18378				
Brett	Walter Thomas	18253		13-Nov-16		Thiepval
Brett	JP	17480				
Brett	JJ	17614				
Bridges	F	17990				
Brigham	Fred	18353				
Broadhurst	WA	18070				
Brock	Edward Clarence	18346	MC			
Brocklebank	O	17507				
Brooks	Joseph	18307		26-Oct-16	Couin British	
Brooks	A	17345				
Brooks	AJ	18264				
Brown	Henry Arthur	18592		13-Nov-16	Serre Road No2	
Brown	Charlie	18012				
Brown	George	17994	MM			
Brown	H	17528				
Brown	A	18163				
Browring	CWD	18352				
Buck	WJ	17166				
Buckley	John	17213				
Bugg	Henry	19369		28-Apr-17		Arras
Bull	Richard	17252		13-Nov-16	Serre Road No2	
Bullen	Charles Frederick	19750		28-Apr-17		Arras
Bullock	JF	17950				
Burden	Willis E	17527				
Burgess	George	18856		30-Jul-16		Thiepval
Burgess	George Harry	18877		30-Jul-16		Thiepval
Burgess	Frederick Ernest	17584		28-Apr-17		Arras
Burke	CE	18345				
Burleigh	C	17736	MM			
Burman	AE	17287				
Busby	Arthur	18029		06-Mar-16	Loos British	
Butler	Nathaniel C	17388				
Cain	James William	17479		28-Jul-16		Thiepval
Callaghan	W	18322				
Calnan	James	17948				
Cameron	Robert	18098		04-May-17	Duisans British	
Cannon	AE	17525				

Surname	Forename	Number	Award	Date	Cemetery	Memorial
Cansdale	Frederick	18445				
Carlile	TW	17168				
Carpenter	Percy Edward	19345		13-Nov-16	Auchonvillers	
Carrington	William Alfred	18035		09-Aug-16	Delville Wood	
Carson	A	18344				
Carter	George William	18355		28-May-16	Cabaret Rouge	
Carter	James Arthur	18535		06-Mar-16	Loos British	
Carter	AE	17577				
Cattanach	J	18252				
Cattermole	George	3 3049	MC MiD			
Caulfield	RCF	18010				
Chace	HJ	18541				
Chandler	Harry	17220		13-Nov-16	Serre Road No2	
Chaplin	Henry John	18028		06-Mar-16	Loos British	
Chapman	SE	18027				
Chappell	WJ	17698				
Charles	John William	19347		09-Aug-16		Thiepval
Charman	Walter	18929				
Churchman	WE	19334				
Clark	James	17270		13-Nov-16	Serre Road No2	
Clark	Edward William	17524		01-Jul-16	Zouave Valley	
Clark	Harry	17570		28-Jul-16		Thiepval
Clark	Desbury	17344				
Clark	J	18333				
Clark	PAR	17161	MM			
Clark	FW	18164				
Clark	JJ	17540				
Clark	EW	18074				
Clark	AW	18110				
Clark	Alf G	18273				
Clarke	William Arthur	17578		03-Jul-16	Delville Wood	
Clements	Ernest George	18362		29-Jul-16		Thiepval
Clements	Walter	3 9391				
Clifford	Johnathon	17148				
Cochrane	John	17454				
Cockrain	W	4 2011	DCM			
Codling	A	19035				
Coe	G	17212				
Coker	William James	17171		16-Aug-16	Etaples Military	
Collingwood	William Charles	18678		28-Apr-17		Arras
Collins	Charles Norris	17387		13-Nov-16		Thiepval
Connelly	WW	18201				
Cook	Ernest William	18329		09-Aug-16		Thiepval

Cook	W	18902	MSM			
Cook	WG	18026				
Cook	FH	21117				
Cook	DR	17386				
Coomes	Wallace	18174				
Cooper	William	18296		09-Aug-16	Delville Wood	
Cooper	Henry Harlock	18827		23-Oct-17	East London Cemetery	
Cooper	Joseph	17958		27-Apr-16	Loos British	
Cooper	Walter Leonard	17687		28-Apr-17	Orchard Dump	
Cooper	Ernest Edward	17696		30-Nov-17		Cambrai
Cooper	J	17703				
Cooper	H	17759				
Cooper	F	18200				
Coram	GE	17306				
Corner	Reuben John	17219		09-Aug-16		Thiepval
Corner	WG	17122				
Cotten	Percy	17492	MM	13-Nov-16		Thiepval
Coulter	Albert	17569		13-Nov-16		Thiepval
Course	AE	18137				
Cousins	Frederick Albert	18850		31-Jul-16		Arras
Cousins	HC	18251				
Cousins	RC	18276				
Coventry	John Levi	17153		13-Nov-16		Thiepval
Coward	GR	17211				
Cowell	Frank Henry	18468		19-Feb-16	Bethune Town	
Cox	G	18025	MM			
Cox	RH	17210				
Cox	G	17269				
Cox	Harry	17268				
Crancher	A	17949				
Crewe	FW	18881				
Crispin	Thomas Edward	18250		01-Jun-16	Cabaret Rouge	
Cross	F	18919				
Cruse	WJ	18199				
Curtis	BA "Ernie"	18814				
Da Costa	John Jacob	18555				
Dabbs	FS	18140				
Dale	AWD	17853				
Dance	WG	17278				
Daniells	Rupert Joseph	18175		28-Apr-17		Arras
Darken	A	17209				
Darrington	Ernest	17585	MM			

David	H	17925					
Davies	Arthur Ley	17521					
Davis	A	17170					
Davis	W	18176					
Dawson	WE	18343					
Day	Albert Henry	18533		17-Aug-16	Heilly Station		
Day	Alf	18820					
Dean	Charles Henry	17997		09-Aug-16	Delville Wood		
Dearsly	J	17385					
Death	A	17609					
Debuse	Edward James	18041		09-Aug-16		Thiepval	
Delaney	John	18748		18-Feb-17	Regina Trench		
Denman	TW	17160					
Derbyshire	Albert	17141					
Desmond	HH	18669					
Dexter	WH	17267					
Digby	F	19022					
Dilloway	P	17343					
Dipple	Henry John	18097		14-Nov-16		Thiepval	
Divver	D	18544					
Doe	Harold George	3 3387		13-Nov-16	Serre Road No2		
Dolby	Robert Bertram	17686		02-Mar-16	Fosse 10		
Dolby	WJ	17567					
Donatz	Conradin	17957		31-Jul-16		Thiepval	
Doo	Samuel Philip	18182		30-Jul-16		Thiepval	
Douglas	WE	17586					
Dove	PA	17140					
Dowdall	J	18300					
Dowling	Daniel Frederick	17617		13-Nov-16	Serre Road No2		
Dowse	Alfred James	18350		29-Jul-16		Thiepval	
Driver	William Henry	18053		29-Jul-16		Thiepval	
Dunn	Joseph	17129					
Durant	JT	17415					
Durrell	J	18254					
Dutton	James William	18052		15-May-16	Loos British		
Eade	Frank	17249					
Earle	William Joseph	17395		13-Nov-16	Serre Road No2		
Eary	Ernest William	17266		14-Nov-16	Bertrancourt		
Eaton	Alf	18532					
Edgley	Charles	17852		02-Aug-16	La Neuville		
Edmunds	Charles Edgar	18807		13-Nov-16	Serre Road No2		
Edwards	Henry Jonathan	17591		01-Jul-16	Zouave Valley		
Edwards	AF	19525	MM				

Edwards	D	17857					
Edwards	AH	18473					
Edwards	AH	18473					
Eeles	Alfred James	18315		29-Jul-16		Thiepval	
Elliott	Walter Edwin	18681		30-Jul-16		Thiepval	
Ellis	Albert Benjamin	17661		01-Jul-16	Barlin		
Ellis	EE	17265					
Ellis	James	17724					
Ellis	CW	17384					
Ellis	FAC	21462					
Embleton	Robert	17304		05-Aug-16	St Sever		
Emerson	AW	17263					
Emmings	WT	18472					
Englefield	Herbert James	17566		29-Mar-17	Cologne Southern		
Enright	JM	17993					
Escott	W	18087					
Evans	Harry William	18111		13-Nov-16		Thiepval	
Fair	James	18009					
Farmer	J	19520	DCM MM				
Farmer	CH	18342					
Farrington	JG	17956					
Farrow	Sidney	18275					
Feasey	JH	18177					
Feasey	JS	18972					
Ferry	J	18295					
Field	A	18323					
Fisher	William	19529		20-Dec-17	Hermies Hill British		
Fitch	John William	17207		13-Nov-16		Thiepval	
Flack	Walter Percy	18808		31-Jul-16	Bronfay Farm Military		
Fleming	James	17248		13-Nov-16	Mailly Wood		
Fleming	A	18153					
Fletcher	William	17410					
Fletcher	Frederick	17756					
Flicker	Walter Harold	18023		13-Nov-16		Thiepval	
Ford	WG	17662					
Foreman	G	17142					
Fox	Charlie	18096					
Francis	A	18166					
Francker	George Thomas	18545		14-Jul-16	Canadian No2		
Fraser	A	17456					
Fray	Charles Frederick	17400		13-Nov-16	Serre Road No2		

Surname	Given	Number	Col5	Date	Location	Memorial
Free	CT	17167				
Freeman	Charles	17128				
French	AG	17247				
French	F	17685				
Furlong	John Clifford	18475		13-Nov-16		Thiepval
Furness	H	17988				
Gannon	R	17311				
Gardiner	Henry	17684				
Garland	GW	17755				
Garnar	L	18375				
Garner	Edward Christopher	18088		09-Aug-16		Thiepval
Garwood	F	17133				
Gear	Fred	17303				
Geveaux	FT	18294				
Gibbon	Cebert Douglas	17520		13-Nov-16	Serre Road No2	
Gibbons	J	18331				
Gibbons	E	17998				
Gibbs	Charles John	17722		13-Nov-16		Thiepval
Gibbs	G	18653				
Gibson	George	17341		30-Nov-17		Cambrai
Giess	Alfred	18089				
Giess	Arthur	17721				
Gilbert	William	18183				
Gilbert	W	18349				
Giles	Albert Charles	18832		30-Jun-16	Cabaret Rouge	
Gill	J	17663				
Gillman	SE	17999				
Girling	EC	17406				
Gladding	G	18095				
Gladdy	CW	17477				
Gladwin	Herbert Henry	17246		13-Nov-16		Thiepval
Glover	AW	19328				
Godfrey	C	17587	MM			
Good	JW	18057				
Goodchild	Cecil	17564				
Goodey	HW	17340				
Goodhew	Alfred Henry	17359		30-Jul-16		Thiepval
Goodman	William James	8650				
Gordon	H	17720				
Gore	RW	17245				
Gormley	B	18687				
Grant	Thomas Charles Escott	18293		29-Jul-16		Thiepval

Gray	Alfred	19773		13-Nov-16	Redan Ridge No2	
Gray	AW	17985				
Gray	W	18168				
Greaves	HE	18292				
Green	Ernest	17457		30-Jul-16	Delville Wood	
Green	George	18949		13-Mar-17		Thiepval
Green	WA	17302				
Green	Fred	17588				
Greeno	George	18040				
Greenwood	Henry	17505				
Gretton	Albert	17719				
Griffiths	WC	17651				
Groome	CW	17244				
Grubb	Edwin Charles	17650		27-Aug-16	St Sever	
Gurr		17339				
Guy	George	17312				
Hackett	BC	18033				
Hales	WA	3 2392				
Hall	SC	17519				
Hall	JT	17205				
Hall	JW	17944				
Halls	Wilfred Cecil	18924				
Halls	H	17589				
Hamilton	FG	17337				
Hardcastle	WC	18303	MM CduG			
Hards	WW	17317				
Harley	SC	18106				
Harris	Alfred George	17381		09-Aug-16		Thiepval
Harris	JW	18133				
Harris	FG	18274				
Harrison	E	17380				
Hartigan	RT	18861				
Harvey	Albert Howard Beckford	17943		25-Jan-19	Mons Bergen	
Harvey	EH	18341				
Harvey	C	17981				
Harwood	LJ	17204				
Hathaway	Sidney John	17379		13-Nov-16	Serre Road No2	
Hauser	WM	18651				
Hawes	Fred	19642		30-Jul-16	Bernafray Wood British	
Hawes	John	18000				
Hawker	G	17983				

Hawkins	Henry	18154		09-Aug-16		Thiepval
Hawtin	Eli John Fox	17665		16-Aug-16	St Sever	
Hayden	WH	18922				
Hayes	J	18278				
Head	WR	17518				
Heath	GR	18480				
Heighway	William Edward	17660		19-Feb-16	Calais Southern	
Hemmings	Henry	18050				
Hendrick	JA	17408				
Henman	AJ	17620				
Hill	EP	19324				
Hill	EL	17203	MM			
Hills	AW	17982				
Hipperson	A	17125				
Hitchcock	CW	17378				
Hobbs	CJ	18210				
Hockley	A	17621				
Hockley	A	18037				
Holden	Thomas	18090		29-Jul-16		Thiepval
Holder	Henry T	17417				
Holder	WA	17476				
Holland	PL	17490				
Holt	Thomas	17475		13-Nov-16	Serre Road No2	
Homewood	Paul	17336		28-Apr-17		Arras
Hookham	Richard	17716				
Hooper	JR	17592				
Hooper	RP	18135				
Hooten	WF	17377				
Hornsby	JA	18478				
Howell	Stanley Charles	17849		13-Nov-16		Thiepval
Howes	GA	17718				
Hudgell	Arthur	18557		28-Jul-16		Thiepval
Hull	Albert A	19075		04-Dec-17		Thiepval
Hume	RW	18006				
Humphries	Edward Abraham	17143		30-Jul-16		Thiepval
Hunt	Frederick Oliver	18477		04-Sep-16		Thiepval
Hunt	BJ	17202				
Hunt	EG	18446				
Hyde	J	17516				
Issacs	N	17144				
Izzat	Arthur	17126				
Jacks	RJ	17941				
Jackson	Frank	18112		20-Jan-16	Bethune Town	

Jaggers	Robert	19527				
Jago	A	17488				
James	Frank	18094	MM+Bar			
Jarman	R	18255				
Jenns	Frank Arthur	19651				
Jepson	E	17473				
Joel	PC	17715				
Johnson	William Edmund	17847		19-Apr-17	Orchard Dump	
Johnson	FN	17401				
Jolley	Joseph Bertie	17846		09-Aug-16		Thiepval
Jolley	William Henry	19420		28-Apr-17		Arras
Jorden	FG	17752				
Kaley	J	18484				
Kaminski	A	17421				
Keeble	WJ	18067				
Keer	George William	17659		28-Apr-17		Arras
Kenefeck	RRJ	18102				
Keys	WTG	17239				
Killby	G	17593				
King	William James	17980		20-Jan-16	Guards Cem Guinchy	
King	George Arthur	18062		13-Nov-16	Serre Road No2	
Kipling	J	18179				
Kirk	B	17416				
Kirvan	S	17918	MM			
Kite	BC	17180				
Knight	John	18483				
Knowles	J	19343	MM CduG			
Kunkel	EW	17917				
Kurtz	EL	18068				
Lancaster	Frederick	18857		28-Apr-17		Arras
Lane	Frederick Charles	17562		28-Jul-16		Thiepval
Lane	William	17375		28-Apr-17		Arras
Langford	WH	17594				
Langley	E	18152				
Lashmar	G	18107				
Latham	William	17938				
Lathangue	Fred	18046				
Lathangue	Sidney	19024				
Lathangue	Harry	18047				
Launder	James Fred John	17260		21-Feb-17		Thiepval
Lawley	Frank	17502				
Lawrence	Frederick Henry	17134		30-Jul-18		Thiepval

Surname	Forename	Number	Medal	Date	Cemetery	Memorial
Leach	FJ	17238				
Leaning	WT	17472				
Legg	Lawrence Stanley	18449	MM			
Leonard	AC	18039				
Lewin	FT	18271				
Lincoln	John Grey	17979		20-Jan-16	Bethune	
Livings	David	17595		13-Nov-16		Thiepval
Lixenfield	Edgar	18048		09-Aug-16	Serre Road No2	
Llewellyn	Percy James	17280		25-Dec-17	Rocquigny-Equancourt Road	
Lloyd	James	19793		23-Feb-18	Tournai	
Lloyd	AL	17200				
Lobley	BF	17937				
Logan	RF	17487				
Longhurst	IW	17154				
Lovegrove	SH	18373				
Lovell	Frederick	17199		02-Aug-16	Dantzig Alley	
Loynes	William Edward	17978		06-Mar-16	Loos British	
Lucas	Charlie	18007	MM			
Luck	Walter	18448				
Lynn	JH	17374				
Mace	JW	18580				
Mackay	JJ	17596				
Maher	J	17333				
Maidwell	EA	17237				
Male	T	17373				
Manly	William Henry	18338				
Mann	H	17300				
Mann	AW	17372				
Mantle	Barrington or Bertram	17645		13-Nov-16	Serre Road No2	
Mantle	A	17916				
Marmoy	Walter Ernest	18060		13-Nov-16	Redan Ridge No3	
Marney	Henry Francis	17535		13-Nov-16	Serre Road No2	
Marney	John William	17127		30-Jul-16		Thiepval
Marsh	William James	17514		09-Aug-16		Thiepval
Martin	Frederick	18450		09-Aug-16	Delville Wood	
Martin	B	18269				
Martin	Michael	18302				
Matthews	RA	17624				
May	William	18595		01-Jul-16	Zouave Valley	
Mayo	Samuel	17121		06-Mar-16	Loos British	
McAllister	F	18661				

McCarthy	Walter	18339				
McDonald	R	17712				
McGarva	John	17361				
McGrath	HD	17459				
Medcraft	CA	17299				
Meddings	George	17460		09-Aug-16		Thiepval
Mellish	James	18655				
Merrett	FE	17642				
Middleton	G	19340				
Mile	CW	17647				
Miles	JG	17598				
Miller	JW	18059	MM			
Milligan	W	17561				
Millin	Fred	19057				
Mills	ET	18247				
Mills	CJ	18867				
Minahan	Thomas	17626		02-Jul-16	Barlin	
Minahan	J	17625				
Mole	WA	17369				
Mooney	JC	17915				
Moore	Harry	18359		13-Nov-16		Thiepval
Moore	George	18677				
Moore	R	17643				
Moore	AT	17298	DCM			
Moore	WG	18058				
Morrison	Harold John	17197		26-Oct-16	Sucrerie	
Morton	H	17461				
Moss	GH	18357		01-Jul-16	Zouave Valley	
Moss	H	18830				
Motton	Arthur Sidney	17235		27-May-16	Cabaret Rouge	
Muhly	HT	18301				
Munday	GE	17368				
Munting	FA	18794				
Murphy	James	18457		30-Jul-16	Sucrerie	
Musgrove	Harold	17749		13-Nov-16		Thiepval
Myers	L	17515				
Neal	William John	18955		13-Nov-16		Thiepval
Newell	Harry James	17332		29-Jun-15	Great Warley	
Newell	Sidney Ernest	19341		13-Nov-16		Thiepval
Newins	H	17976	MM CduG			
Newman	Joseph	18487		02-Jun-16	Cabaret Rouge	
Newson	HG	18931				

Surname	Forename	Number	Medal	Date	Place	Memorial
Newton	Arthur	17608		01-Jul-16	Zouave Valley	
Nicholls	WGT	17679				
Nicholson	Charles	18527		03-Dec-17	Hermies Hill	
Noon	George Benjamin	17678		28-Jul-16		Thiepval
Norris	GEA	17462				
North	William	17977		09-Aug-16	Delville Wood	
Northfield	HG	17513				
Nugent	H	17290				
O'Keefe	T	17413				
Oliver	Herbert	18560				
Olsen	W	17843				
Orton	William Charles	18863		13-Nov-16	Cerisy-Gailly French National	
Osbourne	George William	18812		27-May-16	Abbeville	
Osbourne	AJ	17486				
Outram	FW	18372				
Owens	HA	18337				
Page	Frank Walter	18277		03-Jul-16	Barlin	
Paget	A	17748				
Palmer	Simeon Claydon	19708		13-Nov-16	Serre Road No2	
Park	C	17954				
Parker	Ernest Arthur	18078		06-Mar-16	Fosse 10	
Parsons	FC	18195				
Paxman	Fred Richard Thomas	17471		13-Nov-16		Thiepval
Payne	Charles Andrew	18013		07-Mar-16	Bully Grenay	
Payne	T	17367				
Peacey	D	17974				
Peacock	W	17914	MM			
Pearce	EGP	17297				
Pearman	B	18836				
Pears	J	18015				
Pearson	J	19331				
Peartree	T	13363	DCM MM			
Peek	J	18280				
Pelham	H	18267				
Penn	Philip Henry	17676		11-May-16	St Patricks	
Penny	FJ	18846				
Percival	Alfred Winsper	17181		27-May-16	Caberet Rouge	
Perry	HG	17470				
Pettey	J	17601				
Phelps	WJ	17558				
Philips	G	17316				
Pickett	W	18257				

Picking	J	17557				
Piddington	CH	18167				
Piercy	H	18169	MM			
Pinder	Henry Francis	17607		31-Jul-16		Arras
Place	J	17623				
Plato	FH	18108	MM			
Pleasant	Thomas Henry	18104		13-Nov-16	Serre Road No2	
Pleasants	AE	18005				
Plummer	PB	19999				
Pogson	RB	18844				
Poile	William Philip	17366		19-Apr-17	Achiet-le-Grand	
Pointer	EA	17330				
Pond	Arthur	17746		28-Jul-16		Thiepval
Porter	E	17132				
Porter	GW	18287				
Potts	Henry	17365		28-Apr-17		Arras
Pounds	Samuel	18079		23-May-17	Etaples Military	
Powell	Bertie	17364				
Poynter	Charles Frederick	18548		26-Aug-16	St Sever	
Preston	AE	17675				
Price	Percy Victor	17555		11-Dec-15		Loos
Prickett	AV	18113				
Probyn	Edward	17745		22-Jun-16	Quatre Vents	
Prowse	FJ	18840				
Pugh	JH	18016				
Pullen	JA	17275				
Purton	R	17463				
Quilter	Walter John	17554		13-Nov-16	Serre Road No2	
Randall	William	17196				
Randall	WF	18134				
Rankin	E	17602				
Ranner	W	17501	DCM			
Raven	Harry	17553		30-Jul-16		Thiepval
Rawlings	WG	18336				
Rayment	H	17281	MM			
Regardsoe	AE	17131				
Relland	John Thomas	18159		01-Mar-16	Bully Grenay	
Reynolds	WR	17629				
Richmond	Walter	18017		31-Dec-18	Manor Park	
Riley	John Edwin	18920		30-Jul-16		Thiepval
Roberts	John	17232		13-Nov-16	Serre Road No2	
Rodda	George	18150		13-Nov-16	Waggon Road	
Rodwell	James	17706				

Rollings	Robert 'Reg'	17217					
Rosamond	A	17164					
Roscoe	Harold	18647	MM	17-Dec-18	Barking Rippleside		
Roscoe	W	17469					
Rose	AJ	17500					
Rowe	R	17953					
Rowse	E	18526					
Rugless	Thomas William	18635		09-Aug-16		Thiepval	
Rule	AJ	17258					
Rutty	Edgar George	18860		31-Jul-16		Thiepval	
Ryan	Edward	17972		06-Mar-16	Loos British		
Ryan	WPT	17841					
Sage	Frederick Reginald	19265		01-Jul-16	Zouave Valley		
Sait	Joseph Henry	17231	MM	30-Jul-16		Thiepval	
Saker	A	17512					
Salmon	Arthur Thomas	17674					
Salmon	A	18268					
Saltmarsh		18310					
Salton	JH	18640					
Sampson	Walter	17117	MM				
Sandle	Reuben	17277					
Sarling	William	18332		27-Feb-15	East Ham		
Scales	GH	17933					
Schuler	JA	18198					
Scott	Victor Herbert	17637		09-Aug-16		Arras	
Scott	HC	17552					
Scott	George	17194		31-Jul-16		Thiepval	
Seaman	Herbert William	18457		30-Nov-17		Cambrai	
Shadbolt	AR	17605					
Sharman	G	17603					
Sharp	H	17840					
Shea	TJ	19020					
Shepheard	J	18685					
Shepherd	S	17705					
Shields	HS	17912					
Shillingford	Thomas Henry	18494		30-Jul-16		Thiepval	
Shipp	Walter	17123		13-Nov-16	Serre Road No2		
Shrosbee	WA	18629	MM				
Shuttleworth	Alexander	18549		18-Mar-16		Arras	
Simmonds	Arthur Walter	17550		28-Apr-17		Arras	
Simonds	EH	18018					
Simpson	HG	17838					

Sipple	EWJ	18563					
Skerrit	Alf	17182					
Slate	Frank Cecil	17327		28-Apr-17		Arras	
Smith	Arthur Thomas	18149		28-Apr-17	Le Treport		
Smith	George Thomas	18524		13-Nov-16	Serre Road No2		
Smith	Fred	18105		23-Mar-17	St Sever		
Smith	William	18456		10-Jan-18	St Sever		
Smith	John George	18656		28-Apr-16		Arras	
Smith	Henry Valentine	17970		28-Jul-16		Thiepval	
Smith	Richard	17464		09-Aug-16		Thiepval	
Smith	Charles J	18148		09-Aug-16		Thiepval	
Smith	Fred J	17296					
Smith	JW	17229	MM				
Smith	Joseph	18918					
Smith	John	17192	MM				
Smith	HC	17172					
Smith	Charles A	17193					
Smith	Leslie	17295					
Smith	William J	17315					
Smith	Fritz	17326					
Smith	Charles E	17484					
Smith	CH	17702					
Smith	John A	17910					
Smith	Benjamin	18258					
Smith	Arthur	18632					
Smith	Cecil	18858					
Songhurst	Charles Edward	18061	MM	22-Aug-18	Vis en Artois		
Sparkes	B	18496					
Sparrow	Thomas George	17191		01-Mar-16	Bully Grenay		
Sprod	Herbert George	18668		13-Nov-16		Thiepval	
Spurling	AA	17909					
Stadward	JW	17325					
Stafford	JS	17907					
Standen	RE	18793					
Starie	W	17835					
Stevens	Walter	19066					
Stevens	E	17361					
Stevens	W	18171					
Steward	Stanley Leonard	18455		04-Sep-15	Leyton St Mary		
Steward	William Walter	18652		13-Nov-16	Redan Ridge No1		
Stickley	David F	17360					
Stiff	A	17630					

Stimson	J	18493					
Stone	TR	17640					
Stone	Thomas	18368					
Stoneman	Horace	17169		30-Jul-16			Thiepval
Stuchfield	James	17511		06-Apr-16	Lillers		
Stunt	WR	17657					
Sturman	W	17274					
Sullivan	Michael	18525					
Sullivan	J	17743					
Sullivan	H	17952					
Sumpter	AE	18790					
Swannell	Frederick	17549		28-Apr-17			Arras
Sweet	FK	17559					
Swindell	JE	17639					
Swinnerton	Charlie	18284					
Tarling	F	18283					
Taylor	FC	17742					
Taylor	SG	18662					
Teitjen	F	17737					
Tettmar	David Bloxham	18459		09-Aug-16	Delville Wood		
Therin	George	18203					
Therin	A	18202	MM				
Thomas	Howard	18826		31-May-16	Cabaret Rouge		
Thomas	L	17638					
Thompson	GH	17483					
Thompson	Arthur	18172					
Thorne	W	18796					
Thorogood	Ernest Victor	18870		09-Aug-16			Thiepval
Thurston	AJ	18631					
Tinning	Thomas	18347		19-Apr-17	Orchard Dump		
Todd	FW	18147	MM				
Tomliens	WJ	18550					
Tomlin	Charles	17293					
Tonbridge	G	18576					
Tovery	F	17510					
Towsey	A	18921					
Tozer	Tom	17188	MM				
Tranter	George Frederick	17226		30-Jul-16			Thiepval
Travers	Ernie	18139					
Trotter	CA	17499					
Trower	E	18139					
Tucker	Albert Frederick	18083		31-Jul-16			Thiepval
Tully	JW	17465					

Turner	Edward Henry	17358		01-Jul-16	Zouave Valley	
Turner	WE	17357				
Turner	H	17969				
Turner	F	18980				
Tyler	AF	18158				
Underwood	William Charles	17968		13-Nov-16	Serre Road No2	
Valentine	James Wicks	17548	MM	30-Jul-16		Thiepval
Varley	JA	17967				
Vaus	H	17323				
Vautier	John Raymond	18145		05-Sep-16	City of London	
Viles	George Frederick	18923		28-Apr-17		Arras
Vogt	G	18498				
Wackett	Herbert	18461				
Wade	Albert	17322				
Wade	Alexander	17631				
Wake	William	17175		03-Sep-16	Euston Road	
Walden	Ernest	17966				
Walker	BA	17179				
Walker	TH	18259				
Wall	Charles William	18575		13-Nov-16		Thiepval
Walls	B	17282				
Walsby	James	19045		30-Jul-16		Thiepval
Wanklin	SH	17738				
Ward	John	17610		27-Jun-16	Barlin	
Ward	Samuel	17717				
Ward	Reginald George	17321				
Waring	DA	17906				
Waterman	Charles	17225	MM	30-Jul-16		Thiepval
Watson	W	18084				
Watts	AE	17673				
Watts	Charlie	18441				
Watts	CA	18928				
Watts	Elias	17187				
Waving	W	18333				
Weaver	BJ	19394				
Webb	S	17546				
Webb	HH	17547				
Webb	Albert	17224	MM			
Webber	HE	18334				
Weeden	William Arthur	17606		31-Jul-16	Dive Copse	
Weeden	Ernest	19036		09-Aug-16		Thiepval
Wells	Cecil John	18636		13-Nov-16		Thiepval
West	J	17545				

Surname	Forename	Number	Medal	Date	Cemetery	Memorial
Westoby	Charles Henry	18020		09-Aug-16		Thiepval
Weston	Jack	17929		24-Apr-17	Mory Abbey	
Weston	HG	18499				
Whatley	SG	17286				
White	GW	17186				
White	JS	18916				
White	TW	17155	MM			
White	James	3 2865				
Whitehead	P	17482				
Whittaker	LO	17351				
Wicker	William	18085		13-Nov-16		Thiepval
Wildash	G	17393				
Wilder	William	17284	MM			
Wilding	Edward William	17951	MM			
Wilkinson	JT	17184	MM			
Wilkinson	A	17509				
Williams	Frank Arthur	18157		02-Jul-16	Barlin	
Williams	Walter George	17928		27-Apr-17	Etaples Military	
Williamson	John	17404		02-Jun-16	Cabaret Rouge	
Williamson	Henry William	18660		30-Jul-16		Thiepval
Williamson	JJ	17183				
Wilson	FW	17396				
Wilson	WR	17965				
Wilton	Christopher	17632		04-Feb-16	Bethune	
Windley	PG	18021				
Windsor	L	17318	MSM			
Witherall	A	19332				
Wood	Alfred	17468				
Woollard	G	17544				
Woollard	George	18460				
Woollard	A	18568				
Woolward	Frederick	17633		07-May-16	Loos British	
Worricker	Albert Edward	18262		21-Aug-16	Bus les Artois	
Wright	William	17289		30-Jul-16	Delville Wood	
Wright	William George	18192		19-Apr-17		Arras
Wyman	A	17739				
Yallop	RG	17926				
Yellop	JJ	18309				
Young	F	17839				
Young	David	17137				
Young	Fred	18639				
Zimmer	Henry	18022				

Visiting the battlefields

Today, as more people are becoming keenly interested in the part their family played during the First World War, tours are widely available in France. Many of them incorporate areas fought for by the Hammers, such as Delville Wood and Vimy Ridge. They are very popular. the hotels are regularly pre-booked and full, while the Somme itself is tightly crammed with tourist coaches over the summertime. But, less than forty minutes by car from the Calais Eurostar, is a peaceful little cemetery which isn't a destination of the tours, it's hardly visited at all in fact. If you prefer to pay your respects in a tranquil less touristic way then the whole return trip can be achieved in a few hours along well maintained and uncongested motorways and roads.

In the Loos British CWGC at Grenay you'll find a number of the Originals, all lying close to each other. They include Joe Cooper from the advance party who died while stretcher-bearer Norman Bellinger tried to save his life and got wounded in the process. Close-by lies L/Cpl Bedford who witnessed Samuel Ward blow his foot off. The majority of those men who were gassed in the warm billet cellar in a snowy March of 1916 also lie there. Percy Price, the first overseas casualty of the West Ham Battalion is also named on the surrounding Memorial to the Missing.

Being off the tourist route, there aren't too many cafes or bistros around here so after enjoying your packed lunch head a few minutes away to find the Rue Emile Zola, which the men would have known as West Ham Lane. Around the corner in Rue Brunel are some houses used as billets, including the one where the men were suffocated by carbon-monoxide. In a field at the end of a parallel road, you'll be tracing the footsteps of William Busby and others as they left on the first home-leave along the 'Calonne North' communication trench. On the flat horizon to the east you'll spot the dark pyramids of coal mining slag heaps which would have been a skyline very familiar to the Hammers.

Within a ten minute drive there are two other CWGC, Fosse 10 and Bully Grenay Communal, holding more of the Originals who were killed in early 1916. A few miles away to the East you will find the village of Oppy which caused such chaos for the Hammers in April 1917 on the same day West Ham United won the Southern Combination Championship.

If you do wander the old battlefields, please remember
Do NOT touch anything remotely resembling ammunition!

About the authors:

Barney Alston enjoyed a long career with the blue berets of SO19, the Metropolitan Police firearms unit. Now retired, he maintains a passionate interest in military history and lives in Norfolk.

As a lifelong follower of West Ham United Elliott Taylor was humbled to discover that his Great-Grandfather served and died as an original in the Hammers Battalion and so organised the memorial at the Boleyn Ground and the West Ham Pals blog before embarking on shaping Barney's twelve years of initial research material and getting the book finished.

Acknowledgements
Thanks are due first and foremost to the families for sharing their memories.

Acknowledgements and appreciation for sharing their knowledge, expertise and support are sent to Ian Hook at the Essex Regiment Museum, Lt-Cdr Keith Hook RN (Rtd) RD, Andy Cullen at the Royal Anglian Regiment Association, Tony Jones at the Essex Regiment Association, Ian Tompkins and Tara Warren at West Ham United Football Club, Kay Callaghan at the Royal British Legion, Kenny Hill and the members of the East Ham branch of RBL, Michael Holden, Andrew Riddoch, John Kemp, Anthony Kitchen, Kathy Taylor, Clive Manning, Paul Reed, Newham Archive, Busby Troop of Newham Scouts, Anthony Clarke, Glyn Warwick, Michael Tierens, Ralph J Whitehead, Ron Clifton and members of the great war forum and ww2talk forum.

References
13th Essex War Diary
6th Brigade War Diary
2nd Division Official History
Medal index cards
Enlistment papers
Service and Pension files
The Stratford Express
West Ham Council minutes

When The Whistle Blows – Riddoch & Kemp (2008) ISBN-10: 1844256563
War Hammers – Brian Belton (2006) ISBN-10: 0752441558
The Zeppelin Menace – Ian Castle (2008) ISBN 978 184603 245 5
Somme Battle Stories – AJ Dawson (1916)
Storm of Steel – Junger (1920)

Audio interview with Cpl Manningtree courtesy of John Keeble
Audio interview transcript of Sgt William Gilbert courtesy of Richard Gilbert
Memoir of Ernie Kurtz/Curtis courtesy of the Western Front Association (Essex)
Personal diary of William Busby courtesy of Derek Pheasant
Photographs are courtesy of family members, the Essex Regiment Museum, Michael Holden's collection and the authors own.

Front cover image is detail from "*The Magnificent Last Stand of the Essex*" at the Lock and Sunken Road, by Richard Caton-Woodville which was published as a double page spread in a February 1918 edition of the Illustrated London News.

Copyright: Elliott Taylor & Barney Alston 2012

first published in digital format on Kindle April 27th 2012
This paperback edition first published November 11th, 2012

The right of Elliott Taylor and Barney Alston to be identified as the authors of this work has been asserted in accordance with the Copyright, Designs and Patents Act 1988.

All Rights Reserved. No part of this publication may be reproduced, stored in a retrieval system or transmitted in any form by any means, without the prior written permission of the author, nor to be otherwise circulated in any form of binding or cover.

ISBN 9 781479 279463

Printed in Great Britain
by Amazon.co.uk, Ltd.,
Marston Gate.